Judy Garton-Sprenger
Philip Prowse

new inspiration

MACMILLAN

Student's Book **2**

CONTENTS

CONTENTS

Welcome!

Welcome to London, and hello to all our competition winners! I'm Carrie and I'm a journalist – I work for World2day, the website with all the latest news.

Hi, nice to meet you all. I'm from Izmir in Turkey. This is my first visit to London and I can't wait to see all the sights.

Hello – I'm Jay and I'm from the USA. I'm having a great time here! And this is Leyla.

COMPETITION

Win a fantastic holiday in London!

WORLD2DAY

Try our London quiz –
choose the right answers and you could be a winner!

1   **London is**
     ○ 1,000 years old.   ○ 2,000 years old.   ○ 3,000 years old.

2   **The population of Greater London is**
     ○ 12,500,000.   ○ 10,000,000.   ○ 7,500,000.

3   **London's river is called**
     ○ Trafalgar.   ○ Big Ben.   ○ the Thames.

4   **The London home of the British Prime Minister is**
     ○ 221b Baker Street.   ○ 10 Downing Street.   ○ Buckingham Palace.

5   **The Prime Meridian (0° longitude) runs through the London district of**
     ○ Greenwich.   ○ Wembley.   ○ Wimbledon.

SEND

Hello, I'm Ramón and I live in Granada in Spain. I love music, and I'd love to go to a gig this week.

Hi! I'm Kristin from Switzerland, and I want to meet lots of English people. I can speak German and French, but I'm going to speak English all the time in London.

I'm Emma and I'm British. No, I'm not English, I'm from Edinburgh in Scotland. I like shopping and there are some great markets here.

And I'm Alexey from Russia. This is a beautiful city – I'm going to buy a camera and take lots of pictures!

1   OPENER

Read the World2day quiz and try to guess the answers.

🔘 1.01   Now listen and check.

2   READING

🔘 1.02   Read the dialogue. How many competition winners are there?

3   AFTER READING

Answer the questions.

1   What is Carrie's job?
2   What is the name of the girl from Scotland?
3   Who wants to go sightseeing?
4   Who wants to go to a concert?
5   Who is going to take lots of photos?
6   Who wants to meet lots of English people?
7   Where in Turkey does Leyla live?
8   Which city is Ramón from?
9   Who can speak three languages?
10   Who loves shopping?

Your response Do you want to visit London? Why/Why not?

4   SPEAKING

Ask and answer questions about the people in the photo.

What's his/her name?   Where's he/she from?

Extension   Write sentences about the competition winners.
Ramón is from Granada in Spain.

5   VOCABULARY

What nationalities are the winners? Choose from these words.

Word Bank Nationalities

American   British   French   German   Italian
Russian   Scottish   Spanish   Swiss   Turkish

Leyla is Turkish.

▶ Language File p112

PREVIEW

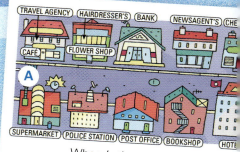

Where's the post office?
It's opposite the bank.

COMMUNICATIVE AIMS
LEARNING HOW TO ...

1 Talk about regular activities
2 Describe what's happening now
3 Talk about possessions
4 Compare things
5 Give advice
6 Say where things are
7 Talk about likes and dislikes
8 Say what people can do

He's good at singing.

TOPICS AND VOCABULARY

Clothes
Colours
Jobs and occupations
Tourist attractions
Carnivals and festivals
Adjectives
Social customs
Prepositions of place
Town facilities
Music

Whose camera is it?

1 Match the communicative aims (1–8) with the pictures (A–H).

2 Put the words into categories.

Music   Town facilities   Colours

It's bigger than any other Brazilian carnival.

jazz green hotel market restaurant salsa soul church café world red hip-hop yellow brown museum purple reggae blue

"I go to the movies on Saturdays."

E

"You should tell me where you're going."

G

"What's happening?"

H

F

I love going to festivals.

5 Do the Birthday Questionnaire with three other students.

BIRTHDAY *Questionnaire*

1 What do you do on your birthday?
Do you:
* stay at home or go out?
* celebrate with your friends or with your family?
* do something special or have an ordinary day?
* have a birthday party?

2 What about food on your birthday?
Do you:
* eat at home or in a restaurant?
* eat something special? If so, what?
* have a birthday cake?

3 What about presents?
Do you get presents:
* from your family? If so, what kind?
* from your friends? If so, what kind?

4 What happens on your ideal birthday?

3 Name the clothes.

1   2   3

4   5   6

What interesting or surprising things did you find out? Tell another group.

4 🔴 1.03 Listen to extracts 1–3 from Units 1 and 2. Match them with A–C below.

A   An interview about personal information
B   A sightseeing guide
C   A description of New Year celebrations

Believe it or not!

In a group of 23 people, there's a 50% chance that two people share a birthday!

9

1 Do you really speak Chinese?

Talking about regular activities
Present simple

1 OPENER

What things do you like? What things don't you like?

2 READING

🔴 1.04 Read the dialogue. Which of these topics do they talk about?

> animals   films   food   languages   school

KRISTIN   Oh, Emma, look at the horses! I love them!

EMMA   Do you? I don't like them at all.

JAY   Really? How about dogs? I love dogs.

EMMA   Dogs are OK, but cats are my favourite. We have two cats at home.

KRISTIN   What else do you like, Jay? I bet you like computer games.

JAY   No, I never play computer games. But I surf the Web and chat to people online.

KRISTIN   What about movies?

JAY   I watch DVDs but I don't often go to the movies.

KRISTIN   I do. I go to the cinema on Saturdays – after yoga.

EMMA   Oh, I do yoga too – every Tuesday. My mum teaches yoga.

KRISTIN   And what languages do you speak?

EMMA   Oh, let's see – Italian, French and Chinese!

JAY   Chinese? Do you really speak Chinese?

EMMA   Of course not. It's a joke, silly!

JAY   Oh, I know a good joke! Why do birds fly south in winter?

KRISTIN   I don't know. Why do they fly south?

JAY   Because it's too far to walk!

3 AFTER READING

True or false? Correct the false sentences.

1   Emma loves horses.
2   Emma likes cats more than dogs.
3   Jay doesn't watch movies.
4   Kristin goes to the cinema every Tuesday.
5   Kristin and Emma do yoga every week.
6   Emma's mother teaches yoga.
7   Emma speaks Chinese.
8   Jay knows a joke about birds.

Your response

Do you like cats more than dogs?
What languages do you speak?
What do you do on Saturdays?
What do you never do?

4 LISTENING

🔴 1.05 Listen and complete the sentences.

WORLD2DAY **WINNERS**

_L_ does gymnastics and goes swimming every Friday.
_A_ plays basketball and does karate.
_R_ loves hip-hop and rap.
_K_ chats online in English and German.

Ramón

Alexey

Leyla

Kristin

7 SPEAKING

Ask other students and complete the chart. You can write the questions first!

> Do you play football every week?

> Yes, I do.   No, I don't.

Find someone who ...	Name
doesn't play football every week.	Zava
drinks tea at breakfast.	Floor
doesn't do yoga.	Lida
speaks three languages.	Cayla
often watches TV.	Nicholas
doesn't go to bed late.	Leonardo/Siphe
often phones friends.	Adrián
doesn't chat online.	Carla

Extension Ask questions about other students.
A Does Mariella do yoga?
B No, she doesn't.
A Do Claude and Jean play football every week?
B Yes, they do.

8 WRITING

Look at the activities in exercise 7, and write sentences about what other students do and don't do.

Mark doesn't play football every week.
Joanna drinks tea at breakfast.

Now write five sentences about yourself.

I play football every week. I don't drink tea at breakfast,
I drink coffee ...

Extension Write three true and two false sentences about another student. Can your partner guess which are false?

5 PRONUNCIATION

🔘 1.06 Listen and repeat.

/s/ chats	/z/ does	/ɪz/ watches
drinks	knows	chooses
eats	loves	finishes

Now listen and write these words in the correct column.

> dances   goes   likes   plays   speaks   teaches

6 GAME

Practise spelling.

A How do you spell 'karate'?
B K-A-R-A-T-E.
A Correct! One point!

LANGUAGE WORKOUT

Complete.

Present simple
I _____ to the cinema on Saturdays.
She **loves** horses.
Emma _____ Italian.
What languages _____ you speak?
Do you really _____ Chinese?
I _____n't often go to the movies.
She _____n't speak Chinese.

We use the present simple to describe states, routines and regular activities.

▶**Answers and Practice**
Language File page 112

11

1
2
You're standing on my foot!

Describing what's happening now
Present continuous
Relative pronouns: *who/that*

1 OPENER

Which of these things can you see in the photo?

> bag camera guitar hat juggler map
> shirt sunglasses trees umbrella

2 READING

🔘 1.07 Read the dialogue. Who can you see in the photo?

STEVE — It's the highest wheel in Europe – it's 135 metres high.

RAMÓN — What's happening?

EMMA — Steve is telling everyone about the London Eye.

RAMÓN — Who's Steve?

EMMA — He's the tour guide. He's standing next to Leyla. He's the one that's wearing a blue jacket.

RAMÓN — What are Alexey and Kristin doing? Oh, look, they're holding hands!

EMMA — No, they aren't holding hands! She's helping him with his camera.

RAMÓN — Let me see!

EMMA — Ow! You're standing on my foot!

RAMÓN — Sorry. Hey, what's that man doing?

EMMA — Who do you mean? The juggler?

RAMÓN — No, the thin man who's standing behind the girl in the orange top. Look!

EMMA — Is he helping her?

RAMÓN — No, he isn't helping her. He's putting his hand in her bag. I think he's taking her wallet.

EMMA — Quick, let's stop him!

RAMÓN — He's running this way!

3 AFTER READING

Match the questions with the answers. There is one wrong answer.

1 Who is standing next to Leyla?
2 Is Ramón wearing a jacket?
3 Are Alexey and Kristin holding hands?
4 Is Kristin taking photographs?
5 Is Kristin helping Alexey?
6 What is Ramón doing when Emma says 'Ow!'?
7 Where is the thin man standing?
8 What is the thin man doing?

a Behind the girl.
b No, she isn't.
c Yes, they are.
d He's putting his hand in her bag.
e Steve.
f No, they aren't.
g No, he isn't.
h He's standing on her foot.
i Yes, she is.

Your response Who is the thin man? Is he really stealing the wallet? Why is he running? What happens next?

🔴 1.08 Now listen and see if you are right.

4 PRONUNCIATION

🔴 1.09 Listen and count the syllables. Mark the stress.

behind   camera   happening   jacket
orange   umbrella   video   wallet

■
behind   2

Now listen again and repeat.

5 VOCABULARY

Look at the photo of the group. Ask and answer questions about who people are.

Who's Emma?

She's the one who's wearing a green top and black trousers.

Who's Alexey?

He's the boy that's standing …

Word Bank Clothes

boots dress hat jacket jeans pullover
shirt shoes shorts skirt sweatshirt top
trainers trousers T-shirt

6 SPEAKING

Ask and answer questions about what people are doing.

A What's the girl in the orange top doing?
B She's watching the juggler.

7 WRITING

Write sentences describing the people in the photo. Don't write their names!

He's the one who's standing on the left, next to Steve. He's wearing a blue T-shirt and he's holding an umbrella.

Now give your sentences to another student. Can he/she guess the names?

Extension Look out of the classroom window and write about what is and isn't happening outside.
It's raining and no one is dancing in the street.

LANGUAGE WORKOUT

Complete.

Present continuous
You're stand**ing** on my foot.
He's _____ a blue jacket.
They're hold**ing** hands.
What _____ they do**ing**?
_____ he help**ing** her?
He _____n't help**ing** her.
They _____n't hold**ing** hands.

We use the present continuous to talk about temporary events and what is happening now.

Relative pronouns: *who/that*
… the thin man **who**'s standing behind the girl …
He's the one **that**'s wearing a blue jacket.

We can use either *who* or _____ to refer to people.

▶ **Answers and Practice**
Language File pages 112–113

3 It's my sister's birthday

Talking about possessions
Possessive adjectives and pronouns
Possessive *'s* and *s'*

1 OPENER

Which of these words do you expect to find in a text about a social networking site?

> account   breakfast   email address   Internet   jacket
> password   text message   mobile phone   username   wallet

2 READING

🔴 1.10 Read the text and check your answers to exercise 1.

Anna

twitter is one of the most popular social networking sites on the Internet. You can use Twitter to send very short messages (up to 140 characters or letters) in answer to the simple question: What are you doing? These messages are called tweets and you send them via the Twitter website or via your mobile phone as text messages.

It's easy to create an account. Ask for your parents' permission to sign up, choose a username and password, and give your email address. Now you can send tweets – tell your friends what you're doing in no more than 140 characters. And lots of famous people are on Twitter, from Barack Obama to Miley Cyrus. Add them to your network and you can follow celebrities' lives day by day!

Luke

Now look at the photos and read these tweets. Which message is ...?

Anna's   Luke's   Rosie's   Bill's   Teresa's   Simon's

Rosie

A   I'm waiting to interview Linkin Park. They're my favourite band, and I'm really excited!

- -

B   I'm writing a song about people's problems and what they can do about them. It's called *You Can Get It Right* – I hope you like it. 😜

- -

C   Our new play starts tomorrow. Everyone else knows ☹ their lines but I'm still trying to learn mine!

- -

D   It's my sister's birthday and we're going to a great restaurant for a meal. I'm taking lots of photos.

- -

E   I'm giving my dog Goldie a health check – she seems fine. I work with hundreds of animals, but I only have one of my own.

- -

F   My boss says I can't go on Twitter at work. But she's in a meeting, and it's my lunch break, so I'm having fun in the office!

- -

Bill

Teresa

Simon

3 AFTER READING

Give short answers to the questions.

1 What is Rosie's favourite band?
2 What is *You Can Get It Right* about?
3 Who doesn't know his lines?
4 Whose birthday is it?
5 Where is Bill's boss?
6 Whose dog is called Goldie?

Your response Write your own tweet using up to 140 characters.

4 SPEAKING

Look carefully at the photos. Ask and answer questions about these things.

> book   camera   dog   glasses   guitar
> laptop   microphone   mobile phones
> pen   pink shirt   stethoscope

> Whose is the book?

> It's Luke's. Whose are the glasses?

> They're …

Now ask and answer these questions.

Bill's guitar?

> Is it Bill's guitar?

> No, it isn't his. It's Anna's.

1 Luke's microphone?
2 Teresa's glasses?
3 Rosie's camera?
4 Bill's pink shirt?
5 Simon's mobile phones?
6 Anna's dog?

5 PRONUNCIATION

🔴 1.11 Listen and repeat.

> break   eat   great   meal   mean
> meet   plane   play   speak   take

Now write the words under /iː/ or /eɪ/ in the chart. Then listen and check.

/iː/	/eɪ/
eat	break

6 VOCABULARY

Match these definitions with jobs from the Word Bank.

a someone who takes pictures
b someone that performs in a play or film
c a person who plays an instrument
d someone who writes or broadcasts news stories
e a doctor for animals
f someone in an office that helps his/her boss

> **Word Bank** Jobs and occupations
>
> actor   firefighter   musician   nurse
> PA (personal assistant)   photographer   pilot
> receptionist   reporter   teacher   vet   waiter

> **Extension** Write definitions of two other jobs. Can other students guess the jobs?

7 SPEAKING

Ask and answer questions about the people in the photos. What do they do, and what are they doing at the moment?

> What does Rosie do?

> She's a reporter. What's she doing?

> She's waiting to interview Linkin Park.

8 WRITING

Write about the people in the photos. Say what they do and what they're doing at the moment.

Rosie is a reporter and she's waiting to interview Linkin Park. They're her favourite band and she's really excited.

> **Extension** Write similar sentences about three celebrities. Say what they do, and what you think they're doing at the moment.

LANGUAGE WORKOUT

Complete.

Possessive adjectives		Possessive pronouns	
my	_____	_____	ours
_____	your	yours	yours
his/her/its	_____	his/hers/its	theirs

Possessive 's and s'	
Singular noun	sister**'s** birthday
Plural noun	parent**s'** permission
	celebritie**s'** lives
Irregular plural noun	people**'s** problems

▶**Answers and Practice**
Language File page 113

Personal Profiles

1 OPENER

Guess: What languages does Leyla speak? What are her favourite colours?

READING

2 Read *Five Minutes With Leyla* and complete the answers with sentences a–e.

a   I listen to music.
b   Turkish, of course, and French. And I'm learning English.
c   That's easy. Pink and black!
d   'Sorry'. The English say 'sorry' all the time!
e   That's difficult. Let me think. I know. I try to help someone every day.

🔴 1.12   Now listen and check.

3 Here are Ramón's answers to some of the same questions. Which questions?

1   Good music.
2   People that don't tell the truth.
3   I play the guitar.
4   My girlfriend. I'm looking forward to seeing her again.
5   I cycle five kilometres before breakfast every morning.

WORLD2DAY

Five Minutes With

Leyla

Leyla is one of the winners of the World2day London holiday competition. What's she like? Find out here!

Hi Leyla. Where do you live?
In Izmir in Turkey, but at the moment I'm staying at the Royal Hotel in London.

What are your favourite clothes?
It depends. I often wear jeans and a sweatshirt, but I like dresses in the summer.

And your favourite colours?
1 _____

What is your favourite English word?
2 _____

What makes you angry?
People who don't listen.

What makes you happy?
Sunshine and blue sky!

How do you relax?
3 _____

What languages do you speak?
4 _____

Is there someone very important to you?
What do you mean? Do I have a boyfriend? I'm not telling you! But my mother is very important to me.

Is there something special you do every day?
5 _____

What are you reading at the moment?
An English book called *This is London*. It's great!

Thank you, Leyla!

4 LISTENING

1.13 Read this profile. Then listen to an interview with Jay and correct six mistakes in the profile.

Jay Serrano

WORLD2DAY

Jay is our winner from the USA and he's from California. He's 17 and lives at home with his parents and sister, Rose. His favourite clothes are shorts and T-shirts.

Jay's favourite colours are red, white and green and his favourite word is 'Yes!' Nothing makes him angry and his friends make him happy.

Jay relaxes by playing with his dog DJ in the park. He speaks English, of course, and he's learning French. His friends are very important to him and he's missing them now he's in London. Finally, Jay watches TV for half an hour every evening.

5 SPEAKING

Ask another student the questions in *Five Minutes with ... Leyla*. Note down the answers.

6 WRITING

Look at the profile of Jay. Match the information in each paragraph with the questions in *Five Minutes with ... Leyla*.

Now write a three-paragraph profile of the student you interviewed in exercise 5.

LEARNER INDEPENDENCE

7 Different people learn in different ways. What is your favourite way of finding the meaning of a word? Order these ways 1–5 (1 = best, 5 = worst).

- Use a bilingual dictionary.
- Use an English–English dictionary.
- Ask your teacher for help.
- Guess from the context.
- Ask another student.
- Use the Internet.

Now compare with another student.

8 Make your own personal phrasebook. Choose English expressions from this unit that you want to learn and write the translation next to each expression.

9 1.14 **Phrasebook:** Find these useful expressions in Unit 1. Then listen and repeat.

> Of course not.
> It's a joke, silly!
> What's happening?
> Let me see!
> Ow!
> Hey!
> I hope you like it.
> It depends.
> What do you mean?

Now write a four-line dialogue using one or more of the expressions.

A *What's happening?*
B *Johnny Depp is outside.*
A *Really?*
B *Of course not. It's a joke, silly!*

LANGUAGE LINKS

Congratulations!

When someone passes a test or is successful at something you can say *'Congratulations!'*. Match the different ways in which people say *'Congratulations!'* with the languages.

Congratulazioni! Felicitats! Felicitaties! Félicitations! Glückwünsche! Parabéns! Tebrikler! ¡Felicitaciones! Pozdravlyayu! (Поздравляю)

Catalan Dutch French German Italian
Portuguese Russian Spanish Turkish

You can say *Please* and *Thank you* in your language and English – what about other languages?

Game *Spelling Chain*

- Form two teams.
- Student 1 from Team A says and spells a word of five or more letters.
- Student 1 from Team B must say and spell a word that begins with the last letter of Team A's word.
- Student 2 from Team A continues …
- Teams score one point for each word they spell correctly. All words must have at least five letters. If a team cannot continue, they lose a point.

A Shirt S-H-I-R-T

B Trousers T-R-O-U-S-E-R-S

A Sister S-I-S-T-E-R

B Relax R-E-L-A-X

A ?!?!?!

SKETCH *The Ticket Inspector*

🔴 1.15 **Read and listen.**

A passenger is sitting on a train. He is reading a newspaper.

WAITER   Coffee?
PASSENGER No, thanks.

The passenger continues reading. The waiter comes back.

WAITER   Seats for dinner?
PASSENGER No, thanks.

The passenger continues reading. The ticket inspector speaks to him.

INSPECTOR Tickets!
PASSENGER No, thanks.
INSPECTOR Pardon?
PASSENGER I don't want a ticket, thank you.
INSPECTOR I'm not *selling* tickets, sir!
PASSENGER No?
INSPECTOR No. I want to *see* your ticket.
PASSENGER Oh, I haven't got one.
INSPECTOR You haven't got a ticket?
PASSENGER No, I never buy a ticket.
INSPECTOR Why not?
PASSENGER They're very expensive.
INSPECTOR Sir, you're travelling on a train. When you travel by train, you buy a ticket.
PASSENGER *I* don't.
INSPECTOR I see. All right. Then please leave the train.
PASSENGER What?
INSPECTOR Leave the train.
PASSENGER I can't leave the train!
INSPECTOR Why not?
PASSENGER It's moving!
INSPECTOR Not now, sir. At the next station.
PASSENGER Oh.
INSPECTOR And we're coming to a station now. Here we are, sir. Please leave the train.
PASSENGER Now?
INSPECTOR Yes, sir. Sorry.
PASSENGER Oh, that's OK.
INSPECTOR What?
PASSENGER That's OK.
INSPECTOR OK?
PASSENGER Yes, this is my station. Goodbye!

Adapted from a sketch by Doug Case

Now act out the sketch in pairs or groups of three.

REVISION

LESSON 1   Look at the conversation on page 10. Write two sentences each about Kristin, Emma and Jay using the present simple.

Kristin loves horses. She goes to the cinema ...

LESSON 2   Look at the photo on pages 12–13. Write questions and answers about what people are doing/ wearing.

What's Steve doing?
He's telling everyone about the London Eye.

LESSON 3   Make a list of clothes and other things that people wear. Use the photos on pages 14–15 to give you ideas.

jacket, glasses, ...

LESSON 4   Look at the profile of Jay on page 17. Write a similar profile of Leyla using information from the webpage on page 16.

Leyla is our winner from Turkey and she lives in Izmir. Her favourite clothes ...

EXTENSION

LESSON 1   Choose two friends or members of your family. Write sentences about:

- what they love
- what they do at weekends
- what they never do
- what languages they speak

My mother loves rock music.

LESSON 2   Look at the photo in Lesson 1 on pages 10–11 and write sentences about Kristin, Emma and Jay using the present continuous. What are they doing/ wearing and where are they standing?

Kristin is talking about horses. She's wearing ...

LESSON 3   Look at the photos on pages 14–15. Write questions and answers about these things.

> purple dress   black jacket   silver ring
> blue top   colourful T-shirt

Whose is the purple dress?
It's ....

LESSON 4   Look at Jay's profile on page 17. Write a similar profile of yourself in the third person singular.

YOUR CHOICE!

WHO AM I?
- Work in a small group.
- Think of a famous person. Write five sentences saying what the person does every day. But don't write the person's name.
- Read out your sentences to the rest of the group. They try to guess who the famous person is.

WHOSE IS THIS?
- Work in a small group and use a coloured plastic bag.
- Choose two small objects and put them in the bag. Don't show your objects to the rest of the group.
- One student takes objects out of the bag one by one and asks *Whose is this?*
- The other students answer *It's Diana's* or *Diana, is it yours?*

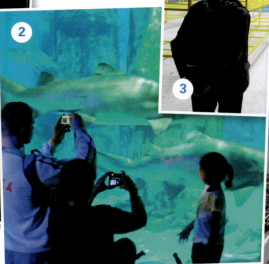

Welcome to

A The London Eye

Ride up in the sky and look down on London. The London Eye is 135 metres high and is the slowest big wheel in the world. It has 32 capsules which carry 25 passengers each. The London Eye is on the South Bank of the Thames in the centre of London.

B The Monument

Another good place to see London from the sky. You can climb to the top of the 300-year-old Monument and look out over the city. It's the tallest stone column in the world. The column is exactly 61.5 metres tall and 61.5 metres from where the Great Fire of London started in 1666.

C St Paul's Cathedral

This famous church, rebuilt after the Great Fire, is near the Monument. It's the fifth cathedral on this site. Visit the famous Whispering Gallery – you can hear people whisper 30 metres away!

D Tate Modern

London has lots of famous art galleries, but Tate Modern is Britain's national museum of modern art. It has exciting and unusual exhibitions, and there are works by many important artists, including Matisse and Picasso. The museum is in a former power station on the River Thames.

E The Museum of London

If you're interested in London's history, then this is the place for you. Learn about life in London from the Romans to the present day. Make sure you see the Lord Mayor's coach, built in 1757 and still in use today. The museum is open seven days a week and, like most London museums, it's free!

London

F Covent Garden

Once London's biggest flower, fruit and vegetable market, the Covent Garden piazza is now a great place for shopping, and also has lots of cafés and restaurants. You can usually listen to buskers and watch street theatre here – but be careful of pickpockets!

G Big Ben

What is Big Ben? Is it a clock? In fact, Big Ben is really the name of one of the clock's bells and it weighs over 13 tonnes. Big Ben is in the clock tower of the Houses of Parliament. The tower is 95.7 metres high and it's on the River Thames.

H Madame Tussaud's

Come here and see models of famous people, from film stars to kings and queens. It's open every day of the year except Christmas Day. A popular attraction is the 'Spirit of London' time ride – you sit in the back of a real black taxi and 'travel' through London's history in five minutes. And don't miss the Chamber of Horrors!

I The London Aquarium

Meet sharks face to face! This aquarium has over 365 kinds of fish – more than one for every day of the year. The aquarium makes its own seawater, and every year it uses salt equal to the weight of nine London double-decker buses. It's on the South Bank of the river, next to the London Eye, and is open every day from 10am–6pm.

1 OPENER

Look at the headings (A–I) of the London sightseeing guide and try to match the places with the photos (1–9).

2 READING

1.16 Read the guide and check your answers to exercise 1. Then find the answers to these questions.

Where can you …
1 see models of film stars?
2 see sharks?
3 watch street theatre?
4 get good views of London?
5 see pictures by Picasso?
6 hear a famous bell?
7 find out about London's history?

3 VOCABULARY

Match the words with their definitions.

1 an attraction
2 an aquarium
3 a busker
4 a cathedral
5 passengers
6 a double-decker
7 a pickpocket

a someone who plays music in the street for money
b someone who steals things from people's pockets
c a place where you can see unusual fish and water animals
d people who are travelling
e something interesting for people to see or do
f the most important church in a city
g a bus with two floors

4 MINI-PROJECT
Sightseeing Guide

Work with another student and write a description of a famous place in your town/country for a sightseeing guide. Use the London sightseeing guide and these questions to help you.

- Where is it?
- What is special about it?
- What can you see/do there?
- How old is it?
- When is it open?

Read your work carefully and correct any mistakes. Then join other students and put your descriptions together to make a sightseeing guide.

Europe's best street party

Comparing things
Comparative and superlative adjectives

1 OPENER

Talk about festivals in your country. Which are the most important? Use these words to help you.

Word Bank Festivals

band   carnival   costume   dancer
music   parade   stage   stall

2 READING

You are going to read about carnivals in Rio de Janeiro and London. Which carnival do you think is bigger?

🔘 1.17   Now read *Carnivals* and check your answers.

CARNIVALS

Carnival in Rio

In Brazil, people celebrate carnival in February or March. Every region has its own festival, but carnival in Rio is the most famous. It lasts four days and millions of people go to it, including 300,000 foreign visitors. It's one of the biggest Brazilian carnivals – and it's the best, say the *cariocas* (the people of Rio).

The *escolas de samba* (samba schools) work all year to prepare for the two nights of parades in the streets and in the giant samba stadium, which holds 90,000 people. Some parades have thousands of dancers, all in the most amazing costumes, and 600 to 800 drummers. Each parade lasts ten to twelve hours and the judges choose the best samba school. There are also all-night carnival balls with non-stop loud samba music.

At carnival, Rio is the most exciting city in the world, but it is also one of the most expensive – hotels and taxis cost four times as much as usual. But that's because Rio has the most spectacular carnival in the world!

Notting Hill Carnival

For most of the year, Notting Hill is a smart quiet part of London. But at carnival time you can see the real cosmopolitan Notting Hill, which is much more exciting – and noisier!

Notting Hill Carnival is smaller than Rio and less well-known, but it's the largest carnival in Europe. It started in 1964 and now over a million people come to the carnival for two days at the end of August each year. More than fifty bands parade through the streets in colourful costumes. There are lots of sound systems playing reggae and other kinds of music, and three stages where bands play. The streets are full of people dancing and following the bands. And when you get hungry, there are stalls selling exotic food from all over the world.

They call Notting Hill Carnival 'The Greatest Show on Earth'. It's Europe's best street party! And it's less expensive than Rio!

3 AFTER READING

True or false? Correct the false sentences.

1 In Rio each carnival parade lasts 24 hours.
2 At carnival time hotels in Rio are much more expensive than usual.
3 Carnival in Rio is longer than Notting Hill Carnival.
4 Notting Hill Carnival is in winter.
5 The carnival in Notting Hill is less famous than the one in Rio.
6 Notting Hill Carnival is the biggest in the world.

Now read *Carnivals* again and complete the chart for Rio and Notting Hill.

	Rio	Notting Hill	Your festival
When?			
How long?			
How many people?			
What kind of music?			
How expensive?			
What's special about it?			

Your response Complete the chart for a festival you know about (in your country or another one).

4 SPEAKING

Look at the chart in exercise 3, and compare the two carnivals and your festival.

A The carnival in Rio lasts longer than Notting Hill Carnival.
B The carnival in my country is smaller than Rio, but it is one of the most …

5 PRONUNCIATION

🔊 1.18 Listen and repeat. Then circle the /ə/ sound.

/ə/ bett**er**
carnival colourful dancer famous longer parade region samba special thousand

6 SPEAKING

Compare three cities in your country. Use adjectives from the Word Bank and talk about:

age size people festivals weather shops sport food attractions atmosphere

Word Bank Adjectives

cheap/expensive cold/hot cool/warm dry/wet exciting friendly good/bad old/modern popular quiet/noisy safe/dangerous

A I think Barcelona is older than Madrid.
B I think Granada is the oldest city in Spain.

Extension Play *Adjective Challenge*.

Good.
Better, the best.
Two points!

7 WRITING

Write sentences comparing cities in your country.

Barcelona is bigger than Granada, but Madrid is the biggest city.

Extension Write a paragraph for a tourist brochure about your favourite city. Say what's special about it and why it's the best place to visit. *London is the coolest city in the world …*

LANGUAGE WORKOUT

Complete.

Adjective	Comparative	Superlative
small	small___	the small**est**
large	larg**er**	the _____
big	big**ger**	___ _____
noisy	_____	the nois**iest**
famous	**more** famous	the _____ famous
exciting	_____ exciting	the _____ exciting
expensive	**less** expensive	the **least** expensive

Irregular

| good | better | ~~the best~~ |
| bad | worse | the worst |

The opposite of *more* is ~~less~~.
The opposite of *most* is *least*.

We use comparative adjectives to compare two things.
We use superlative adjectives to compare _____ or more things.

▶**Answers and Practice**
Language File page 114

We should stay together

Giving advice
Saying where things are
should and *shouldn't*

1 OPENER

What can go wrong at a festival or carnival? Think about:

crowds   food and drink   money
safety   transport   weather

Pickpockets can be a problem in crowds.

2 READING

1.19 Read the dialogue. Why does Steve get angry with some of the group at Notting Hill Carnival?

STEVE   It's really easy to get lost here. We should stay together. Where are Emma and Alexey?

JAY   Oh, I don't know.

LEYLA   They're dancing next to the band – in front of the Mexican food stall.

STEVE   Hey, you two – come here! You shouldn't go away like that.

EMMA   Why not? It's a carnival. We're on holiday.

STEVE   You should tell me where you're going. I'm looking after you.

EMMA   I can look after myself. Bye!

JAY   Emma, you shouldn't go off on your own – it isn't safe. I'm coming with you!

STEVE   Now listen, the rest of you. Stay together and meet me in half an hour at the Gate Café. It's opposite the police station, OK? Emma, Jay, come back!

3 AFTER READING

Answer the questions.

1 Who is dancing next to the band?
2 Why should they tell Steve where they are going?
3 Does Emma agree with Steve?
4 Why does Jay go with Emma?
5 When does Steve ask the others to meet him?
6 What is opposite the police station?

Your response Do you think Emma and Jay should do what Steve says?

4 SPEAKING

Read the *Getting it right!* questionnaire. What should/shouldn't you do in your country?

GETTING IT RIGHT!
What should/shouldn't you do when ...

1 ... **you visit someone's home for the first time?**
A   Take flowers.
B   Arrive half an hour early.
C   Arrive a little late.
D   Take your own food with you.

2 ... **you meet someone's parents?**
A   Kiss them once on the cheek.
B   Kiss them twice on the cheek.
C   Shake hands.

3 ... **someone gives you a present?**
A   Say thank you and open it immediately.
B   Say thank you and open it later.

4 ... **you answer the telephone?**
A   Say hello.
B   Say your name.
C   Say your number.
D   Say your address.

5 ... **you are a guest at a meal?**
A   Start eating first.
B   Wait until others are eating.
C   Eat everything on your plate.
D   Leave some food on your plate.

5 PRONUNCIATION

🔘 1.20 Listen and repeat.

/s/ /ʃ/

She's got sixty shirts and sixty-six skirts – she should stop shopping!

6 VOCABULARY

Look at the carnival photo and complete with prepositions from the Word Bank.

1 Ramón is standing _____ Leyla.
2 Steve is standing _____ the group.
3 Leyla is _____ Ramón and Kristin.
4 Kristin is _____ Steve.
5 Jay is _____ Kristin.
6 The group are _____ the carnival parade.

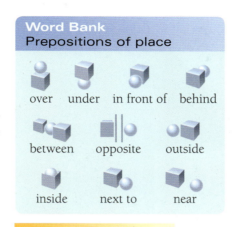

Word Bank
Prepositions of place

over   under   in front of   behind

between   opposite   outside

inside   next to   near

▶ **Language File page 114**

Extension Play *What is it?*
Describe objects you can see in the classroom but don't say their names. Can other students guess what you are describing?

It's near the computer and over the teacher's desk.

The clock!

7 VOCABULARY

Ask and answer questions about the town facilities.

Word Bank Town facilities

bank bookshop café chemist's flower shop hairdresser's hotel
newsagent's police station post office supermarket travel agency

Where's the bank?

It's opposite the post office.

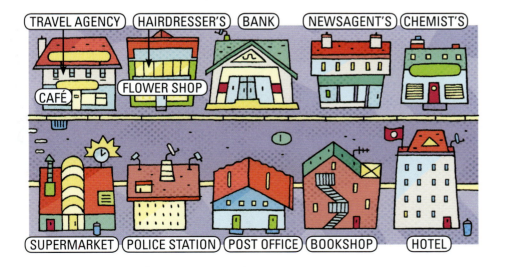

8 ROLE PLAY

You are in the street in exercise 7. Act out a conversation between a visitor and a local (someone who knows the town) using the phrases in the box.

Excuse me. Where can I buy some medicine?

There's a chemist's opposite the hotel.

Thank you. And where can I …?

buy some medicine
buy some stamps
find the police
book a flight
buy some flowers
get some bread
get a haircut
change some money
get a cup of coffee
buy some magazines

Extension Act out a similar conversation between a visitor and a local about facilities in your town.

9 WRITING

Write a paragraph giving advice to a visitor to your country. Use the topics in the questionnaire and add others.

When you visit someone's home for the first time, you should take flowers.

LANGUAGE WORKOUT

Complete.

should and ***shouldn't***
We **should** stay together.
You _____ tell me where you're going.
You _____ go off on your own.
Why _____ they tell Steve?

We can use *should* or *shouldn't* to give advice.

▶**Answers and Practice**
Language File page 114

I love going to festivals

Talking about likes and dislikes
Saying what people can do
Verb/Preposition + gerund

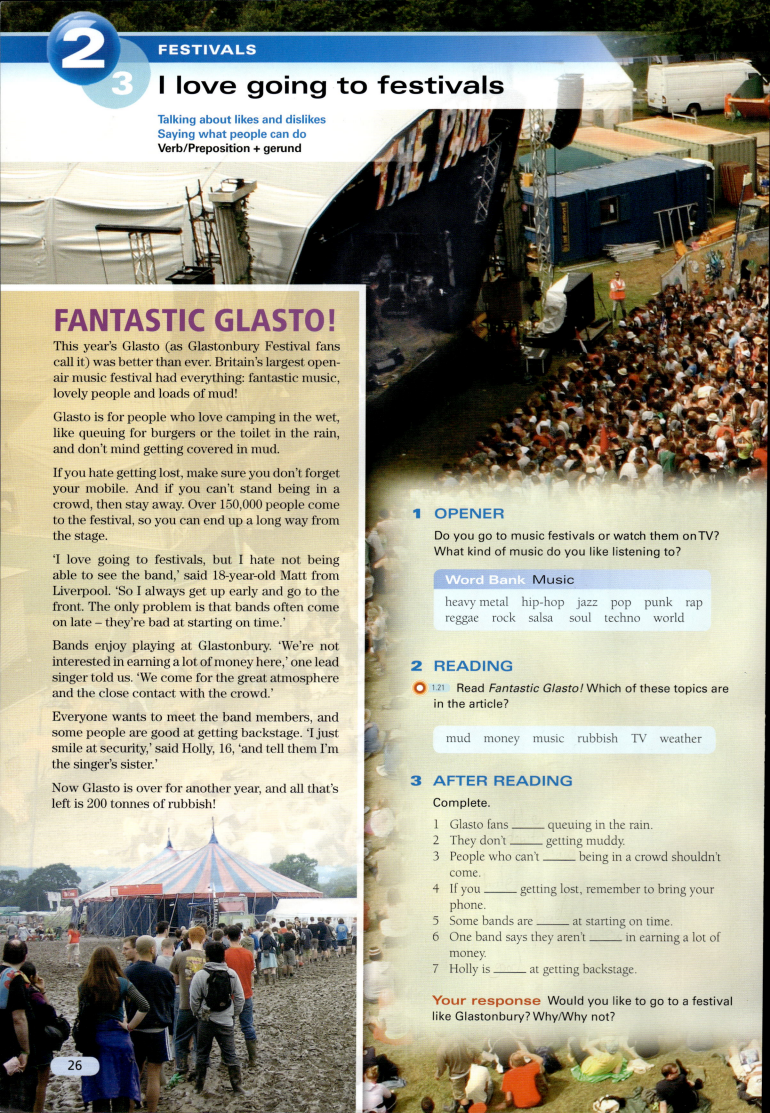

FANTASTIC GLASTO!

This year's Glasto (as Glastonbury Festival fans call it) was better than ever. Britain's largest open-air music festival had everything: fantastic music, lovely people and loads of mud!

Glasto is for people who love camping in the wet, like queuing for burgers or the toilet in the rain, and don't mind getting covered in mud.

If you hate getting lost, make sure you don't forget your mobile. And if you can't stand being in a crowd, then stay away. Over 150,000 people come to the festival, so you can end up a long way from the stage.

'I love going to festivals, but I hate not being able to see the band,' said 18-year-old Matt from Liverpool. 'So I always get up early and go to the front. The only problem is that bands often come on late – they're bad at starting on time.'

Bands enjoy playing at Glastonbury. 'We're not interested in earning a lot of money here,' one lead singer told us. 'We come for the great atmosphere and the close contact with the crowd.'

Everyone wants to meet the band members, and some people are good at getting backstage. 'I just smile at security,' said Holly, 16, 'and tell them I'm the singer's sister.'

Now Glasto is over for another year, and all that's left is 200 tonnes of rubbish!

1 OPENER

Do you go to music festivals or watch them on TV? What kind of music do you like listening to?

Word Bank Music

heavy metal hip-hop jazz pop punk rap
reggae rock salsa soul techno world

2 READING

🔘 1.21 Read *Fantastic Glasto!* Which of these topics are in the article?

mud   money   music   rubbish   TV   weather

3 AFTER READING

Complete.

1 Glasto fans _____ queuing in the rain.
2 They don't _____ getting muddy.
3 People who can't _____ being in a crowd shouldn't come.
4 If you _____ getting lost, remember to bring your phone.
5 Some bands are _____ at starting on time.
6 One band says they aren't _____ in earning a lot of money.
7 Holly is _____ at getting backstage.

Your response Would you like to go to a festival like Glastonbury? Why/Why not?

6 LISTENING

1.23 Festival Radio interviewed people at Glastonbury. Listen and complete the chart for Holly and Matt. Use these phrases.

dancing   getting wet   being lost   getting up early
making new friends   meeting old friends
staying up late   talking to girls

	Holly	Matt	Another student
Loves	meeting old friends	staying up late	
Hates	getting wet	being lost	
Good at	dancing	making new friends	
Bad at	getting up early	talking to girls	

Now complete the chart for another student.

What do you love/hate doing?

What are you good/bad at?

7 WRITING

Write sentences about Holly and Matt using the information in the chart. Then write about the student you interviewed.

Holly loves meeting old friends, but she hates ...
She's good at ... She's bad at ...

Extension Write about things you love and hate, and what you are good and bad at.

LANGUAGE WORKOUT

Complete.

Verb + gerund
I love go**ing** to festivals.
Bands enjoy play___ at Glastonbury.
They like _____ for burgers in the rain.
If you hate _____ lost ...
If you can't stand _____ in a crowd ...
They don't mind _____ covered in mud.

Preposition + gerund
Some people are good **at** get**ting** backstage.
We're not interested ___ earn**ing** a lot of money.

▶**Answers and Practice**
Language File page 115

4 PRONUNCIATION

1.22 Listen and repeat. Mark the stress.

atmosphere   dangerous   enjoy   fantastic
festival   interested   lovely   security

■
atmosphere

5 SPEAKING

Make a list of questions beginning *Do you like ...?* and *Do you mind ...?* Use the phrases in the box and add your own ideas. Ask two other students the questions and note down the answers.

sleep in a tent   stand all day   listen to live music
be in a large crowd   pay a lot for a ticket
hear new bands   be a long way from the stage
queue for the toilets   get covered in mud

Do you like sleeping in a tent?

Do you mind standing all day?

Extension Write sentences about the two students you interviewed.
Kurt likes sleeping in a tent and doesn't mind standing all day.

New Year Around the World

Here are some amazing New Year facts!

The **Chinese** celebrate the start of the Chinese New Year in January or February and it is the longest, the noisiest and the most exciting holiday of the year. On New Year's Eve all the children wear new clothes and everyone eats special food. New Year celebrations last 15 days, and there are dragon parades and lion dances in the streets.

In **Brazil**, people wear white clothes on New Year's Eve (31 December) because it brings good luck. At midnight people go to the beach and jump over the waves seven times. Then they throw flowers into the sea and make wishes for the new year. Some people light candles and there are lots of parties.

One of the most unusual festivals is in **Thailand**. People celebrate the Thai New Year on 13 April with 'Songkran Day'. On this day people play games with water and throw it over each other! They also visit their grandparents and ask them for good luck.

In **Japan** most people celebrate New Year with their family. They eat special noodles on 31 December, and at midnight they listen to the bells, which ring 108 times. On New Year's Day people drink *sake*, traditional Japanese rice wine, and eat a special kind of soup. Children get envelopes with money inside, and everyone sends New Year greetings cards.

On 31 December in **Venezuela**, people wear yellow underwear to bring good luck! At midnight they listen to the church bells and drink champagne. Each time they hear the bell they eat a grape and make a wish. People who want to travel in the new year carry a suitcase around the house. Other people write their wishes in a letter, and then burn it.

Like many other European countries, **Italy** celebrates the arrival of the new year with fireworks. On New Year's Eve everyone eats lentils at a large meal that starts late in the evening and goes on even later. Some people also put lentils in their purse or wear red clothes for good luck. Another tradition is to put a candle in the window for every member of the family.

1 OPENER

Choose one of the photos A–F (don't say which one!) and describe it to another student. Can your partner identify the photo?

2 READING

1.24 Read the descriptions of New Year and match the paragraphs with the photos.

Now answer these questions.

1 Where do people eat special noodles at New Year?
2 Where do they drink champagne?
3 What do people in Brazil wear at New Year?
4 What else do people in Brazil do at New Year?
5 Where do people eat lentils at New Year?
6 When do they celebrate New Year in Thailand?
7 How long do New Year celebrations last in China?
8 Where are fireworks important at New Year?

Then ask and answer similar questions.

> Where do people eat grapes at New Year?

> What do people in Venezuela wear at New Year?

3 LISTENING

1.25 Listen to a description of New Year's Eve in England, and choose the correct answer.

1 What do people often do on New Year's Eve?
  A have parties
  B go on holiday
2 What do they do at midnight?
  A go to London
  B listen to Big Ben
3 What do they do after midnight?
  A shake hands
  B sing a song
4 What do people drink?
  A champagne
  B tea
5 What do they say to each other?
  A Good luck!
  B Happy New Year!

4 SPEAKING

Look at the questions in exercise 3.
Ask another student about New Year's Eve traditions in his/her family.

5 WRITING

Write a paragraph about New Year's Eve in your country. Use the texts in this lesson to help you. Notice that the texts usually:

- begin by giving the name of the country and festival, and the date
- continue by describing food and drink, and what people do
- sometimes talk about children and presents
- use prepositions of time: on (date) in (month) at (time)

LEARNER INDEPENDENCE

6 What is your favourite way of learning a word? Order these ways 1–7.

- Writing the word again and again.
- Saying the word aloud again and again.
- Revising the word every week.
- Thinking of similar words.
- Testing yourself once a week.
- Using the word as soon as possible.
- Keeping a vocabulary notebook.

Now compare with another student. Try a new way of learning words.

7 How are your English skills? What are you good at? Assess yourself on this scale for Listening, Speaking, Reading and Writing.

4 = Very good.
3 = Good.
2 = Not sure.
1 = Not very good.

Listening 3

Now compare with another student. Choose a skill which needs more work. What can you do to get better?

8 1.26 **Phrasebook**: Find these useful expressions in Unit 2. Then listen and repeat.

Oh, I don't know.
Come here!
Why not?
Bye!
It isn't safe.
I'm coming with you.
Now listen!
OK?
Come back!
The only problem is …

Now write a four-line dialogue using two or more of the expressions.

A *Where's my music magazine?*
B *Oh, I don't know.*
A *Yes, you do! Come here!*
B *Bye!*

PROJECT Festivals and celebrations

1 Work in a group and look at Unit 2 Lessons 1 and 3 again. Think about festivals and public celebrations (for example, Independence Day or National Day) in your country or another country. Then choose one to write about.

2 Research: Find out information about the festival or celebration:

- What is it called? Where is it? When is it and how long does it last?
- Who goes to it? What do people do there? What kind of food is there? Is there music? What is special about it? What should you take?
- How do you get there? Where can you stay? Any problems?

3 Work together and write about the festival or celebration. Read your work carefully and correct any mistakes. Draw pictures or find photographs from magazines or online. Show your work to the other groups.

Cherry blossom festival

There are festivals all over Japan from March to May when the cherry trees come into flower in different regions.

People have picnics with their family and friends during the day or at night under the *sakura* (cherry trees). They eat a special kind of sweet dish called *dango*, and they sing and play music. There are often lights on the trees at night and that is very special. Don't forget to take your camera!

Would you like to go to a cherry blossom festival? You can get there by train – travel around Japan is easy on the *Shinkansen* high-speed trains. There are lots of good hotels and you can also stay in a *ryokan*, a traditional Japanese inn. The only problem is choosing which of the many festivals to go to!

Game Write a poem!

Love/Hate poem

I *love* reading.
I *love* football.
I *love* fireworks.
But I *hate* homework!

I *love* _____.
I *love* _____.
I *love* _____.
But I *hate* _____!

GOOD/BAD POEM

I'm good at dancing.
I'm good at rap.
I'm good at sleeping,
But I'm **bad** at writing letters!

I'm good at _____.
I'm good at _____.
I'm good at _____,
But I'm **bad** at _____!

PREPOSITION POEM

Over the crowd,
Under the stage,
Inside the singer's head,
The song was everywhere.

Preposition + noun
Preposition + noun
Preposition + noun
Sentence

Give your poems to your teacher and listen. Can you guess who wrote each poem?

REVISION

LESSON 1 Look at the chart below and write sentences comparing the three cities.

City	NEW YORK	LONDON	ATHENS
Age	400 years old	2,000 years old	6,000 years old
Population	8 million	7.5 million	3.5 million
Winter	January 4°C	January 5°C	January 9°C
Summer	July 30°C	July 18°C	July 27°C

London is older than New York, but Athens is the oldest city.

LESSON 2 Look at the Word Bank for prepositions of place on page 25. Write sentences describing the position of people and things in your classroom. Use all the prepositions!

The teacher is standing in front of us.

LESSON 3 Look at the chart and write sentences about Leyla and Alexey.

	Leyla	**Alexey**
Loves	swim	take photos
Hates	lose things	fly
Good at	write poems	play the guitar
Bad at	get up early	dance

Leyla loves swimming. She hates ...

LESSON 4 Look at the text on page 28 and read the paragraph you wrote about New Year's Eve in your country. Write a paragraph about Christmas or another family celebration in your country. Think about:

food drink clothes presents what people do

EXTENSION

LESSON 1 Choose three bands, pop stars, film stars or sports stars and write sentences comparing them using comparative and superlative adjectives.

The Black Eyed Peas are better than Linkin Park, but I think The Strokes are the best band.

LESSON 2 Write sentences about things you should/shouldn't do:
in class in the street at home

In class you should listen to the teacher. You shouldn't throw paper planes!

LESSON 3 Choose two friends or members of your family. Write sentences about:

- what they love doing
- what they hate doing
- what they're good at
- what they're bad at
- what they're interested in

Petra loves talking to boys.

LESSON 4 Write a list of questions to find out about another student's favourite festival or celebration. Then interview each other.

YOUR CHOICE!

MUSIC FESTIVAL ADVICE

Read the advice and then write sentences with *should* or *shouldn't*.

MUSIC FESTIVAL DOS AND DON'TS

✓ Make sure you have enough money.
✗ Don't leave valuable things in your tent.
✓ Carry a bottle of water.
✗ Don't drop rubbish on the ground.
✓ Remember to take your mobile.
✗ Don't take a heavy rucksack.

You should make sure you have enough money.

SUPERLATIVE YOU!

- Work in pairs, but don't show each other your work.
- Complete these sentences about your partner.

  Your best time of the day is …
  You think the greatest band in the world is …
  Your best school subject is …
  Your worst lesson of the week is …
  Your best friend's name is …
  Your most valuable possession is …

- Now discuss the sentences.

  A It says my best time of the day is the morning. That's right.

  B My best friend isn't Olivia. It's Toni.

REVIEW

1 Read and complete. For each number 1–10, choose word or phrase A, B or C.

LONDON CELEBRATIONS

Some of London's many celebrations are very British, but others, like Notting Hill Carnival, __1__ that London __2__ very cosmopolitan.

Up to 100,000 people celebrate the Chinese New Year in London's West End in January or February. There are lion dances, fireworks and stages with traditional Chinese music and dance. It is the __3__ important festival of the Chinese year.

Tourists __4__ try to see 'The Trooping of the Colour' in June. The Queen __5__ in an open carriage, and watches a __6__ of soldiers __7__ Buckingham Palace in central London.

There are fireworks in Southall in west London in October when Hindus celebrate Diwali, the Hindu festival of lights. This festival is also the start of the Hindu New Year and lots of families enjoy __8__ the celebrations.

Guy Fawkes' Night with bonfires and fireworks is on 5 November. People celebrate Guy Fawkes' failure to kill the king in 1605. Many children think this is the __9__ night of the year!

Finally, at Christmas there is a huge Christmas tree in Trafalgar Square. It is a present from Norway and it is the __10__ famous Christmas tree in Britain.

1	**A** show	**B** shows	**C** are showing
2	**A** are	**B** have	**C** is
3	**A** more	**B** most	**C** much
4	**A** should	**B** shouldn't	**C** don't
5	**A** ride	**B** rides	**C** is riding
6	**A** dance	**B** parade	**C** walk
7	**A** on	**B** off	**C** near
8	**A** watch	**B** to watch	**C** watching
9	**A** most	**B** best	**C** better
10	**A** much	**B** more	**C** most

2 Complete with the correct form of the present simple of these verbs.

> be   chat   do   drink   eat   get   go
> like   phone   play   speak   watch

1 In the evening Kristin _chats_ online to her friends.
2 I (not) _____ interested in going to the cinema.
3 Alexey _watches_ TV every evening.
4 _Does_ Leyla _speak_ four languages?
5 Ramón _phones_ his parents every day.
6 Emma (not) _likes_ horses.
7 I _go_ swimming on Mondays.
8 _Does_ Jay _drink_ coffee at breakfast?
9 Ramón (not) _do_ yoga.
10 Leyla never _eats_ chips.
11 Alexey (not) _play_ volleyball.
12 The children _get_ envelopes with money inside.

3 Complete with the correct form of the present continuous of these verbs.

> help   hold   listen   make   stand   tell

1 Steve _is telling_ the group about the London Eye.
2 _Are_ Alexey and Kristin _holding_ hands?
3 Kristin _is helping_ Alexey with his camera.
4 _Is_ Steve _standing_ on Emma's foot?
5 The actors _are making_ a film.
6 _Are_ you _listening_ to me?

4 Write questions and answers.

camera/Alexey
Whose camera is this? It's Alexey's. It's his.

1 watch/Ramón
2 bag/Carrie
3 book/Leyla
4 jacket/Steve
5 videos/my parents
6 sandwiches/the dancers

5 Complete with comparative or superlative adjectives.

1 Rio carnival is _the largest_ carnival in the world. (large)
2 Notting Hill Carnival is _most exciting_ street party in Europe. (exciting)
3 Leyla is a _better_ dancer than Alexey. (good)
4 Jay is _worse_ than Emma at learning languages. (bad)
5 Who is _the most popular_ singer in the world? (popular)
6 London is _the biggest_ city in Britain. (big)
7 Hotels in Rio are _more expensive_ at carnival time. (expensive)
8 Notting Hill Carnival is _less well-known_ than Rio carnival. (well-known)

6 Rewrite this safety advice using *should* and *shouldn't*.

> ### When you go out in the evening …
> ▲ Never take lifts from strangers, or get into a stranger's car.
> ▲ Don't stay out very late and don't walk home on your own.
> ▲ Remember to carry a mobile.
> ▲ Make sure you've got enough money for a taxi home if necessary.
> ▲ Don't forget to check the times of the last trains and buses.

You shouldn't take lifts from strangers …

7 Look at the photo on pages 12–13 and complete with these words.

> behind   between   in front of   near   next to   over

1 Steve is standing _between_ Jay and Leyla.
2 Kristin is standing _next to_ Alexey.
3 The thin man is _behind_ the girl in the orange top.
4 The girl in the orange top is _in front of_ the thin man.
5 The group are _near_ the London Eye.
6 The big wheel is _over_ their heads.

8 Complete with the gerund of these verbs.

> be (x3)   dance   give   go   learn   queue   wait

1 Some people don't like _being_ in large crowds.
2 Leyla is good at _dancing_ to all kinds of music.
3 I can't stand _waiting_ for people.
4 The fans don't like _queue_ in the rain.
5 Emma thinks she's bad at _learn_ languages.
6 Holly doesn't enjoy _being_ late.
7 Kristin likes _going_ to the cinema.
8 Carrie loves _giving_ presents.
9 Matt hates _being_ lost.

VOCABULARY

9 Match ten of these words with their definitions.

> candle   chemist's   costume   crowd   guide
> joke   medicine   newsagent's   outside
> parade   pickpocket   pilot   remember

1 someone that steals things from people's pockets
2 something you burn to give light
3 when people walk or dance in the street at a carnival
4 short funny story
5 shop where you can buy medicine
6 shop where you can buy newspapers
7 opposite of *inside*
8 clothes that you wear in a play or at a carnival
9 someone who shows tourists around
10 opposite of *forget*

10 Match the verbs in list A with the words and phrases in list B.

	A	B
1	change	hands
2	chat	a language
3	do	online
4	get up	yoga
5	hold	games
6	make	glasses
7	play	some money
8	speak	early
9	stay at	a hotel
10	wear	a wish

11 Find the odd word.

1 (cost) band parade stage
2 expensive famous exciting (costume)
3 under (street) behind opposite
4 carnival (hotel) festival party
5 newsagent's supermarket chemist's (bank)
6 (suitcase) website password email

LEARNER INDEPENDENCE
SELF ASSESSMENT

Look back at Lessons 1–3 in Units 1 and 2.

How good are you at …?	✓ Fine	? Not sure
1 Talking about regular activities Workbook pp4–5 exercises 2–4	☐	☒
2 Describing what's happening now Workbook pp6–7 exercises 2, 4 and 5	☒	☐
3 Talking about possessions Workbook pp8–9 exercises 2 and 5	☒	☐
4 Comparing things Workbook p17 exercises 3–6	☐	☒
5 Giving advice Workbook p18 exercises 1 and 2	☒	☐
6 Saying where things are Workbook p19 exercise 3	☒	☐
7 Talking about likes and dislikes Workbook p20 exercises 1 and 3	☒	☐
8 Saying what you can do Workbook p20 exercise 2	☐	☒

Not sure? Have a look at Language File pages 112–115 and do the Workbook exercise(s) again.

Now write an example for 1–8.

1 I go to the cinema on Saturdays.

PREVIEW

COMMUNICATIVE AIMS
LEARNING HOW TO ...

1 Talk about past events
2 Describe what was happening
3 Ask for and give reasons
4 Talk about future plans and intentions
5 Make predictions
6 Talk about the way people do things

TOPICS AND VOCABULARY

Buildings and places
Inventions
Transport
Time reference words
Jobs and occupations
American English
Recorded music
Feelings
Performance
Adverbs
TV programmes
Grammar words

A Why do most meteorites land in water?

B What will replace MP3 players?

C What is Dan going to do next?

1 Match the communicative aims (1–6) with the pictures (A–F).

2 Put the words into categories.

[Transport] [Jobs and occupations] [Feelings]

worried car happy
actor plane loud pilot musician
tired angry
bicycle teacher
doctor
boat pleased bus
scared scientist train

Actors work really hard.

F

The Great Fire of London destroyed most of the city.

My ears were ringing for hours afterwards.

E

3 Write three more words for each of these word families.

Buildings
museum _____ _____ _____

Performance
band _____ _____ _____

TV programmes
news _____ _____ _____

4 🔘 1.27 Listen to extracts 1–3 from Units 3 and 4. Match them with A–C below.

A A description of a TV series **3**
B A description of a historical event **1**
C A conversation about an accident **2**

5 Do the questionnaire with three other students.

FIRST TIME LAST TIME
Questionnaire

When was the FIRST time you …

When I was seven.

* went to the cinema?
* went on a train?
* rode a bicycle?
* used a computer?
* had an English lesson?

In 2002.

Last year.

I can't remember.

When was the LAST time you …

At nine o'clock.

* watched TV?
* saw a film?
* listened to music?
* read a book?
* bought a CD?

Last night.

Yesterday.

Two days ago.

What interesting or surprising things did you find out? Tell another group.

Believe it or not!

The word *time* comes first in the list of most common nouns in English! Third on the list (after *person*) is *year*, and *day* is fifth.

3 1 The fire started at a baker's

Talking about past events (1)
Past simple: affirmative and negative

The Great Fire

1 OPENER

Look at the picture of the Great Fire of London. Use these words to describe what you can see.

> boats   a bridge   buildings   burn   a church
> escape   flames   a river   smoke

2 READING

🔘 1.28   Read *The Great Fire*. What is the most surprising information in the text?

3 AFTER READING

True or false? Correct the false sentences.

1 The Great Fire of London was in 1665.
2 The fire started at a baker's.
3 The fire crossed the River Thames.
4 Samuel Pepys wrote about the fire in his diary.
5 Pepys and his wife left their home on Tuesday.
6 Pepys buried things in his garden.
7 The fire burnt for five days.
8 The fire destroyed 12,000 houses.
9 Most people escaped to the sea.
10 Under five people died in the fire.

Your response   Which of your possessions would you most like to save from a fire?

When the Romans came to Britain in the first century AD, they built a town called Londinium – London – on the river Thames. London became the most important city in Britain. But in 1666, the Great Fire of London destroyed most of the city …

The people of London were asleep when the Great Fire started early on Sunday, 2 September 1666. The fire started at a baker's in Pudding Lane, near London Bridge. After many weeks of hot weather and no rain, everything was very dry, and the wind quickly carried the flames to the River Thames. Luckily the fire didn't cross the river, but it reached tall buildings full of inflammable things like oil, sugar, butter and brandy.

Samuel Pepys wrote about the fire in his famous diary. When he got up on Sunday morning, he walked to the Tower of London and he saw houses on fire at the end of London Bridge. The fire wasn't near his house then, but Pepys went home and started to pack. At 4am on Monday the fire was much closer, and Pepys and his wife left their home in their nightclothes. They didn't have time to take a lot with them, and later that day Pepys returned and buried his wine and cheese in the garden!

The fire burnt for four days. By the evening of Wednesday, 5 September, there weren't many buildings left in London. The fire destroyed 13,300 houses in 400 streets, and most of the churches. Some people climbed into boats, but most people escaped to the fields outside the city, and only four people died in the fire.

4 VOCABULARY

Find the past tense of these verbs in the text. Which ones are irregular?

become   build   burn   bury   carry   climb   come   destroy   die
escape   get   leave   reach   return   see   start   walk   write

5 SPEAKING

Look at the quiz and make sentences using the past simple. Then match them with the people.

He built the first car.   *Karl Benz!*

QUIZ Who was the first?

1   He (build) the first car.
2   He (make) the first phone call.
3   He (be) the first person to travel in space.
4   He (make) the first cartoon film with sound.
5   He (design) the first helicopter.
6   They (show) the first films.
7   He (invent) the first ball-point pen.
8   He (take) the first photograph.
9   He (print) the first book in English.

1895
The Lumière brothers

1860
Antonio Meucci

1928
Walt Disney

1939
Igor Sikorsky

1885
Karl Benz

1961
Yuri Gagarin

1826
Joseph Niepce

1938
László Bíró

1475
William Caxton

1.29   Listen and check. Then write sentences.

In 1885, Karl Benz built the first car.

6 LISTENING

1.30   Listen and find five mistakes in the text.

Walt Disney was born in New York in 1901 and he studied at art school there. He started Walt Disney Studios with his sister on 16 October 1923. He married Lillian Bounds in 1928, and it was she who thought of the name Mickey Mouse. Disneyland, one of the world's first theme parks, opened in California on 27 July 1955. Disney planned another park in Florida, but he died on 15 November 1966 before it opened.

Now correct the mistakes in the text.

He was born in New York.   *No, he wasn't born in New York. He was born in _____ .*

Extension   Make more false statements about events in *The Great Fire.*

The fire started at a supermarket.   *No, it didn't! It started at a baker's.*

7 PRONUNCIATION

1.31   Listen and write the verbs in the correct column.

carried   crossed   designed
destroyed   escaped   invented
showed   started   walked

/d/	/t/	/ɪd/
designed	*crossed*	*carried*

Now listen and check. Repeat the words.

8 WRITING

Imagine you were in London at the time of the Great Fire. Write your diary! Use the text in exercise 2 to help you.

- What time did you get up?
- Who were you with?
- What did you see?
- What did you do?

Extension   Think about last weekend, and write answers to the questions above, including some false information. Then read out your sentences to another student. Can he/she guess which are false?

LANGUAGE WORKOUT

Complete.

Past simple of *be*: was/were
Everything **was** very dry.
The people _were_ asleep.
The fire w___n't near his house.
There _____n't many buildings left.

Past simple: regular verbs
The fire start__ at a baker's.
Most people escape__.
The wind carr__ the flames.
The fire **didn't** cross the river.

Past simple: irregular verbs
Samuel Pepys **wrote** about the fire.
They _____n't have time.

Regular and irregular verbs form the negative in the same way.

▶Answers and Practice
Language File page 115
Irregular Verbs page 127

Did you have fun?

Talking about past events (2)
Past simple: questions and short answers
Adverbial phrases of time

1 OPENER

Read *London Facts* and match the landmarks with the photos A–D.

2 READING

Read and complete the conversation with the places from exercise 1.

The group meet for a picnic lunch in a park.

ALEXEY Hi, guys. Did you have fun this morning?

KRISTIN Yes, we did. It was brilliant! First we went to the __1__.

JAY And we saw a great exhibition about the theatre in Shakespeare's time.

KRISTIN Then we walked from Tate Modern across the river over the __2__. And we spent an hour in __3__.

ALEXEY Did you climb up to the Whispering Gallery?

KRISTIN No, we didn't. But we climbed to the top of the __4__!

JAY Emma didn't. She was really lazy!

EMMA I wasn't lazy – I was thirsty! I sat outside and had a long cold drink! And the others were exhausted when they came down.

KRISTIN Well, there were hundreds of steps and it took ages! Ow, my feet hurt!

EMMA And what happened to you, Alexey? Were you asleep all morning?

ALEXEY No, I wasn't!

🔴 1.32 Now listen and check.

LONDON *Facts*

* The old **St Paul's Cathedral** burnt down in 1666, and the famous architect Christopher Wren designed the present cathedral. Building work started in 1675, but Wren didn't receive the second half of the payment for his work until the cathedral was complete in 1710 – 35 years later!

* Christopher Wren also designed the **Monument** to the Great Fire of London. It stands near London Bridge and there is a spectacular view from the top – but there are 311 steps to climb!

* The **Millennium Bridge** is the newest bridge over the Thames. It opened in 2000 and crosses the river from Tate Modern to St Paul's Cathedral.

* The **Globe Theatre** is a copy of Shakespeare's original Globe Theatre of 400 years ago, It's next to Tate Modern, and it's the first building in London with a thatched roof since the Great Fire! The first performance in the new Globe was on 21 August 1996.

3 AFTER READING AND LISTENING

Answer the questions.

1 What did the group do first this morning?
2 Did they see a play?
3 How did they cross the river?
4 Where did they spend an hour?
5 Did Emma climb the steps?
6 Was she hungry?
7 Were the others tired?
8 Was Alexey asleep all morning?

Your response Which of the places would you most like to visit? Why? Which do you think is the least interesting? Why?

A

B

4 PRONUNCIATION

🔵 1.33 Listen and count the syllables. Mark the stress.

architect brilliant cathedral exhausted
exhibition gallery millennium monument
original performance spectacular

■
architect 3

5 LISTENING

🔵 1.34 Listen to Alexey and match the actions with the times.

9.00–10.00	go to a music shop
10.00–11.00	have an ice cream in a café
11.00–12.00	sit in the park
12.00–1.15	surf the Internet

Now ask and answer.

> What did Alexey do between nine and ten o'clock?

> Did he go to a music shop?

> No, he didn't. He …

Extension Play *Past Simple Challenge.*

> see   saw

6 SPEAKING

What did you do last weekend? Think about Saturday and Sunday – morning, afternoon and evening. List six different things, but don't write the times!

I went swimming.   I bought some jeans.

Exchange lists with another student. Ask questions to find out when he/she did things. You can only ask 20 questions! Note down the answers.

> Did you go swimming on Saturday morning?

> No, I didn't.

> Did you go swimming in the afternoon?

> Yes, I did!

7 WRITING

Write your diary for last weekend.

Saturday
In the morning I went shopping and bought some jeans. At 2.30pm I went swimming ...

Extension Read *London Facts* again and think about landmarks in your town. Find out information and write one or two sentences about each of them.

LANGUAGE WORKOUT

Complete.

Past simple: questions and short answers
What **did** you do?
How _did_ they cross the river?
Did you have fun?   Yes, we **did**.
Did they see a play?   No, they _didn't_.
Was Alexey asleep all morning? No, he **wasn't**.
Were they exhausted?   Yes, they _were_.

Regular and _irregular_ verbs form questions in the same way.

Adverbial phrases of time
on Saturday (morning)   **on** 21 August
in the morning **in** August **in** 1666
at 9am **at** night

▶**Answers and Practice**
Language File pages 115–116

3 It was coming straight towards him

Describing what was happening
Asking for and giving reasons
Past continuous
Why? because

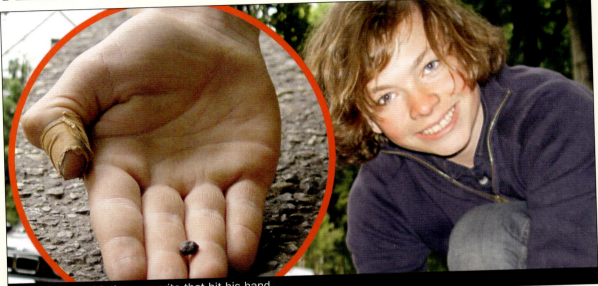

TEENAGER HIT BY METEORITE

Gerrit Blank with the mereorite that hit his hand

On 5 June 2009, Gerrit Blank was walking to the school bus when he saw a ball of light in the sky. It was coming straight towards him – a meteorite! The red-hot rock burnt the schoolboy's hand and hit the ground so hard that it made a 30cm-long hole in the road.

The meteorite crashed to Earth in Essen in Germany. 14-year-old Gerrit told reporters: 'I saw a large ball of light and then I suddenly felt a pain in my hand. A moment later, there was an enormous bang, like thunder! The noise was so loud that my ears were ringing for hours afterwards. After the meteorite hit me, it was still falling fast enough to make a hole in the road.'

Gerrit took the tiny piece of rock to school and told the story of his lucky escape. His classmates believed him. 'I'm really keen on science and my teachers discovered that the rock is magnetic,' he added. Experts think it was travelling at about 500 kilometres per hour when it hit Gerrit.

Most meteorites don't actually reach Earth because they burn up in the atmosphere. Some of them hit the ground, but most of them land in water. It's extremely rare for meteorites to hit people – the chance is about 1 in 100 million. As far as we know, there's only one other case where a person survived a meteorite strike. In November 1954 a rock crashed through the roof of a house in Alabama, USA. It landed on housewife Ann Hodges, who was asleep on the sofa because she wasn't feeling well.

1 OPENER

Look at the newspaper headline and photos. Which of these words do you expect to find in the newspaper article?

atmosphere ball bridge crash escape
ground helicopter hit hole magnetic
rock roof suitcase water

2 READING

🔘 1.35 Read the newspaper article and check your answers to exercise 1.

3 AFTER READING

Answer the questions.

1 What was Gerrit doing when a meteorite hit him?
2 What did he see in the sky?
3 What did he feel, and what did he hear?
4 Was the meteorite large? How do you know?
5 How fast was it travelling when it hit Gerrit?
6 Do meteorites often hit people?
7 Did the meteorite kill Ann Hodges?
8 Was she reading when the meteorite hit her?

Your response Do you believe Gerrit's story? Why/Why not?

4 SPEAKING

Ask questions 1–5 and choose the correct answers from reasons a–e.

1 Why were Gerrit's ears ringing for hours?
2 Why did the meteorite make a hole in the ground?
3 Why are most meteorites magnetic?
4 Why don't most meteorites reach the Earth?
5 Why do most meteorites land in water?

a Because they contain iron.
b Because they burn up in the atmosphere.
c Because water covers more than two-thirds of the Earth.
d Because it was falling so fast.
e Because there was an enormous bang when the meteorite hit the ground.

Now write sentences with *because*.

1 Gerrit's ears were ringing for hours because ...

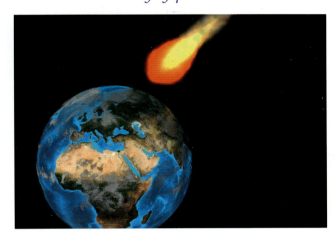

5 LISTENING

🔘 1.36 Emma's brother, Lee, had a lucky escape. Listen and decide: true or false?

1 Lee fell overboard last month.
2 He was sailing with a friend off the coast of Spain.
3 At first the sun was shining.
4 Then the weather got better and there was a storm.
5 It was dangerous because they were sailing in a big boat.
6 Lee called the emergency number on his mobile phone.
7 They were swimming back when the boat hit a rock.
8 A speedboat rescued them.
9 Lee wasn't happy because he lost his watch.

Correct the false sentences. Then write a paragraph about Lee's lucky escape.

Lee fell overboard last year. He was sailing ...

6 PRONUNCIATION

🔘 1.37 Listen and repeat.

/w/

Why was the white whale whistling when it was swimming in the wonderful warm water?

7 VOCABULARY

Make a word map for transport. Use these words and add other words you know.

Word Bank Transport

bicycle boat bus car helicopter plane
rocket ship spaceship speedboat taxi train

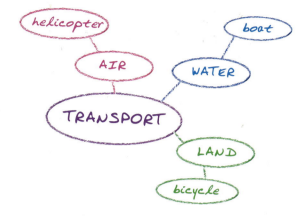

Extension Play *Word Association*.

boat river water swim fish chips

8 WRITING

Write a paragraph about a lucky escape.
Where were you? What were you doing?
What happened? Why did it happen?

I was near the station. I was cycling to school. I nearly fell off because a bus stopped suddenly in front of me.

Extension Write about what you were doing and how you felt when you heard some dramatic news.

I was playing football in the park when I heard about ....

LANGUAGE WORKOUT

Complete.

Past continuous: *was/were* + present participle
He **was** walking to the school bus when he saw a ball of light.
It _____ travelling at about 500 km/h when it hit him.
My ears _____ ringing for hours.
She _____ n't feeling well.
What _____ he doing?
_____ she reading?   No, she wasn't.

We use the past continuous to say what was happening at a particular time in the past.

***Why? because* (reason)**
Why was she asleep   She was asleep on the sofa
on the sofa?   **because** she wasn't feeling well.

▶**Answers and Practice**
Language File page 116

1 OPENER

You are going to read about William Shakespeare. Which of these words do you expect to find in the text?

actor architect meteorite performance play playwright roof spaceship tragedies

READING

2 Read the text about Shakespeare and match four of these topics with paragraphs 1–4.

Fame and fortune   Marriage problems
Later life   Foreign travel
Early career   The first years

3 Complete the text with these words.

Word Bank
Time reference words

after between by finally for in later on next soon until when

🔊 1.38 Now listen and check.

4 Answer these questions about Shakespeare.

1 When and where was he born?
2 When did he get married? Who did he marry?
3 How many children did they have?
4 When did he start writing plays?
5 How many plays did he write?
6 What else did he write?
7 When did he die?
8 Why is he important today?

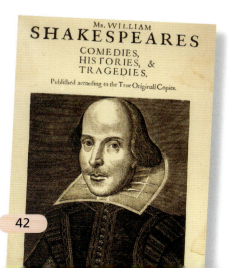

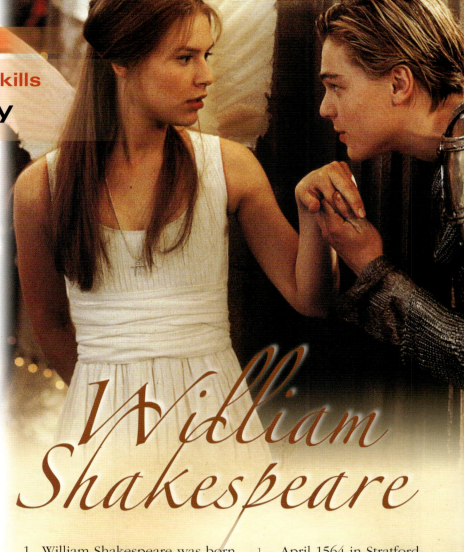

William Shakespeare

1 William Shakespeare was born __1__ April 1564 in Stratford-upon-Avon, in the centre of England. He went to school in Stratford and he probably became a teacher. In 1582, __2__ he was 18, he married Anne Hathaway and they soon had three children.

2 In the late 1580s, he decided to leave Stratford and try to find work in London. __3__ this time, there were several theatres in the city – the first public theatre opened in London in 1567. Shakespeare joined an acting company, and soon he was also writing plays. He quickly became a well-known actor and playwright.

3 __4__ 1589 and 1600, Shakespeare wrote about 20 plays, including *A Midsummer Night's Dream* and *Romeo and Juliet*. His plays were extremely popular and there were even special performances for Queen Elizabeth I! Shakespeare __5__ became the most important playwright in the country. He was now a rich man, and was a part-owner of the Globe Theatre, which opened in 1599. He lived and worked in London __6__ many years, but he often went home to see his wife and children in Stratford.

4 Shakespeare's success continued into the __7__ century, when he wrote some of his most famous tragedies, including *Hamlet* and *Othello*. In all, he wrote 37 plays, and he also wrote many beautiful poems. __8__, he returned to Stratford in 1611, and he lived there __9__ he died, aged exactly 52, __10__ 23 April 1616. In his will, he left his wife his second-best bed! __11__ his death, two actor friends collected all his plays and published them in 1623. Today, 400 years __12__, he is one of the most famous writers in the world, and there are many films of his plays.

5 LISTENING

1.39 Listen to a description of the life of Charles Dickens, the English novelist, and complete the chart with dates and numbers.

Charles Dickens

Date	
7 February 1812	Born in Portsmouth, on the south coast of England.
1823	Family moved to London.
1824	Left school, started working in a factory.
1836	First novel: *The Pickwick Papers*.
1836	Married Catherine Hogarth, had 10 children.
1842	Visited the USA and wrote *American Notes*, which criticised slavery.
1836–65	Wrote 14 major novels, including *Oliver Twist*, *David Copperfield*, and the ghost story *A Christmas Carol*.
9 June 1870	Died suddenly after a tour of the USA. Most popular English writer of the 19 th century.
Over 140 **years later**	His books are still bestsellers, many films of his novels.

6 SPEAKING

Ask and answer questions about the life of Charles Dickens. Use the questions in exercise 4 to help you.

> When was he born? — On 7 February 1812.

7 WRITING

Find out information about a famous person in your country: for example, a writer, a musician, or an artist. Make notes about the person's life, similar to the chart in exercise 5.

Now write four paragraphs about the person. Use some of the topics from exercise 2 and time reference words from exercise 3.

LEARNER INDEPENDENCE

8 When you want to learn new words, you can make associations. For example, you can associate a word:

- with a picture in your mind
- with a sound or a colour
- with other words in the same category
- with a word in your language
- with a person or a story

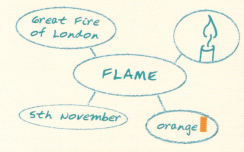

Choose some words and try to learn them by making associations.

9 Word maps are a great way to organise vocabulary. In lesson 3 you made a word map for transport. Now make a word map for jobs and occupations.

10 1.40 **Phrasebook:** Find these useful expressions in Unit 3. Then listen and repeat.

> Did you have fun?
> It was brilliant!
> It took ages!
> Ow, my feet hurt!
> What happened to you?
> There was an enormous bang!
> I'm really keen on …
> It's extremely rare.
> As far as we know, …
> She wasn't feeling well.

Now think of other situations where you could use each of the four exclamations.

'It was brilliant!'
Talking about a film.

Inspiration EXTRA!

LANGUAGE LINKS

Read and find out what these dates and numbers refer to.

1604   250 million   1620s   1475   6 million

English past and present

In Shakespeare's time, around 6 million people spoke English and they all lived in Britain. Then people emigrated to North America in the 1620s, and to Australia and New Zealand in the 1770s and 1790s. Today there are about 60 million English-speakers in Britain, 250 million in the USA, 27 million in Canada, 18 million in Australia and nearly 4 million in New Zealand.

Books and spelling

William Caxton printed the first book in English in 1475. In Caxton's time different people spelt words in different ways. Caxton himself spelt *book* sometimes *booke* and sometimes *boke*. The first dictionary appeared in 1604, but it only contained 3,000 words. It wasn't until 100 years later that everyone agreed on how to spell English words.

How many words are there in English today?

A 10,000   B 100,000   C At least 1,000,000

SKETCH *Shakespeare*

🔴 1.41 Read and listen.

Two tourists are visiting the exhibition at the Globe Theatre.

WOMAN   Look at all these things from the theatre in Shakespeare's time!

MAN   Yes, isn't it exciting! There's Shakespeare's computer!

WOMAN   No, that's impossible!

MAN   What do you mean?

WOMAN   Well, Shakespeare didn't use a computer.

MAN   Didn't he?

WOMAN   No, they didn't have computers in those days. Shakespeare used a typewriter.

MAN   Oh, yes, of course.

WOMAN   Do you think that's Shakespeare's TV?

MAN   Where?

WOMAN   Over there. It's very old.

MAN   No, Shakespeare didn't have a TV.

WOMAN   Why not?

MAN   Because he went to the theatre every night. He didn't have time to sit at home and watch TV.

WOMAN   No, of course not.

MAN   Look at these! CDs of all Shakespeare's plays!

WOMAN   Did he have a CD recorder?

MAN   Yes, I'm sure he did. I expect he recorded all his plays at the Globe Theatre.

WOMAN   Oh, and here's an old telephone!

MAN   Hey, why don't we call Shakespeare!

WOMAN   Don't be silly! We can't call him.

MAN   Why not?

WOMAN   Because we don't know his phone number!

Based on a sketch in English Sketches 2 by Doug Case and Ken Wilson

Now act out the sketch in pairs.

Game *Link-up*

- Form two teams.
- One team chooses a letter square from the game board. The teacher asks a question about a word beginning with the letter. If the team guesses the word, they win the square.
- Then the other team chooses a letter square …
- The first team to win a line of *linked* squares from top to bottom or from left to right is the winner. You can go in any direction, but all your squares must touch!

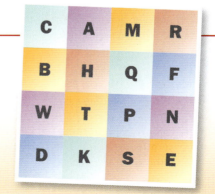

LESSON 1 Choose ten verbs from page 37, exercise 4. Write a sentence with each verb in the past simple.

Karl Benz built the first car.

LESSON 2 Look at *London Facts* on page 38. Write questions beginning *When ...? What ...?* or *Who ...?* about the four landmarks, and answer the questions. Use the past simple.

When did the old St Paul's Cathedral burn down?
In 1666.

LESSON 3 Look at the photos on page 40. Write questions about what Gerrit was doing/wearing, and then answer them.

Was Gerrit crying?
No, he wasn't crying, he was ...

LESSON 4 Imagine you are interviewing Shakespeare's ghost. Look at the Reading text on page 42 and the questions in exercise 4. Write an interview between yourself and Shakespeare's ghost.

Me: When and where were you born?
Ghost: I was born in April 1564 in
*   Stratford-upon-Avon.*

LESSON 1 Write your diary for yesterday, saying what you did and didn't do.

LESSON 2 Look at the conversation on page 38 and your answers to exercise 5. Write a similar conversation between yourself and Alexey.

Me: Hi, Alexey! Did you have fun this morning?

LESSON 3 Look back at the photo in Unit 1 Lesson 2. Write sentences about what people were doing/wearing and where they were standing.

Steve was telling everyone about the London Eye. He was wearing ...

LESSON 4 Look at the Reading text on page 42 and at your completed chart in Listening exercise 5. Write four paragraphs about the life of Charles Dickens.

YOUR CHOICE!

SIMPLY THE BEST!

- Work in a small group.
- Think about the best things that happened to you last week. Make a list, for example:

  At home: *the best meal I had / the best TV programme I saw / the best game I played / the best song I heard / the best surprise I had was ...*

  At school: *the best lesson I had / the best piece of work I did / the best homework I had / the best book I read / the best website I visited was ...*

- Take turns to ask and answer questions about the best things that happened last week.

  A   What was the best meal you had?
  B   Spaghetti – I love pasta.

SURVEY: TRANSPORT

- Work in a small group.
- Each group member interviews three other students and notes down the answers. Ask these questions:

  How did you get to school today?
  Is it the same every day?
  How did your parents get to work today?
  Is it the same every day?
  How did you travel when you last went on holiday?
  What's your favourite way of travelling?

- Now work together and use your notes to write a summary of the interviews. Compare your summary with another group.

  Today five students walked to school, three cycled, six came by bus, and the rest came by car.

HELLO New York! Quiz

1 In 1624 the first people came to live in New York from Europe. They were

Ⓐ French   Ⓑ Dutch   Ⓒ English   Ⓓ Italian

2 New York City is on the

Ⓐ Kennedy River   Ⓑ Times River
Ⓒ Hudson River   Ⓓ Liberty River

3 Manhattan is

Ⓐ a forest   Ⓑ a person
Ⓒ an island   Ⓓ a river

4 The population of New York City is

Ⓐ 6,000,000   Ⓑ 8,000,000
Ⓒ 10,000,000   Ⓓ 12,000,000

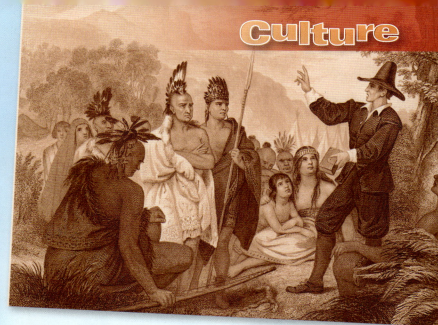

1 OPENER

How much do you know about New York?
Try our New York quiz on page 46.

2 READING

🔵 1.42 Read *The first New Yorkers* and check
your answers to the quiz. Then number
these events to show the order in which
they happened.

A An Italian sailed into New York harbour.
B The English changed the name to New York.
C The Algonquian Indians lived on the island
of Mannahatta.
D An Englishman discovered the Hudson River.
E A Dutchman bought Manhattan.

VOCABULARY

3 Match the words with their definitions.

1 native   4 explorer
2 forest   5 boss
3 island   6 nonsense

a piece of land with water around it
b something that isn't true or an idea that
seems very stupid
c people who were born in the place
d person in charge at work
e someone who travels to new places to find
out what they are like
f large area covered with trees

4 Match these British and American words.

British English	American English
car park	apartment
chemist's	cellphone
chips	drugstore
film	French fries
flat	garbage, trash
mobile phone	movie
railway	sneakers
rubbish	parking lot
trainers	railroad
shop	store

5 MINI-PROJECT
Town History

Work with another student and write a
short history of your town. Use *The first
New Yorkers* and these questions to
help you.

● Where is your town?
● When did people first live there?
Where did they come from?
● What was the town called at that time?
Did it have the same name as now?
● What are the important dates in your
town's history? Why are they important?

Read your work carefully and correct any
mistakes. Then show your *Town History* to
other students.

The first New Yorkers

Only a few hundred years ago, the only people to live
in New York were Native Americans – the Algonquian
Indians. They lived in a forest on an island, which they
called Mannahatta. Then Giovanni da Verrazano, an Italian
explorer, discovered New York harbour in 1524 and in 1609
an Englishman, Henry Hudson, found the Hudson River. But
it was the Dutch who came to live in New York in 1624. In
1626 a Dutchman called Peter Minuit bought Mannahatta
island from the Algonquian Indians for $24 – today the island
is called Manhattan. The Dutch name for their town was
New Amsterdam, but in 1664 the English took the town and
changed the name to New York after the English town of York.
At that time, the population of New York was about 1,500 –
now there are eight million New Yorkers!

People continued to speak Dutch in parts of New York well
into the nineteenth century. Many words in American English
came from the Dutch who lived in New York. These include:
boss, Yankee, cookie (= biscuit), *nitwit* (= stupid person) and
poppycock (= nonsense). The question *How come?* (meaning
Why?) also comes from a Dutch word, *hoekom*. The grammar
of American English is very similar to British English but
the vocabulary is often different. For example, *pants* is the
American English word for *trousers*, but in British English
pants are what you wear under trousers.

He isn't going to go to university

Talking about future plans and intentions
going to: future

1 OPENER

Who is the actor in the photos? Do you know the names of any of his films? Do you like the books which the films come from?

2 READING

2.01 Read *Dan the Man*. What are the three most interesting facts in the text?

Dan the Man

Daniel Radcliffe (Dan to his friends) was a boy wizard at 11 and he spent his teen years making the eight Harry Potter films. He became one of the world's two highest earning teenagers (the other was Miley Cyrus) and the Potter films overtook James Bond as the most successful movie series in film history.

Is JK Rowling going to write any more Harry Potter novels? No. So what is Dan going to do next? One thing he wants is for people to take him seriously as a stage actor. He's now having singing and dancing lessons because he's going to star in a musical in New York.

Acting is Dan's life and he isn't going to go to university, unlike his co-star Emma Watson – she's going to study in the USA. In fact, Dan wasn't always happy at school, and some of the other boys bullied him.

A little-known fact is that Dan can't ride a bike or swim because he suffers from dyspraxia, which affects his coordination. It means, for example, that it's hard for him to do up his shoes, or write neatly. He's also sensitive about his height – he's 1 metre 65.

And what does he think of JK Rowling? 'She is fantastically attractive. Very, very beautiful. And so intelligent, it's frightening.'

3 AFTER READING

Answer the questions.

1 How old was Dan when he first played Harry Potter?
2 Are there going to be any new *Harry Potter* books?
3 Why is Dan having singing and dancing lessons?
4 Is Dan going to continue with his education?
5 What happened to him at school?
6 Why does Dan have bad handwriting?
7 What three adjectives does Dan use to describe JK Rowling?

Your response Why do you think some boys bullied Dan at school? What causes bullying?

4 LISTENING

2.02 Listen to Steve. What are the competition winners going to do in the afternoon?

a have a tour of a film studio ✓
b watch a *Harry Potter* film
c watch a rehearsal
d visit other studios
e interview the actors
f rehearse
g act in a film
h appear on a TV quiz
i have a party with the actors
j meet Daniel Radcliffe

5 SPEAKING

Ask and answer questions about the afternoon's plans.

A Are they going to have a tour of a film studio?
B Yes, they are.

Now write ten sentences about the afternoon.

They're going to have a tour of a film studio.
They aren't ...

6 PRONUNCIATION

Match the words in box A with their rhymes in box B.

A	B
friend	break
height	choose
make	fight
quiz	here
shoes	his
teen	mean
tour	send
year	sure

2.03 Now listen and check.

Extension Think of more rhyming words with different spellings. Make a list and then play rhyming pairs with another student.

speak   week   course   horse

7 SPEAKING

Think about your next holiday – real or imaginary! Ask other students about their holiday plans.

● Where are you going to go? Who with? For how long?
● How are you going to get there?
● Where are you going to stay?
● What are you going to do on your holiday?

Extension Write about what other students are going to do on holiday.

Emilia is going to go to California with her best friend for a month.

8 WRITING

Read this email from a friend and write a reply. Use the questions in exercise 7 to help you.

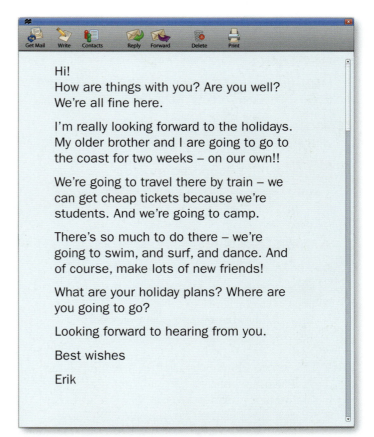

Get Mail Write Contacts Reply Forward Delete Print

Hi!
How are things with you? Are you well? We're all fine here.

I'm really looking forward to the holidays. My older brother and I are going to go to the coast for two weeks – on our own!!

We're going to travel there by train – we can get cheap tickets because we're students. And we're going to camp.

There's so much to do there – we're going to swim, and surf, and dance. And of course, make lots of new friends!

What are your holiday plans? Where are you going to go?

Looking forward to hearing from you.

Best wishes

Erik

LANGUAGE WORKOUT

***going to:* future**
He**'s going to** star in a musical.
She's _____ _____ study in the USA.
He **isn't going to** go to university.
_____ JK Rowling _____ _____ write any more *Harry Potter* novels?
What _____ Dan _____ _____ do next?

We use *going to* to talk about plans and intentions.

▶**Answers and Practice**
Language File page 116

2 Which will we choose?

Making predictions
Future simple: will/won't

MUSIC TO YOUR EARS
-the history of recorded music

1 OPENER

When and where do you listen to music? Do you download it or listen to CDs?

2 READING

Match the photos 1–5 with these ways of listening to music: cassette, CD, LP, MP3 player, phonograph.

2.04 Now read *Music to your Ears* and complete it with these words. Then listen and check.

> **Word Bank** Recorded music
>
> cassette tapes   CDs   LPs   MP3 players   records

3 AFTER READING

True or false? Correct the false sentences.

1 In the 19th century cylinders were more popular than records.
2 Thomas Edison invented the tape recorder.
3 Tape recorders weren't available in the USA until 1948.
4 LPs became less popular after the invention of the Walkman.
5 CDs were very expensive when they first appeared.
6 Most people think that CDs will replace MP3 players.

Your response What do you think will replace MP3 players? How will we listen to music in ten or twenty years' time?

4 PRONUNCIATION

2.05 Listen and repeat.

/ɪ/ will	/iː/ we'll
live	leave
fit	feet
it	eat
sit	seat
tin	teen
fill	feel

Now listen and write the words you hear.

1877

Thomas Edison invented the phonograph, which recorded sound on cylinders. Four years later Charles Tainter invented the first flat disc record. Which were the most popular: cylinders or records? Surprisingly, __1__ weren't popular for another fifty years. Until the 1920s most people listened to music on cylinders on a phonograph.

1928 and 1948

In 1928 Dr Fritz Pfleumer invented tape recording in Germany, but tape recorders weren't available in the USA until twenty years later. Also in 1948 the invention of the LP (long-playing record) meant that people could hear more music on each record – around 23 minutes a side. Which did people choose: tapes or LPs? Most people chose __2__, but after Sony introduced the Walkman in 1979 more and more people listened to __3__.

1982

Compact discs appeared in 1982. At first they were very expensive, but by the 1990s they were more popular than both LPs and cassettes. But how much longer will CDs be popular? Apple introduced the first iPod in 2001 and more and more people bought internet-based MP3 players.

The Future

MP3 or CD: which will we choose? Most people think that __4__ will soon replace __5__. The big question is: what will replace MP3 players? We won't know the answer to that question for a few years.

5 SPEAKING

What do you think will happen next? Choose A, B, or C.

> I think Emma will say she's got no money.

> I don't agree – I think she'll say it's a great idea because she loves shopping

1 Leyla and Kristin want Emma to go shopping with them. Will Emma …
   A say no because she's got no money?
   B say no because she's too tired?
   C say it's a great idea?

2 Steve brings his dog to the hotel. Will Jay …
   A say he's afraid of dogs?
   B say he prefers cats?
   C say he wants to take the dog for a walk?

3 It's Leyla's birthday. Kristin gives her a black T-shirt as a present. Will Leyla …
   A say thank you and then try and change it?
   B say she loves black?
   C say thank you and not wear the T-shirt?

4 Ramón is playing the guitar. Will Alexey…
   A start dancing?
   B start singing?
   C take some photos?

2.06 Now listen and check.

> **Extension** What will happen to the characters in Units 5–8? Look at the pictures and lesson titles and make predictions.
>
> *I think they'll go to a pizza restaurant.*

6 WRITING

What do you think will happen to you in the future? What are your hopes? Think about travel, work, home and relationships, and write predictions.

I'm sure I'll travel a lot but I don't think I'll work abroad.

Now compare your predictions with other students.

LANGUAGE WORKOUT

Complete.

Future simple: *will/won't*
MP3 players _____ soon replace CDs.
We _____ know the answer for a few years.
What _____ replace MP3 players?
Which _____ we choose?

We can use *will/won't* to say what we predict or hope about the future.

▶**Answers and Practice**
Language File page 117

3 You spoke too fast

Talking about the way people do things
Adverbs of manner

1 OPENER

Look at the photo of the group at the film studio.
Which of these adjectives describe how they are feeling?

Word Bank Feelings

angry   comfortable   happy   nervous   pleased   sad

Guess: What is Steve saying?

2 READING

🔘 2.07 Read the dialogue and check your answers to exercise 1.

STEVE   Is everyone sitting comfortably? Well, I've got some bad news for you. The director isn't going to use your scene in the film.

JAY   Oh, no! What a shame! Why not?

STEVE   I'm afraid she thinks you acted badly.

EMMA   But I don't understand – it doesn't make sense. We weren't acting, we were being ourselves.

STEVE   I know, and I thought you did very well. But the director thinks you spoke too fast.

EMMA   That's absurd! We just spoke normally, that's all.

RAMÓN   I think it's because we didn't have enough time to rehearse properly.

STEVE   It's not just a question of rehearsing, Ramón. Actors work extremely hard – they spend hours doing drama exercises.

LEYLA   Can you do some of these exercises with us?

STEVE   Of course. Does everyone want to try?

ALL   Yes, please.

3 AFTER READING

Match the questions with the answers.
There are two wrong answers.

1   Why isn't the director going to use the group's scene?
2   What does the director think about the way they spoke?
3   How did the group speak?
4   What does Ramón think the problem was?
5   How do actors spend a lot of their time?
6   What is Steve going to do with the group?

a   In the way that they usually do.
b   Doing drama exercises.
c   They're going to rehearse the scene again.
d   She thinks they spoke too quickly.
e   Some drama exercises.
f   Steve thinks they spoke too slowly.
g   He thinks they needed a longer rehearsal.
h   Because she didn't like their performance.

Your response How do you feel when you are performing in front of people – for example, acting in a role play, playing music, doing gymnastics? Do you enjoy it? Why/Why not?

4 PRONUNCIATION

🔘 2.08 Listen and write the words in the correct column.

> comfortably director exercise extremely happily
> normally properly rehearsal tomorrow

comfortably

Now listen and check. Repeat the words.

5 LISTENING

🔘 2.09 Steve explains two drama exercises to the group. Listen and choose the correct answer.

1 In the first exercise Steve tells them how to run/walk/ move.
2 In the second exercise he tells them to sing/talk/play.

Now listen to the second drama exercise and guess the adverb of manner before the group! Choose from the adverbs in the Word Bank.

1 Alexey 2 Emma 3 Jay 4 Kristin 5 Leyla 6 Ramón

> **Word Bank** *Adverbs of manner*
>
> angrily happily loudly nervously politely
> quickly quietly rudely sadly slowly

> **Extension** Do the drama exercises using the adverbs in the Word Bank.

6 VOCABULARY

Match the definitions 1–6 with six of these nouns.

> **Word Bank** Performance
>
> actor band character concert drama
> director film musician play rehearsal
> scene stage studio show theatre

1 place where people make a film or TV/radio programme
2 short part of a film or play
3 practice of a play, piece of music, etc before a performance
4 person in a film, book or play
5 part of a theatre where actors/musicians perform
6 person who tells the actors what to do

> **Extension** Write definitions of five more words from the Word Bank. Then read out your definitions to another student, but don't say the words. Can he/she guess the words?

7 WRITING

Write a paragraph describing a character in a film or TV series.

- Who is the character and where does he/she live?
- What does he/she do?
- What does he/she usually wear?
- How does he/she talk and behave?
- Why do/don't you like the character?

> ## LANGUAGE WORKOUT
>
> Complete.
>
> **Adverbs of manner**
>
> | Regular | | Irregular | |
> |---|---|---|---|
> | **Adjective** | **Adverb** | **Adjective** | **Adverb** |
> | bad | ____**ly** | early | early |
> | normal | ____ | fast | ____ |
> | proper | ____ | good | ____ |
> | quick | quick**ly** | hard | hard |
> | comfortab**le** | comfortab**ly** | late | late |
> | angr**y** | angr**ily** | | |
> | happ**y** | happ**ily** | | |
>
> We use adverbs of manner to describe how we do something.
>
> ▶**Answers and Practice**
> Language File page 117

TV programmes

CLASSIC **TV** SERIES

1 _____

The imaginary city of Springfield, USA is the setting for one for the world's most successful TV series. People in over 70 countries follow the activities of the cartoon characters in *The Simpsons*, a satire of middle-class American life. Matt Groening created the Simpson family – he named Homer, Marge, Lisa and Maggie after his own parents and sisters, and substituted Bart for his own name. The first broadcast was in 1989, and the show is now the longest-running American sitcom.

2 _____

Medical drama series are always popular and one of the best is *Scrubs*, which takes place in a hospital and a medical school. The lives and loves of doctors, nurses and their patients are what a hospital series is all about. There's both comedy and tragedy in this fast-moving show, which is action-packed with accidents, serious illnesses and emergencies, as well as romance.

3 _____

In *Ugly Betty,* clever, friendly Betty Suarez works in an office for a fashion magazine. She isn't pretty and she doesn't wear fashionable clothes, but she's a lovely character. There's often trouble in the office and Betty always helps her boss with his many problems. The first broadcast was in 1999 in Colombia – now the soap is very popular all over the world, from India to Mexico, and from Italy to Japan.

4 _____

Millions of people around the world watch *Heroes*. In this science fiction series, ordinary people suddenly discover that they can do extraordinary things: for example, an artist can paint pictures of the future, a police officer can hear other people's thoughts, a businessman can travel through time, and a politician can fly. They come together to try to save the world – but will they succeed?

1 OPENER

What are the names of popular TV programmes in your country? What kinds of programmes are they? Choose from these words. Can you think of an example of each kind of programme?

Word Bank TV programmes

cartoon   chat show   drama   documentary   game show
music programme   news programme   reality show
science fiction programme   sitcom   soap (opera)
sports programme   talent show   thriller

2 READING

Read the descriptions of TV series and match the paragraphs with the pictures. Then choose a title for each paragraph.

Office Favourite   Extraordinary People   Family Life   Life and Death

🔘 2.10 Now listen and check.

3 LISTENING

🔘 2.11 Carrie talks about her favourite TV series. Listen and choose the correct answer.

1 What's the name of Carrie's favourite TV series?
   A *Changing Times*.
   B *Changing Places*.
2 What's it about?
   A People in a big city.
   B People in a small town.
3 Where does it take place?
   A In Santa Lucia.
   B In San Lorenzo.
4 How often is it on?
   A Every day.
   B Five times a week.
5 What was the most exciting episode?
   A Two people escaped from a fire.
   B Two people escaped from prison.
6 And what's happening at the moment?
   A They're looking for a mother.
   B They're looking for a murderer.

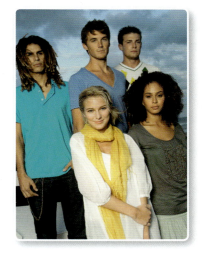

4 SPEAKING

Look at the questions in exercise 3. Ask another student about their favourite TV series.

What's your favourite TV series?

5 WRITING

Write a paragraph about a popular TV series. Use the texts in this lesson to help you.

- What's the TV series about?
- Where does it take place?
- What happened in a recent episode?
- What's happening at the moment?
- What do you think will happen next?

LEARNER INDEPENDENCE

6 It's important to know which words can go together. Match the verbs with as many adverbs as possible.

Verbs
eat   drink   listen   look   speak
understand   walk   write

Adverbs
angrily   carefully   easily   happily
hungrily   quickly   slowly   thirstily

When you find useful word combinations, write them in your vocabulary notebook.

Verb + Adverb	Verb + Noun
eat hungrily	take place

7 To use a dictionary properly, you need to know the meanings of grammar words. Match these words with the grammar words in the Word Bank.

at   boring   camera   dancing
make   slowly   they   to see

Word Bank
Grammar words

adjective   adverb   gerund
infinitive   noun   preposition
pronoun   verb

Look at the Language File for Units 1–4 on pages 112–117 and find the grammar words.

8 🔘 2.12 **Phrasebook:** Find these useful expressions in Unit 4. Then listen and repeat.

How are things with you?
The big question is …
I've got some bad news for you.
What a shame!
I'm afraid …
I don't understand.
It doesn't make sense.
That's absurd!

Now write a four-line dialogue using two or more of the expressions.

A   *I've got some bad news for you.*
B   *What?*
A   *I'm afraid I can't get tickets for the concert.*
B   *Oh, what a shame!*

PROJECT *TV programmes*

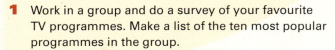

1 Work in a group and do a survey of your favourite TV programmes. Make a list of the ten most popular programmes in the group.

2 Look again at Unit 4 Lesson 4 and at the work you did in exercise 5 about your favourite TV series. Then look at your group's list of the most popular TV programmes and choose three to write about.

3 Make notes about each programme:
- What kind of programme is it? Who is in it?
- What channel is it on? When is it on? How often is it on?
- Who do you watch it with? Why do you like it?
- Do you know a surprising fact about it?

4 Work together and write about the programmes. Read your work carefully and correct any mistakes. Find photographs for each programme from magazines or online. Show your work to the other groups.

Strictly Come Dancing is one of the world's most popular TV talent shows, with viewers in over 30 different countries. In the show, celebrities have a week to learn and perform a new dance. It's on once a week, on Saturday evenings. All the family watch it and enjoy seeing the celebrities and their professional dance partners. A surprising fact about the programme is that it appeals to people of all ages, from five to 90.

Game *Word Square*

- Work in pairs.
- Write down as many English words as possible, using the letters in the square. You can go in any direction, but all the letters must touch. So, for example, you can make PLAY, but you can't make PART. And you can only use each letter once in any word.
- The pair that finds the most (correct!) words is the winner.

S	T	C	E
O	A	Y	A
R	P	L	R
O	E	N	I

REVISION

LESSON 1 Look at the email in exercise 8 on page 49. Write five questions about the brothers' holiday plans and answer them. Write questions with *going to*: Where ... (go)? For how long ... (go)? How ... (travel)? Where ... (stay)? What ... (do)?

Where are they going to go?
They're going to go to the coast.

LESSON 2 Look at exercise 5 on page 51. Write sentences saying what will and won't happen in each situation.

Emma won't say no. She'll say it's a great idea.

LESSON 3 Write a sentence using each adverb from the Word Bank on page 53, exercise 5.

He shouted angrily at the boy who hit him.

LESSON 4 Look at the questions on page 55, exercise 5. Write a conversation between yourself and a friend.

Me: What's your favourite TV series?

EXTENSION

LESSON 1 Write a paragraph about your plans for next weekend. Say what you are and aren't going to do.

I'm going to watch ... on TV. I'm not going to watch ...

LESSON 2 Write sentences about your next birthday.

- How old will you be?
- What will you do to celebrate?
- What do you think and hope will happen?

LESSON 3 Write about three films which you enjoyed.

- What were they called?
- Who was in them?
- What were they about?
- Why did you like them?

LESSON 4 Make a word map for television.

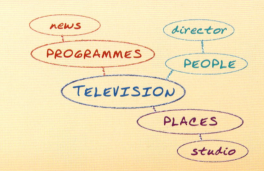

YOUR CHOICE!

HALF MINUTE TALKS

- Work in a small group. Choose a letter of the alphabet (e.g. T). Each student says an 'interesting' noun (singular or plural) beginning with that letter (e.g. *television, trees, teenagers*). Make a list of the nouns.
- One student chooses a noun from the list and talks for half a minute on that topic. The rest of the group can ask questions if the speaker can't think of anything more to say.
- Then choose another letter and speaker.

SAYING WORDS IN TWO WAYS

- Work in a small group. Make a list of five English words which you like, and think about why you like them. Is it their sound, or appearance, or meaning?
- Show your list to the group and say why you like the words.
- In turn, ask the rest of the group to say the words on their list in one of these pairs of ways:
  quickly/slowly   loudly/quietly   happily/sadly   politely/rudely
  Hanna, say the words on your list first quickly, then slowly.

1 Read and choose the best words.

HOLLYWOOD HERE I COME!

Is there life after soap? TV star Tamsin Gold thinks so. She is leaving the UK for a new career in Hollywood. When I met her in her London flat, she (1) got/was getting ready for the trip to California.

'Everything is working out (2) beautiful/beautifully,' Tamsin said. 'I (3) finished/was finishing filming here last week and I start work in Hollywood next month. But I (4) will/am going to have a holiday first!'

She (5) will/is going to play the part of a pop star in the movie. 'I nearly (6) didn't accept/wasn't accepting the part (7) so/because there's a lot of singing in the film.' Tamsin explained. 'Everyone says that I sing quite (8) good/well but I'm (9) nervous/nervously about it. I know that things won't be easy there at first, but I enjoy working (10) hard/hardly.'

Tamsin hopes that her boyfriend Nick (11) will/is going join her in Hollywood. 'We (12) will/are going see what happens!'

Good luck, Tamsin!

2 Complete with the past simple of these verbs.

> be describe destroy die go
> live marry work write

1 Shakespeare _____ Anne Hathaway in 1582.
2 When Shakespeare _____ in 1616, he _____ exactly 52 years old.
3 Charles Dickens _____ in Portsmouth until 1823.
4 He _____ in a factory at the age of 12.
5 He _____ 14 very successful novels.
6 The Great Fire of London _____ St Paul's Cathedral.
7 Samuel Pepys _____ the fire in his famous diary.
8 People _____ to the fields outside London to escape the fire.

3 Ask and answer.

Alexey/visit the theatre ✗/go to a music shop ✓

> Did Alexey visit the theatre?   No, he didn't.
> Did he go to a music shop?   Yes, he did.

1 Jay/cross the bridge ✓/fall into the river ✗
2 Ramón and Kristin/visit a museum ✓/see an exhibition ✗
3 Leyla/lose her camera ✗/take lots of photos ✓
4 the group/have a picnic ✓/go to a restaurant ✗
5 Emma/climb the Monument ✗/wait outside ✓

Now write sentences using the past simple.

Alexey didn't visit the theatre. He went to a music shop.

4 Complete with the correct preposition of time.

1 _____ July
2 _____ Monday
3 _____ 5.30
4 _____ 2004
5 _____ the evening
6 _____ Friday afternoon
7 _____ midnight
8 _____ 5 May
9 _____ winter

5 Write sentences using the past continuous + *when* + past simple.

Lee/sail/fall overboard
Lee was sailing when he fell overboard.

1 Alexey/take photos/he/drop his bag
2 Leyla/do exercises/she/hurt her foot
3 Jay and Emma/dance/see Steve
4 Carrie/record an interview/the phone/ring
5 Ramón/listen to music/he/fall asleep

6 Write sentences using the past simple + *because* + past continuous.

Carrie/go home early/she/not feel well
Carrie went home early because she wasn't feeling well.

1 Steve/stay in the hotel/he/look after the group
2 Emma/get lost/she/not think
3 Jay and Leyla/not play tennis/it/rain
4 Ramón/have a hot shower/he/feel cold
5 Kristin/not dance/her feet/hurt

7 Ask and answer.

you/watch The Simpsons ✗
A Are you going to watch *The Simpsons*?
B No, I'm not.

1 Leyla and Kristin/have dinner now ✓
2 the group/do drama exercises ✓
3 Emma/miss her favourite soap ✗
4 Alexey/buy a new jacket ✓
5 Ramón/get a new mobile ✗

8 Write sentences using *going to*.

I/watch TV ✗
I'm not going to watch TV.

1 Tamsin/appear in another soap ✗
2 Tamsin/leave London ✓
3 we/have a tour of the studio ✓
4 Steve/watch *Ugly Betty* ✗
5 the actors/come to the party ✓

9 Complete this phone conversation with *will* or *won't*.

TAMSIN I hope nothing __1__ go wrong when I'm in Hollywood.
NICK Don't worry. You __2__ have a great time, you know that. And I promise I __3__ come and join you as soon as I can.
TAMSIN I hope you __4__ forget me.
NICK Of course I __5__. I __6__ phone you once a week.
TAMSIN Once a week! Why __7__ you phone every day? You know how much I __8__ miss you.
NICK Because there's eight hours' time difference between London and California. You __9__ want to talk to me in the middle of the night!
TAMSIN __10__ you think about me every day?
NICK Of course I __11__. But I expect you __12__ be too busy to think of me!

10 Complete with adverbs of manner formed from these adjectives.

early   easy   good   happy   late
nervous   polite   quiet   slow

1 Sh! Please talk _____.
2 The bus left _____ and they missed it.
3 Everyone enjoyed the drama exercises and smiled _____.
4 Leyla danced _____ and everyone watched her.
5 Kristin was worried about pickpockets and looked around _____.
6 'Excuse me, please can you help me?' Ramón asked _____.
7 You feel tired when you go to bed _____.
8 Please say that again _____.
9 I can do this exercise _____!

VOCABULARY

11 Complete with six of these words.

best-seller   building   career   chance
documentary   harbour   intelligent   tragedy

1 Last night we watched a TV _____ about meteorites.
2 She always does well at school – she's very _____.
3 Hamlet is a famous _____ by Shakespeare.
4 St Paul's Cathedral is a beautiful _____.
5 It's hard to make a successful _____ as an actor.
6 It's a very popular novel – it's a _____.

12 Match these words with their definitions.

architect   boat   century   exhausted   occupation
playwright   rescue   roof   rudely   whisper

1 speak very very quietly
2 someone who designs buildings
3 opposite of *politely*
4 very very tired
5 top of a building
6 save someone from danger
7 something you sail in
8 job
9 someone who writes plays
10 hundred years

13 Match the verbs in list A with the words and phrases in list B.

	A	B
1	do up	a bike
2	have	a play
3	make	hard
4	rehearse	place
5	ride	sense
6	take	a story
7	tell	fun
8	work	your shoes

LEARNER INDEPENDENCE
SELF ASSESSMENT

Look back at Lessons 1–3 in Units 3 and 4.

How good are you at …?	✓ Fine	? Not sure
1 Talking about past events Workbook pp28–29 exercises 1–5 and pp30–31 exercises 2–4	☐	☐
2 Describing what was happening Workbook pp32–33 exercises 2–4	☐	☐
3 Asking for and giving reasons Workbook p33 exercise 5	☐	☐
4 Talking about future plans and intentions Workbook p40–41 exercises 1–4	☐	☐
5 Making predictions Workbook p42–43 exercises 2 and 3	☐	☐
6 Talking about the way people do things Workbook p44 exercises 1–3	☐	☐

Not sure? Have a look at Language File pages 115–117 and do the Workbook exercise(s) again.

Now write an example for 1–6.

1   Walt Disney made the first cartoon movie with sound in 1928.

PREVIEW

COMMUNICATIVE AIMS
LEARNING HOW TO ...

1 Talk about future arrangements
2 Describe a sequence of events
3 Order a meal in a restaurant
4 Give directions
5 Talk about recent events
6 Talk about experiences
7 Say what's wrong with something

TOPICS AND VOCABULARY

Food
Satellite navigation
Prepositions of direction
Luggage and clothes
Dictionary words
Animals
Transport
Town facilities
Famous landmarks

Have you got any pizzas with mushrooms?

Have you ever been on a high-speed train?

Who is taking them to the Science Museum?

1 Match the communicative aims (1–7) with the pictures (A–G).

2 Put the words into categories.

[Animals] [Landmarks] [Directions]

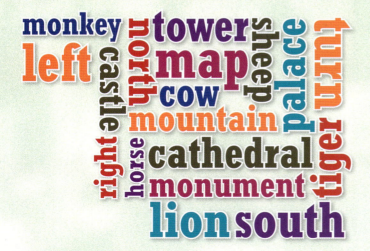

monkey tower sheep turn
left castle north map palace
cow mountain
right horse cathedral tiger
monument
lion south

3 Write three more words for each of these categories.
Dictionary words
noun _____ _____ _____

Drinks
juice _____ _____ _____

Adjectives meaning *fantastic*
wonderful _____ _____ _____

There are too many tourists.

She's just told me.

When you get off the bus, cross the road.

5 Do the Holiday Questionaire with three other students.

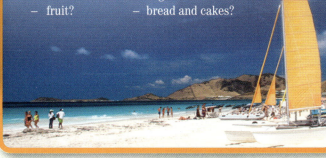

HOLIDAY QUESTIONNAIRE

1 When did you go on holiday this year or last year?
– For how long?
– Was it in your country or abroad?
– Did you stay in one place or travel around?
– Did you camp, or stay with family or friends, or stay in a hotel?

2 How many different ways did you travel during the holiday?
– Did you take a bus, train or plane?
– Did you walk or cycle?
– Did you travel by car, taxi or motorbike?
– Did you go on a motorboat, or sail?

3 What food did you eat on holiday? What kinds of …
– meat and fish?   – vegetables?
– fruit?   – bread and cakes?

What interesting or surprising things did you find out? Tell another group.

Saturday

This is a perfect holiday!
We're going to 'The Lion King'
this evening! And there's
lots happening tomorrow.
First we're .... Next we're
.... Then .... and after
that .... Finally ....!
See you next week.
Love,
Emma xx

Mr and Mrs Newman
8 Forth Street
Edinburgh
EH1 3LD

G

4 2.13 Listen to extracts 1–3 from Units 5 and 6.
Match them with A–C below.

A An email about a holiday
B A description of a famous place
C An announcement about arrangements

Believe it or not!

Tomatoes and cucumbers are over 90% water.
Meat and cheese are 40–60% water.
Even bread can be 35% water.
And about 60% of your body is water!

What's happening tomorrow?

Talking about future arrangements
Describing a sequence of events
Present continuous: future
Sequencing adverbs

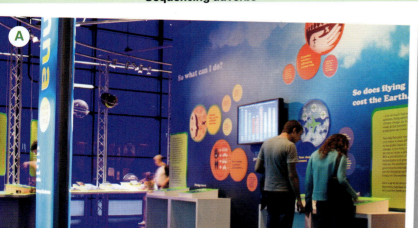

A

B

C

D

1 OPENER

Look at the timetable for Saturday and match the photos A–D with four of the events.

What's happening on Saturday?

8.30am	Leave the hotel and walk to the South Bank.
10am	Go for a ride on the London Eye.
11am	Take a boat trip down the Thames.
1.15pm	Have lunch in Pizza Paradise restaurant.
2.30pm	Take the underground to South Kensington.
3pm	Visit the Science Museum with Steve: Jay, Emma, Ramón.
	Visit the Natural History Museum with Carrie: Kristin, Alexey, Leyla.
5.30pm	Return to the hotel.
6.45pm	Leave for the Lyceum Theatre: *The Lion King.*

2 LISTENING

🔴 2.14 Listen to Steve and look at the timetable. Note down three changes to the arrangements for Saturday.

3 AFTER LISTENING

Answer the questions.

1 What time are the group leaving the hotel on Saturday morning?
2 When are they going for a ride on the London Eye?
3 Where are they having lunch?
4 Who is taking them to the Science Museum?
5 Which museum is Leyla going to?
6 Is Alexey going to the Science Museum?
7 How long are they spending at the museums?
8 When are they leaving for the theatre?

Your response Which do you think is the best event of the day?

4 SPEAKING

Ask and answer questions about what's happening tomorrow.

> Are they going for a ride on the London Eye tomorrow morning?

> Yes, they are.

> Are they leaving the hotel at half past eight?

> No, they aren't. They're leaving at …

5 LISTENING

 2.15 Steve is talking about arrangements for Sunday. Listen and number A–E in the right order.

A Have lunch in Camden Market.
B Visit London Zoo.
C Take a canal boat trip.
D Go shopping in Camden Market.
E Walk along Regent's Canal.

Now complete the timetable.

What's happening on Sunday?

10am	*Visit London Zoo*
Midday	
12.30pm	
2pm	
4–4.45pm	

6 SPEAKING

Ask and answer questions about Sunday.

A When are they visiting London Zoo?
B At ten o'clock on Sunday morning.
A How long are they staying there?
B For two hours.

Now tell each other what the group are doing on Sunday, using *first, next, then, after that, finally.*

> **Extension** Tell each other about your arrangements for next Saturday and Sunday.

7 WRITING

Complete Emma's postcard to her parents.

> Saturday
>
> This is a perfect holiday! We're going to 'The Lion King' this evening! And there's lots happening tomorrow. First we're ………. Next we're ………. Then ………… and after that, …………. Finally …………! See you next week.
> Love
> Emma XX
>
> Mr and Mrs Newman
> 8 Forth Street
> Edinburgh
> EH1 3LD

8 PRONUNCIATION

2.16 Listen and repeat.

/ŋ/ -ing	/n/ in
going	go in
rang	ran
sung	sun
thing	thin
wing	win

Now listen and write the words you hear.

9 WRITING

What's happening in your town/ region/country this weekend? Think about concerts, sports events and famous people, and make notes under these headings.

Who/What?   Where?   When?

Now write sentences.

Arsenal are playing Manchester United at the Emirates Stadium at three o'clock on Saturday.

> **Extension** Plan a day out in your town/city for a group of tourists. Choose interesting places and events, and write a timetable.

LANGUAGE WORKOUT

Complete.

Present continuous: future
Steve is tak**ing** people to the Science Museum.
We're _____ to the hotel at 5.30pm.
They aren't _____ lunch at the hotel.

What time _____ they _____ lunch?
Who _____ _____ them to the Science Museum?
How long _____ they _____ at the museums?

Sequencing adverbs
First they're visiting London Zoo.
Next …   **Then** …
After that, …   **Finally** …

▶**Answers and Practice**
Language File page 117

5.2 OUT AND ABOUT

Could I borrow some money?

Ordering a meal in a restaurant
some and *any* How much/many?
Countable and uncountable nouns
can/could for requests

1 OPENER

What toppings can you have on a pizza? Make a list and compare it with the menu.

2 READING

Look at the menu and complete the conversation with the names of the pizzas.

Emma, Jay and Kristin are in Pizza Paradise.

EMMA   Let's choose something to eat. I'm starving!
WAITER   Are you ready to order?
EMMA   Yes, could I have a __1__ pizza, please?
JAY   What's that?
EMMA   It's a pizza with cheese, tomatoes, olives and garlic.
JAY   Oh, could I have that too? But I don't want any olives.
KRISTIN Have you got any pizzas with mushrooms?
WAITER   There's a __2__ pizza – with cheese, tomatoes, mushrooms, ham …
KRISTIN No, I don't want any meat. I'm vegetarian.
WAITER   Then why don't you have a __3__ pizza? It's got mushrooms and there isn't any meat in it.
KRISTIN OK, I'll have that. And I'd like some garlic bread, please.
WAITER   And what would you like to drink?
KRISTIN A cola, please.
WAITER   How many colas?
EMMA   Two.
JAY   And can I have a glass of water, please?
WAITER   Certainly, coming right up.
JAY   Emma … how much money have you got?
EMMA   About £25. Why?
JAY   Because I haven't got any. Could I borrow some?
EMMA   Honestly, you're hopeless!

🔴 2.17   Now listen and check.

3 AFTER READING

Complete the sentences.

1 We know that Emma is very hungry because she says '_____.'
2 Jay doesn't want any _____ on his pizza.
3 Kristin wants _____ on her pizza.
4 Kristin doesn't want any meat because she's _____.
5 Kristin also orders some _____.
6 How many colas do they order? _____
7 How much money has Emma got? _____
8 Jay wants to borrow some _____.

Your response Which pizza would you like to order from the menu? Why?

4 VOCABULARY

Make a word map for food. Use words from the pizza menu and add other words you know or find in a dictionary.

Extension Play *Food and Drink Tennis.* Say 'countable' or 'uncountable'.

Water. | Uncountable.
One point!

PIZZAS

RIGINAL	Cheese, tomatoes	£7.50
EDITERRANEAN	Cheese, tomatoes, olives, garlic	£7.75
ROPICAL	Cheese, ham, pineapple	£7.50
OUR SEASONS	Cheese, tomatoes, mushrooms, ham, olives	£8.00
URPRISE	Cheese, tomatoes, spinach, a fried egg	£7.75
OUNTRY	Cheese, onions, peppers, mushrooms	£7.50
	Garlic bread	£1.50

5 PRONUNCIATION

Write these words under *good* or *food*.

choose cook could fruit group	
juice look through took would	

/ʊ/ good	/uː/ food

2.18 Now listen and check. Repeat the words.

6 ROLE PLAY

Act out a conversation between two customers and a waiter in Pizza Paradise. You can use the phrases in the boxes.

A Are you ready to order? What would you like to eat?
B Can I have a Tropical pizza, please?
C What's a Tropical pizza?

Waiter	Customers
Are you ready to order? What would you like to eat/drink? It's a pizza with _____. How much/many _____ do you want? Certainly.	What's _____? Can/Could I have a/some _____, please? I'd like a/some _____, please. I don't want any _____. Have you got any _____?

7 WRITING

Write out the conversation between the customers and the waiter in Pizza Paradise. Use the phrases in the boxes in exercise 6 to help you.

Extension Write your ideal restaurant menu. Then exchange menus with another student. Take turns to be the waiter and the customer in each other's restaurant.

LANGUAGE WORKOUT

Complete.

some and ***any***
I'd like **some** garlic bread.
Could I borrow _____ money?
I don't want **any** olives/meat.
Have you got _____ pizzas with mushrooms?

We use *some* and *any* with both plural and uncountable nouns.
We use _____ in affirmative sentences, and in requests and questions when we want/expect the answer 'yes'.
We use _____ in negative sentences and neutral questions.

How much/many?
How _____ money have you got?
How _____ colas?

We use *How* ___much___ with uncountable nouns.
We use *How* ___many___ with plural countable nouns.

Countable nouns	Uncountable nouns
a tomato tomatoes	~~a~~ money some water~~s~~
an olive olives	

▶**Answers and Practice**
Language File page 118

How do they do it?

1 OPENER

What do you know about satnavs? Why do people use them?

2 READING

🔘 2.19 Read the article. How do satnavs work out their position?

3 AFTER READING

True or false? Correct the false sentences.

1 Satnavs use satellites like explorers used the stars.
2 The GPS satellites have clocks which tell the exact time.
3 A satnav can calculate its position from one satellite's signals.
4 A satnav checks its position very frequently.
5 A man who followed satnav directions drove off a cliff.
6 A taxi-driver drove into a river because he didn't listen to his satnav.

Now look at these sentences from the text. Who or what do the words in *italics* refer to?

1 They used the stars to show *them* their position.
2 Drivers can use satnavs to tell *them* their route.
3 But the satnav user needs to give *it* accurate information.
4 The satnav told *me* to keep going.

Your response Imagine you are in a world without mobile phones, the Internet or GPS. How do you communicate and find your way around?

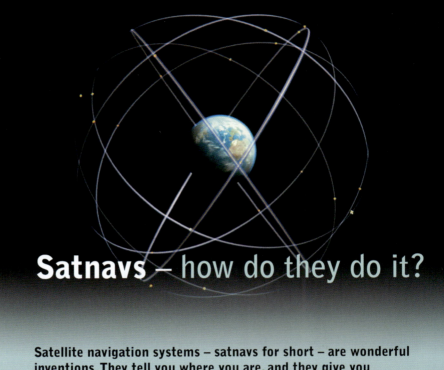

Satnavs – how do they do it?

Satellite navigation systems – satnavs for short – are wonderful inventions. They tell you where you are, and they give you directions. But how do they do it?

When early explorers sailed round the world, they used the stars to show them their position. Now drivers can use satnavs to tell them their route in exactly the same way. The only difference is that satnavs use artificial stars – satellites.

There are more than 20 satellites in the Global Positioning System (GPS). The GPS satellites are about 20,000 kilometres above the Earth. They have atomic clocks which tell the time to an accuracy of one second in 300,000 years.

The satnav compares the positions of three or four satellites and works out exactly where it is. It does this several times a second and is usually accurate to 20 metres anywhere in the world. But the satnav user needs to give it accurate information. Drivers sometimes get lost and end up in the wrong street, the wrong town, or even the wrong country.

And there are stories of extremely lucky escapes. A man using a satnav found himself on the edge of a cliff and a young woman drove onto a railway line in front of a train. A taxi-driver followed satnav directions into a river and carried on driving until his taxi got stuck in the mud. He explained: 'The satnav told me to keep going, so that's what I did.'

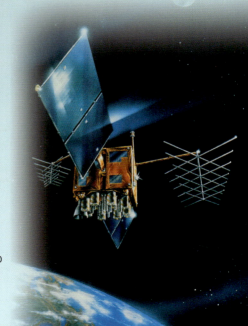

4 LISTENING

🔘 2.20 Look at the London map and find Covent Garden underground station 🚇. Then listen to the directions and follow the route on the map. Where do you get to?

5 VOCABULARY

🔘 2.20 Listen again and complete the directions with prepositions from the Word Bank.

When you come __1__ the underground, turn right __2__ James Street and then turn left. Walk __3__ Floral Street __4__ Bow Street and turn right. Go straight on __5__ Bow Street and Wellington Street. Walk __6__ the London Transport Museum, go __7__ Exeter Street, and it's on the right. It isn't far.

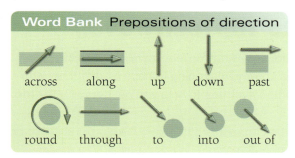

Word Bank Prepositions of direction

| across | along | up | down | past |
| round | through | to | into | out of |

▶ Language File page 119

6 SPEAKING

🔘 2.21 Look at the map. You are outside the Theatre Museum. Ask and answer the question, putting sentences A–D in the correct order. Then listen and check.

> Excuse me, can you help me – how do I get to the National Gallery?

A It's a big building on the left. You can't miss it!
B Walk down to the Strand and turn right.
C Walk through the market and turn left into Southampton Street.
D Go straight on and when you get to Trafalgar Square, turn right.

Now point at places on the map to show where you are, decide where you want to go, and ask each other for directions. Use the Word Bank to help you.

> Excuse me, can you tell me the way to the post office?

Extension Use the map to give each other directions to mystery destinations.

7 PRONUNCIATION

Write these words under *walk*, *stop*, or *go*.

| across | along | clock | fall | four | lost |
| more | post | road | show | talk | told |

/ɔː/ walk	/ɒ/ stop	/əʊ/ go

🔘 2.22 Now listen and check. Repeat the words.

8 WRITING

Write directions from your school to your home.

Turn left outside the school and walk to the bus stop. Catch a bus to … . When you get off the bus, cross the road. I live in the fourth street on the right.

Now read out your directions. Don't say the name of your street. Can other students guess where you live?

LANGUAGE WORKOUT

Complete.

Object pronouns

Singular	Plural
me	us
_____	you
him, her, it	_____

Verb + indirect and direct object
Can you tell **me the way**?
… they give **you directions**.
… show **them their position**.

▶**Answers and Practice**
Language File page 118

4 Integrated Skills
Suggestions and advice

1 OPENER

What do you pack when you go on holiday? Make a list and compare with another student.

READING

2 🔴 2.23 Read *Welcome to TopTeenTravel!* and match five of these topics with paragraphs 1–5.

> Travel light   Keep in touch
> Make a list   Think small
> Enjoy long journeys
> Buy new clothes
> Don't take too much

3 Find the highlighted words in the text which mean:

1 pullover
2 books
3 suggestions
4 cloth made from artificial material
5 travelling cheaply as a tourist
6 does not let water through
7 extremely large
8 small rucksack for use in the day
9 rucksack
10 (group of) things

LISTENING

4 🔴 2.24 Steve is telling Leyla and Ramón about his planned round-the-world trip. Listen to the first part of their conversation and number the countries in the order Steve is visiting them.

> Australia   Brazil   Chile
> New Zealand   Peru   Singapore

Welcome to TopTeenTravel!

Thank you very much for choosing TopTeenTravel for your African adventure holiday – we know you're going to have a great time with us! Here are our favourite travel **tips** to help you get ready for the trip.

1 You know that there won't be room in the minibus for a big suitcase or **backpack**. Also remember that you're flying to Africa, so a **massive** backpack isn't a good idea.

2 How much should you take with you? Put everything you want to take on your bed – remember you'll be away for six weeks. Then look at your things and choose only a third of them! Check that all your **stuff** fits in your bag.

3 And it's not just a question of how many things you take. Choose clothes which are light and easy to wash and dry. So go for a **polyester** T-shirt, not a cotton one, lightweight trousers instead of jeans, and a fleece, not a wool **sweater**. Forget your raincoat and pack a **waterproof** jacket – it's much lighter.

4 You'll often travel for 10 to 12 hours a day. It's a good idea to have some things in your **daypack** to help you pass the time – your MP3 player, **paperbacks** or some playing cards.

5 And last but not least, don't forget your mobile – you'll want to tell your family and friends how the trip is going.

See you soon on our adventure holiday! And happy **backpacking**!

The TopTeenTravel Team

5 ⊙ 2.25 Listen to the second part of the conversation and check your answers. Then tick (✓) the things Steve is taking with him.

> cotton T-shirts   jeans   raincoat   rucksack   shirts
> suit   swimming trunks   tie   umbrella   wool sweater

6 SPEAKING

Read *Welcome to Top Teen Travel!* again and look at the things that Steve is taking with him. Then role play a conversation between Steve and either Leyla or Ramón. You can use the phrases in the box.

Leyla/Ramón   **Steve**

Ask Steve what he is taking on his trip.
                                                   Reply.
Make a suggestion.
                                                   Ask why.
Explain. Ask what else he is taking.
                                                   Reply.
Make a suggestion and explain.
                                                   Agree.

> **Making suggestions and giving advice**
> Do you think that's a good idea?
> Can I make a suggestion?
> Maybe you should …
> Why don't you …?
> What about …?
> It's a good idea to …

7 WRITING

Write the dialogue between Leyla or Ramón and Steve which you practised in the role play.

OR Write an email giving advice to a friend who is going backpacking.

LEARNER INDEPENDENCE

8 What does 'knowing' a word mean? Which of these answers do you agree with? Compare with another student.

- Being able to understand it.
- Remembering it when I need it.
- Being able to pronounce it correctly.
- Being able to spell it properly.
- Knowing how to use it grammatically.
- Knowing which other words I can use it with.

9 Dictionaries use abbreviations to give you information about words. Match these abbreviations with their meanings below.

> abbrev   adj   adv   aux
> C   pl   sb   sing   sth   U

> **Word Bank**
> **Dictionary words**
>
> countable   singular   abbreviation
> adverb   plural   something
> auxiliary verb (like *be*)   adjective
> uncountable   somebody

Compare these abbreviations with your own dictionary.

10 ⊙ 2.26 **Phrasebook**: Find these useful expressions in Unit 5. Then listen and repeat.

> What's happening on Sunday?
> I'm starving!
> Are you ready to order?
> I'll have that.
> What would you like to drink?
> Certainly, coming right up.
> Honestly, you're hopeless!
> It isn't far.
> Excuse me, can you help me?
> You can't miss it!
> Last but not least …

Now match these replies with the four questions in the box.

a   Yes, can I have a pizza, please?
b   We're staying at home.
c   Yes, of course. What's the problem?
d   A glass of milk, please.

69

LANGUAGE LINKS

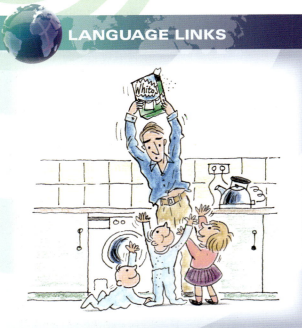

This is a warning on a packet. Do you recognise some words in the different languages?

CAUTION
Keep out of the reach of children.

PRÉCAUTION
Conserver hors de la portée des enfants.

VORSICHT
Darf nicht in die Hände von Kindern gelangen.

PRECAUCIÓN
Manténgase fuera del alcance de los niños.

ATTENZIONE
Tenere fuori dalla portata dei bambini.

Look at packets and bottles in your home. Find more words that you recognise in other languages.

Puzzle

Read and find the word.

My first is in *theatre* and *school* and *shop*
My second is in *go* and it's also in *stop*
My third is in *left* but it isn't in *right*
My fourth is in *evening* and it's also in *night*
My fifth is in both *food* and *drink*
My sixth is in *hear* and *say* but not *think*
My last is at the end of *day*
And my whole is free time – let's go away!

Choose a word from this unit and make up a similar puzzle.

SKETCH *The Restaurant*

2.27 Read and listen.

WOMAN   A table for two, please.
WAITRESS Certainly, madam. This way please.
The man and woman sit down. A waiter comes over.
MAN   Can we see the menu, please?
WAITER   Yes, of course sir. But this table's no good. Much too small.
The waiter takes the table away and brings another, larger, table.
MAN   Now, can we see the menu, please?
WAITER   Of course, sir. Here you are.
The waiter leaves and the waitress comes over.
WAITRESS Are you ready to order?
WOMAN   Yes, please. I'd like steak and chips.
MAN   And I'd like some fish, please.
WAITRESS I'm afraid there isn't any steak or fish.
MAN   Well, what is there then?
WAITRESS Just our special pizza, sir.
WOMAN   Never mind, we'll have two special pizzas, please.
WAITRESS Two special pizzas coming right up!
WAITER   Here we are. Be careful – they're very hot.
He puts the pizzas on the table and leaves. The waitress comes over.
WAITRESS Oh dear, I'm sorry. You've got the wrong knives and forks.
The waitress takes away the knives and forks. She does not come back.
MAN   Well, I'm not waiting any longer. I'm eating with my fingers.
The waiter comes over and feels the plates.
WAITER   Oh dear. I'm sorry. The pizzas are too cold now.
The waiter takes away the pizzas. The waitress returns with knives and forks.
MAN   Thank you, but where are our pizzas?
WAITRESS I don't know, sir. They were here a minute ago.
The waitress leaves and the waiter returns, but without the pizzas.
WOMAN   Excuse me. Where are our pizzas?
WAITER   I'm sorry, madam, but the restaurant is closed now!
The man and woman leave. The waitress comes in with two hot pizzas and the waiter and waitress sit down to eat.

Now act out the sketch in groups of four.

Limerick

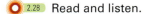

2.28 Read and listen.

There was a young woman called Ida
who found in her soup a huge spider.
Said the waiter, 'Don't shout
and wave it about!'
So now the spider's inside her.

REVISION

LESSON 1 Look at the timetable on page 62 and write sentences about what the group are doing on Saturday:

> in the morning   at lunchtime
> in the afternoon   in the evening

In the morning, they're going for a ride on the London Eye.

LESSON 2 Look at the conversation on page 64 and at the Pizza Paradise menu. Write a similar conversation between the waiter and Ramón and Alexey. Ramón likes spinach, and Alexey doesn't want any tomatoes or peppers on his pizza.

Waiter: Are you ready to order?
Ramón: Yes, could I have a …?

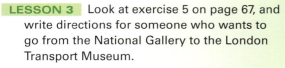

LESSON 3 Look at exercise 5 on page 67, and write directions for someone who wants to go from the National Gallery to the London Transport Museum.

Walk across Trafalgar Square and turn left into the Strand.

LESSON 4 Look again at pages 68–69 and make lists of items under these headings:

Luggage   *rucksack*

Clothes   *T-shirt*

EXTENSION

LESSON 1 Make lists of words for places in a town under these headings.

Places to visit	Performance	Shopping	Food and drink
museum	*theatre*	*market*	*restaurant*

LESSON 2 Look at the word map you made in exercise 4 on page 64, and add at least ten more words to the map. You can also add more categories, such as FISH AND SEAFOOD. Use a dictionary to help you.

LESSON 3 You are outside your school. Write short conversations where you give directions to a tourist who is looking for:

- a place for lunch.
- the nearest hotel.

Tourist: Excuse me, can you help me? I'm looking for a place for lunch.

LESSON 4 Imagine you are going on a round-the-world trip. Write an email to a friend explaining where you are going and what you are taking. Begin like this:

Great news! I'm going on a round-the-world trip. I'm leaving on …

YOUR CHOICE!

SUGGESTIONS

- Work in a small group.
- Think of a problem situation, for example:

  You're lost in a big city.   You're stuck in a lift.
  You're afraid of heights.   You're always late.

- Take turns to tell the rest of the group about the problem and give each other advice.

  Maybe you should …   Why don't you …?
  What about …?

I NEVER TRAVEL WITHOUT IT

- Work in a small group.
- Think of an item which you always take with you when you travel. Don't say what it is!
- In turn, mime using or wearing the item to the rest of the group. They ask *Yes/No* questions to find out what your essential item is.
- Finally, explain why you think your item is essential.

1 OPENER

How much do you know about teenagers in Britain? Try our Teenage Life Quiz!

2 READING

2.29 Read *Girls* and find the answers to these questions.

Who …

1 doesn't enjoy being 15?
2 has a boyfriend?
3 plays two instruments?
4 knows people who are worried about how they look?
5 thinks designer clothes are too expensive?
6 wants more independence?
7 enjoys dancing?
8 likes movies?

Teenage Life Quiz

		A	B	C
1	How many British teenagers want to be famous when they're older? Over …	A 10%	B 30%	C 50%
2	What percentage of teenagers say they are very happy?	A 20%	B 40%	C 60%
3	What percentage of teenagers think it is important to wear designer clothes? The answer for the total population is 20%.	A 20%	B 40%	C 80%
4	What percentage of teenagers eat a healthy diet?	A 30%	B 50%	C 70%
5	How many hours a week do teenagers spend online?	A 10	B 20	C 30
6	In 1821 just under half the population were under 20. How about today? Just under …	A a quarter.	B half.	C two thirds.

What do you think the answers to the quiz are for teenagers in your country?

Girls

Naomi

I quite like being 15. I love shopping and going to the cinema. And I often watch DVDs with friends, because there isn't much to do in this town for people of our age. Computers? I mainly use my computer for homework and revising for exams, and chatting on the Internet. But I know a guy – he's my boyfriend, actually – and he spends hours playing computer games, they're really addictive.

Isabel

Some girls want to look like models, so they go on diets when they don't need to and get much too thin. And I have friends who spend loads of money on designer clothes, even boys. They buy expensive jeans and trainers and stuff. It's a waste of money, really. And others get upset because they can't afford the latest fashions. I just make my own clothes – I'd like to be a fashion designer.

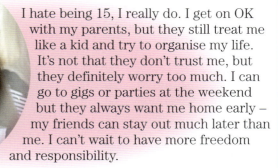

Alice

I hate being 15, I really do. I get on OK with my parents, but they still treat me like a kid and try to organise my life. It's not that they don't trust me, but they definitely worry too much. I can go to gigs or parties at the weekend but they always want me home early – my friends can stay out much later than me. I can't wait to have more freedom and responsibility.

Josie

I listen to music in my free time – I really love it – and I play the violin and the guitar. I like classical music best, actually. Some people think it's rubbish, but I think it's really cool. Of course, when you go to clubs or the disco it's all hip-hop, rap and R&B, and that's fine, too. Anyway, you can't dance to classical music, and I love dancing.

3 VOCABULARY

Match the words with their definitions.

1 kid
2 upset
3 cool
4 addictive
5 rubbish
6 guy

a difficult to stop
b great
c man or boy
d terrible
e child
f worried and unhappy

4 MINI-PROJECT
Teenage Life

Are the things that Naomi, Isabel, Josie and Alice say also true about life for teenage girls in your country? Discuss the similarities and differences with another student.

> Naomi says there isn't much to do in her town. But in our town …

Now work together to write about teenage life for girls and/or boys in your country. Read your work carefully and correct any mistakes. Then compare your *Teenage Life* report with other students.

Have you recorded everything?

Talking about recent events
Present perfect
Present perfect with *just*

1 OPENER

The competition winners are all making two-minute videos about London. What would you like to make a two-minute video about?

2 READING

○ 2.30 Look at the photo and guess who Kristin and Ramón are talking about. Then read the dialogue and check.

Emma, Kristin and Ramón are in Hyde Park.

KRISTIN   Good. Emma is practising with the camera. Now we can talk.

RAMÓN   Look at all those squirrels!

KRISTIN   Forget about the squirrels, Ramón! Listen, why aren't you talking to Emma? Have you had an argument with her?

RAMÓN   No, I haven't! I *have* tried to talk to her, but she's been horrible to me.

KRISTIN   But I think that's because she really likes you.

RAMÓN   You're pulling my leg! She hasn't said a word to me all day – she's so rude.

KRISTIN   I'm not joking. Emma likes you a lot – she's just told me. Hey, cheer up!

RAMÓN   Sh! Here she comes.

EMMA   I've just worked out how to use the camera!

KRISTIN   Great! Have you recorded anything?

EMMA   Yes, I have – I've just filmed you two. I couldn't hear you, but this camera has fantastic sound.

RAMÓN   What? Have you recorded everything we said?

3 AFTER READING

True or false? Correct the false sentences.

1   Ramón has had an argument with Emma.
2   He has tried to talk to Emma.
3   Emma has been friendly to Ramón.
4   Emma has talked to Ramón today.
5   She has just filmed Kristin and Ramón.
6   She hasn't recorded their conversation.

Your response What do you think Emma has recorded?

○ 2.31 Now listen and see if you are right.

4 LISTENING

○ 2.32 Listen to Carrie's interviews with Leyla and Alexey and look at the chart. Tick (✓) the things they've done this week, and put a cross (✗) by the things they haven't done.

	Leyla	Alexey	Another student
Taken any photos?	✗	✓	Licla
Bought any presents?	✓	✗	Silvia
Done any sport?	✓	✗	Michael
Sent any emails?	✗	✓	Stella
Been to a party?	✓	✗	Silphe
Had fun?	✓	✓	Silvia

5 SPEAKING

Check your answers to exercise 4.

A Has Leyla taken any photos?
B No, she hasn't. Has Alexey taken any photos?
A Yes, he has.

Now interview another student and complete the chart.

6 SPEAKING

🔘 2.33 Listen and say what has *just* happened. Use these phrases.

> break a plate   open a present   answer the phone   make a silly noise
> tell a joke   have a shower   send an email   kiss someone

> Someone has just made a silly noise.

7 VOCABULARY

Read *Animals in London*. Where can you see the animals in the photos?

Animals in London

London has more parks and open spaces than most other large cities. So when you've finished sightseeing, take a walk in a park. You'll be surprised how many animals you can see!

Hyde Park is a good place to see squirrels in the trees and people riding horses. There are also ducks and other wild birds in the Serpentine Lake in the middle of the park. Richmond Park has lots of wild animals, including large numbers of red deer.

In Regent's Park there is London Zoo, one of the oldest zoos in the world, with lions, tigers, hippos, monkeys, giraffes and many other species. The zoo works hard to protect wildlife in danger on our planet. London also has several city farms, such as the Kentish Town City farm, where you can see sheep, pigs, cows and goats.

> **Extension** Describe animals but don't say their names. Can other students guess which animals you are describing?

8 PRONUNCIATION

Which words contain the sound /f/?

> bought   enough   laugh
> lightweight   photograph
> right   thought

🔘 2.34 Listen and check. Repeat the words.

9 WRITING

Write sentences about what you have and haven't done this week. Use the list of irregular verbs on page 127 to help you.

This week I've played football three times but I haven't been swimming.

> **Extension** Write sentences about the student you interviewed in exercise 5.
> *Maria hasn't taken any photos this week, but she's bought some presents.*

LANGUAGE WORKOUT

Complete.

Present perfect: *have/has* + past participle
I **have tried** to talk to her.
She has _____ horrible to me.
She _____n't _____ a word to me all day.

_____ you recorded anything?
Yes, I _____.
_____ you _____ an argument?
No, I _____.
What _____ Emma recorded?

We can use the present perfect to talk about recent completed actions or events.

I've just worked out how to use the camera.
I _____ _____ filmed you two.

We can use the present perfect with _____ to talk about *very* recent events.

▶**Answers and Practice**
Language File page 119
Irregular Verbs page 127

Have you ever ...?

Talking about experiences
Present perfect with *ever/never*
Indefinite pronouns and adverbs

Maglev, train of the future?

Have you ever been on a high-speed train (HST)?
Probably, because HSTs are everywhere. France has the TGV with a top speed of 350 kilometres an hour, as fast as the famous Japanese Shinkansen bullet trains. The TGV Lyria travels between France and Switzerland, and the Eurostar links the UK with France and Belgium. Russia has the Velaro RUS, Turkey has the HSR, Germany has the ICE, and Spain has the AVE. The world has never had so many fast trains.

But many people think that HSTs are yesterday's technology and the future lies with Maglev trains. Maglev stands for magnetic levitation. Imagine a train with no engine, wheels or brakes which does over 500 km/h!

The idea behind Maglev trains is very simple. Have you ever played with two magnets? As you know, magnets have north and south poles. Opposite poles attract, so north and south poles stick together. But poles that are the same repel each other, so when you put two north or south poles together they push each other away. Powerful magnets in the Maglev track and on the trains lift them and move them forward – so the trains float on a cushion of air!

Maglev transport has been a dream for over 100 years, but there has never been so much interest in it before. And now it is a reality: Shanghai in China has the first high-speed commercial Maglev train in the world. It takes people to the airport 30 kilometres away in 7 minutes 20 seconds, at an average speed of 250 km/h, and has a top speed of over 500 km/h.

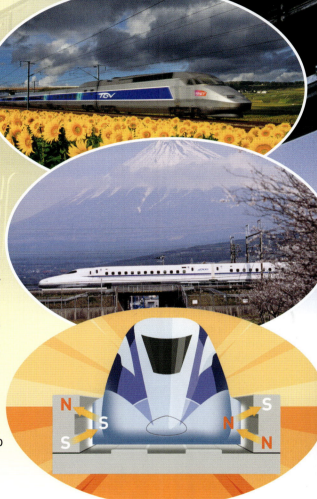

1 OPENER

Look at the photos. Which of these high-speed trains has no wheels? Why?

2 READING

2.35 Read *Maglev, train of the future?* What do you think is the most surprising information in the article?

3 AFTER READING

Choose the best answer.

1 The Japanese HST has a speed of
   A 350km/h.   **B** 500 km/h.   **C** 431 km/h.
2 Maglev trains have
   A engines.   **B** brakes.   **C** magnets.
3 How many poles do magnets have?
   A One.   **B** Two.   **C** Three.
4 '... they push each other away.' What does *they* refer to?
   A Poles that are the same.   **B** Opposite poles.   **C** North and south poles.
5 Maglev transport uses magnets
   A only in the trains.   **B** only in the track.   **C** in both the trains and the track.
6 The Shanghai Maglev train can
   A not go as fast as a TGV.   **B** go faster than a TGV.   **C** go as fast as a TGV.

Your response What are the arguments for travelling by train rather than by car or plane?

4 SPEAKING

Ask other students and note down their answers.

LIFE QUESTIONNAIRE

Have you ever ...

* won a competition?
* been on TV?
* met anyone famous?
* lost anything important?

* found anything valuable?
* flown anywhere?
* travelled on a high speed train?

A Have you ever ...?
B Yes, I have./No, I haven't./No, never.

Now tell a partner about other students' experiences.

> **Extension** Write about three students.
> *Martha has never won a competition or been on TV, but she has met someone famous – Barack Obama!*

5 LISTENING

2.36 Listen to Kristin and Ramón and number the London Transport Museum pictures in the order you hear about them. Then listen again and choose the correct words or dates.

LONDON TRANSPORT MUSEUM

A This tram/bus is around 50/100 years old.

B The world's first electric underground railway is more/less than 100 years old.

C You can practise bus/train driving on this simulator.

D The tube is the oldest/biggest underground railway in the world and this engine is from 1863/1866.

6 VOCABULARY

Match the words in box A with as many words as possible in box B.

bus driver, railway track

Word Bank	Transport	
A	**B**	
bus	driver	stop
car	engine	ticket
railway	line	timetable
train	park	track
	station	

7 PRONUNCIATION

2.37 Listen and check your answers to exercise 6. Repeat the compound nouns. Where is the main stress in compound nouns – on the first word or the second word?

8 GAME

Play *Past Participle Tennis.* You have three seconds!

buy — bought

9 WRITING

Look at the Life Questionnaire in exercise 4 and write about your own experiences.

I have won a competition.

> **Extension** Write three true and two false sentences about yourself using *never*. Show the sentences to another student. Can he/she guess which are false?
> *I've never eaten a hamburger.*

LANGUAGE WORKOUT

Complete.

Present perfect with *ever/never*

_____ you _____ been on a high-speed train?
Have _____ _____ played with two magnets?
The world has _____ _____ so many fast trains.
There _____ _____ been so much interest in it before.

We can use the present perfect with *ever* and *never* to talk about experiences at an indefinite time in the past.

Indefinite pronouns and adverbs

anyone	any_____	anywhere
everyone	everything	every_____
no one	nothing	nowhere
some_____	something	somewhere

▶**Answers and Practice**
Language File pages 119–120

Too many tourists

Saying what's wrong with something
too much/too many   (not) enough

1 OPENER

Which of these can you see in the photos?

> crowds   fruit   grass   meat   models
> a museum   queues   a shop
> a stadium   tourists   traffic

2 READING

🔴 2.38   Read the dialogue. What is the video about?

Leyla and Alexey are introducing their video to the group.

LEYLA   Hello, everyone. We've made a video about London called *City Sights*, and we hope you like it. When people visit London, they want to see all the sights. But sometimes there are too many tourists, too many queues and there isn't enough time to see everything.

ALEXEY   That's why we've made a video about places we haven't all had enough time to visit. We want to thank Steve for helping us – it's his voice you can hear on the video. Please listen carefully and don't make too much noise. Is that loud enough?

3 AFTER READING

Match the questions with the answers. There are two wrong answers.

1   Leyla says 'We hope you like *it*.' What is *it*?
2   What do tourists in London want to see?
3   Why can't they see everything?
4   Why do Alexey and Leyla thank Steve?
5   Alexey asks 'Is that loud enough?' What?

a   Because there isn't enough time.
b   There's too much noise.
c   Their video about London.
d   The sound on the video.
e   All the sights.
f   His voice is too loud.
g   Because he's helped them.

Your response   Imagine you are making a video about your town. Which four places will you choose for the video and why?

4 LISTENING

🔊 2.39 Listen to the video commentary, and number the pictures in the order you hear about them. Then do the City Sights quiz.

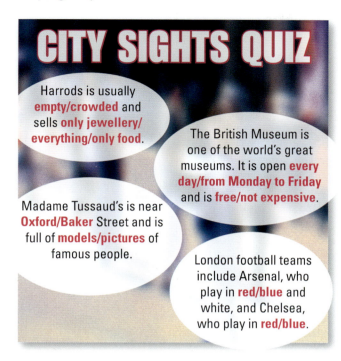

CITY SIGHTS QUIZ

Harrods is usually **empty/crowded** and sells **only jewellery/ everything/only food**.

The British Museum is one of the world's great museums. It is open **every day/from Monday to Friday** and is **free/not expensive**.

Madame Tussaud's is near **Oxford/Baker** Street and is full of **models/pictures** of famous people.

London football teams include Arsenal, who play in **red/blue** and white, and Chelsea, who play in **red/blue**.

5 WRITING

Complete the sentences using *too much/many* or *enough*.

1 Alexey and Leyla are in Trafalgar Square. It's very noisy and Leyla can't hear what Alexey is saying. Why not? There's …
2 Ramón and Emma want to go to a gig. But they can't because the tickets are very expensive. What's the problem? They haven't got …
3 Jay has bought lots of presents for his family, but now he can't close his suitcase. Why not? He has …
4 Kristin always makes mistakes when she plays computer games. Why doesn't she ever win the games? She makes …
5 Steve has satellite TV at home with over 100 channels. But it's hard to choose which channel to watch. What's his problem? There are …
6 Carrie and Steve need time to relax, but they work very hard all day. What's their problem? They haven't got …

6 PRONUNCIATION

🔊 2.40 Listen and repeat.

/tʃ/ much	/ʃ/ shop
cheese	she's
choose	shoes
chair	share
watch	wash

Now listen and write the words you hear.

Extension Write six more words for each sound. Compare your words with other students.

7 SPEAKING

Describe places in your town without saying their names. Say what is good and bad about them. Ask the other students to guess which places you are describing. Think about:

| shops | cafés | cinemas and theatres | churches |
| parks | markets | museums | restaurants | stadiums |

A It's near the centre of town and it has great coffee and cakes. But it's quite small and there aren't enough tables.
B The Brazilian Coffee House!

Extension Have a discussion about your town.
● Where can teenagers meet in your town?
● What can you do there?
● What other teenage facilities would you like?

8 WRITING

Write a description of one or two of the places you talked about in exercise 7.

The market is a great place for shopping. But at weekends there are too many people there …

LANGUAGE WORKOUT

Complete.

too much/too many
They cost **too much** money.
Don't make _____ much noise.
There are too _____ tourists.
There are _____ _____ queues.

We use *too* _____ with uncountable nouns.
We use *too* _____ with plural countable nouns.

(not) enough
There isn't enough time.
Is that loud _____?

enough goes before nouns and after adjectives/adverbs.

▶**Answers and Practice**
Language File page 120

Favourite places

Jay

I've lived in New York all my life and my favourite place is the Statue of Liberty. It's in New York Harbour and it's world-famous. The statue was a present from France to the people of the USA and it's over a hundred years old – it arrived by ship in 1885. The statue is 46 metres high and there are 354 steps to the top. There are ferries to the statue every half hour in summer, and the trip takes twenty minutes. It's very popular, and there are often too many visitors in the afternoons, so you can't go right up to the top.

Leyla

Last year I went to Ephesus, which is in the west of Turkey near the coast, about 80km from Izmir. It's very, very old, and 2,500 years ago it was one of the most important cities in the world. My favourite building is the Library of Celsus, built between AD110 and 135. It's 21m wide and over 16m high. Don't spend too much time at the library, though, because there are lots of other things to see – including the ruins of the Temple of Artemis, one of the seven wonders of the ancient world. You can take a minibus to Ephesus from the nearby town of Selçuk, or it's a 30-minute walk. But in summer it gets extremely hot in the middle of the day.

Steve

My favourite place is in Brazil – it's the Cristo Redentor statue on top of the Corcovado mountain in Rio. A French artist, Paul Landowski, created the statue in 1931 and it's absolutely stunning – it's one of the wonders of the modern world. It's 30 metres high and weighs over 1,000 tonnes. You can drive up the mountain in a car or taxi, but the best way to get there is by train! Yes, there's a little train which climbs up the side of the steep mountain – make sure you sit on the right-hand side going up because the view is better. But when there are too many passengers, the train takes a very long time to reach the top.

Ramón

Come to Granada in Spain, and you can visit the Alhambra – it's the most fabulous place I've ever seen! It's a fortress with beautiful palaces, and many of the buildings are from the 14th century. It also has lovely gardens with fountains and waterfalls – it's like paradise. It's on a hill on the edge of the city and covers an area of 142,000 square metres. The easiest way to get there is to walk up the hill from the city centre. But there's one problem – visitor numbers are limited, so, if you want to be sure of getting in, it's a good idea to buy your ticket in advance.

1 OPENER

Guess: Where are the places in the photos on page 80?

READING

2 (2.41) Read the descriptions on page 80 and match them with four of the photos. Then complete the chart for Leyla, Steve and Ramón.

	Jay	Leyla	Steve	Ramón	Emma
Place	*Statue of Liberty*				
Country	*USA*				
Date	*1885*				
Size	*46m high*				
Getting there	*Ferry*				
Problems	*Too many visitors*				

Now ask and answer questions about the places.

What is ___'s favourite place?
Where is _____?
How old is it?
How big/high?
How do you get there?
Are there any problems?

3 Find *and, but,* and *because* in the texts on page 80.
Then choose the correct words to complete this text.

Carrie

My favourite place is the Eiffel Tower in Paris. It's on the River Seine ___1___ I like it ___2___ I went there with my boyfriend! Alexander Gustave Eiffel designed the 324-metre-high tower for an exhibition in 1889 ___3___ it's the best-known monument in the world. It was also the tallest monument in the world until 1930, when they built the Chrysler Building in New York. ___4___ the real reason so many tourists go to the Eiffel Tower is ___5___ there's a fantastic view from the top. You can take a lift up the tower ___6___ see the whole of Paris. You can also walk up to the top, ___7___ that's hard work ___8___ there are 1,665 steps! It's a good idea to go up the tower early in the morning when it's quiet ___9___ the queues get very long – there are six million visitors every year!

4 LISTENING

(2.42) Listen to Emma talking about her favourite place. Find the photo on page 80 and make notes to complete the chart in exercise 2 for Emma.

5 SPEAKING

Look at the questions in exercise 2. Ask another student about their favourite place.

6 WRITING

Think about your favourite place and write a paragraph describing it. Use the texts in this lesson to help you.

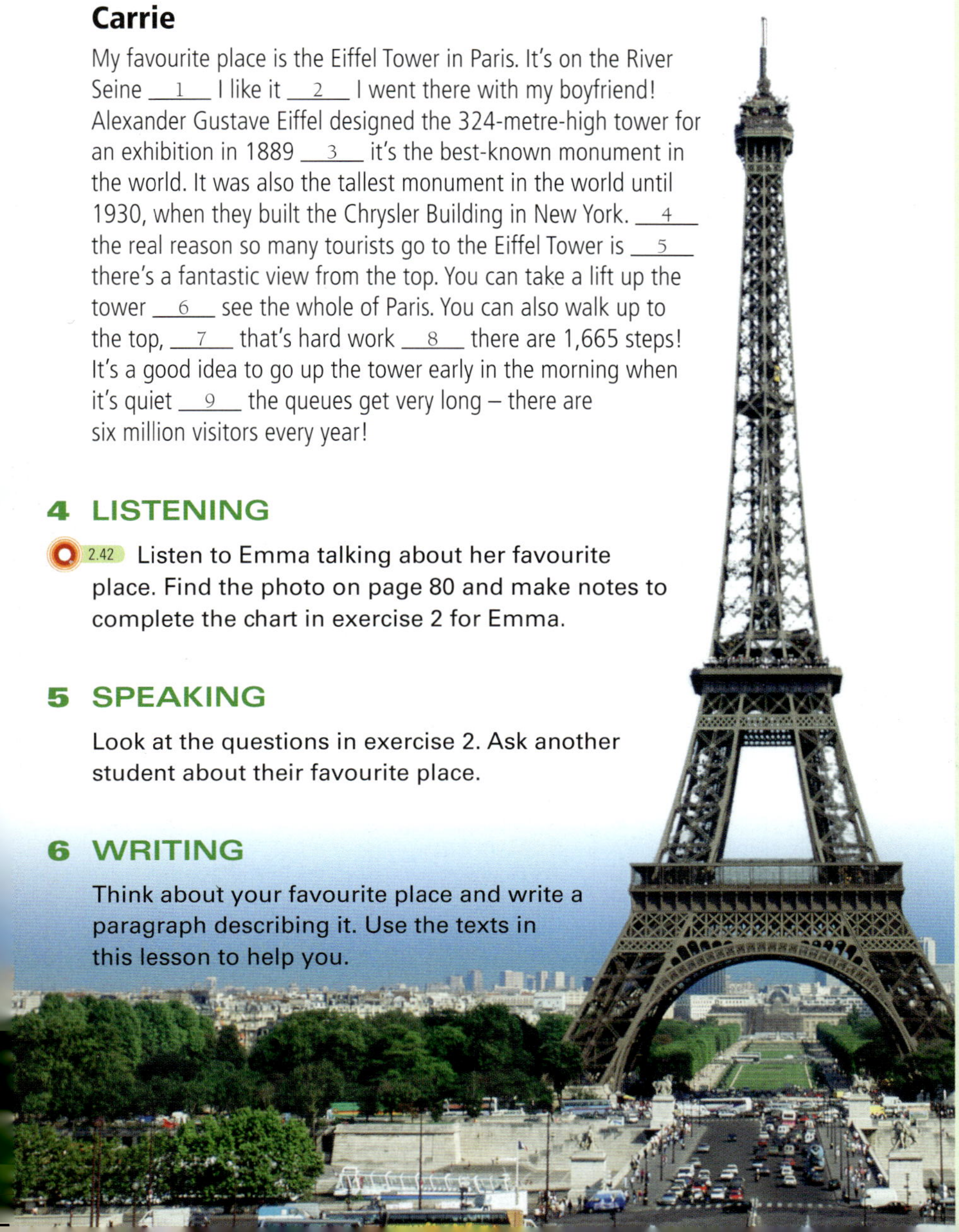

LEARNER INDEPENDENCE

7 Working with other students outside class is a good way to improve your English. You can talk to each other in English or play games like *Word Race*.

> **WORD RACE RULES**
> 1 Play with another student.
> 2 Choose a topic (like Transport, Food or Animals).
> 3 Write down as many words as you can about the topic in one minute.
> 4 Who has the most words?

8 How good a language learner are you? Assess yourself and then ask another student to assess you.

> **How good are you at …?**
> understanding grammar 3
> using a dictionary
> increasing vocabulary
> listening to others
> working with other students
> doing homework 3

> 4 = Very good.
> 3 = Good.
> 2 = Not sure.
> 1 = Not very good.

Now compare your scores with your partner's assessment of you. Are there any differences? What are you going to do about them?

9 (2.43) **Phrasebook**: Find these useful expressions in Unit 6. Then listen and repeat.

> You're pulling my leg!
> I'm not joking.
> Hey, cheer up!
> Here she comes.
> Don't make too much noise.
> It's absolutely stunning.
> The best way to get there is …
> But there's one problem …
> It's a good idea to …

Which expression:

a is something you say to someone who is unhappy?
b is a reply to something very surprising?
c is a suggestion?
d means something is really amazing?

PROJECT *Wonders of the world*

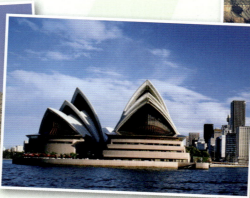

1 Work in a group and make a list of wonders of the world. They can be ancient wonders like the Pyramids, modern wonders like the Sydney Opera House, or natural wonders like the Grand Canyon. Then choose one to write about.

2 Research: Find out information about your wonder of the world and make notes:

- What is it called and where is/was it?
- What is it/was it?
- How old is it?
- What is/was it like?
- What's special about it?

3 Work together and use your notes to write about your wonder of the world. Read your work carefully and correct any mistakes. Find photographs from magazines or online for your project. Show your work to the other groups.

THE PHAROS

The Pharos in Alexandria, Egypt, was one of the seven wonders of the ancient world. It was a great lighthouse which showed ships where the city and harbour of Alexandria was. They built the Pharos in the third century BC – more than 2,200 years ago. The lighthouse was probably 180 metres high. There was a fire at the top which burnt 24 hours a day. Earthquakes damaged the lighthouse but it stood for over 1,500 years. Then in 1303 there was a massive earthquake and the lighthouse fell into the sea. In 1994, Asma el-Bakri, an Egyptian diver, found 3,000 stones and statues from the Pharos in the harbour. Now you can dive and see the remains of the lighthouse underwater.

Game *Alphabet poem*

Write an alphabet poem. Use the list of irregular verbs on page 127 to help you.

Things I've done …
I've …
Answered lots of questions
Been to Brazil
Climbed a lot of hills
Done my homework and
Eaten a lot of meals
Found a friend
Given her a present
Had a haircut and
Ironed my jacket
Just sung a song
Kept a notebook
Lost some money
Made some mistakes
Never been sad
Often been happy
Played lots of games
Quickly and slowly
Read a hundred books and
Seen fifty films
Tried to play tennis and
Usually lost
Visited London
What a lot to see!
X is too difficult
You know and so is
Z

Give your poems to your teacher and listen. Can you guess who wrote each poem?

REVISION

LESSON 1 Write sentences about the group's time in London. Look back at Units 1–6, and use some of these phrases.

> visit the Globe Theatre   visit the British Museum
> watch a football match   watch a juggler
> see the Trooping of the Colour
> go for a ride on the London Eye
> visit a film studio
> dance at Notting Hill carnival
> cross the Millennium Bridge
> visit the Tower of London

They've visited the Globe Theatre but they haven't visited the British Museum.

LESSON 2 Write five questions beginning *Have you ever…?* using these verbs.

> made   been (to)   read   seen   played

Have you ever made a cake?

Now answer the questions for yourself.

No, I haven't./I've never made a cake. Or Yes, I've made lots of cakes!

LESSON 3 Some people can't stand big cities. Why not? Write three sentences using *too much* and three sentences using *too many*.

There's too much noise.

LESSON 4 Write questions and answers about a place in your country.

Where is … ? It's in …
What's it like? It's …

EXTENSION

LESSON 1 Write five sentences about things you have done this week, and five sentences about things you haven't done this week.

I've played tennis twice.
I haven't watched a football match.

LESSON 2 Read what happened to Carrie's sister, Jenny. Then look at the Life Questionnaire on page 77, exercise 4, and write an interview between a magazine reporter and Jenny.

Jenny Grant won a painting competition last year, and the prize was a weekend in New York. On the plane, she sat next to a man wearing sunglasses – it was Jay-Z! He dropped two valuable CDs on the floor. Jenny found them and gave them to him. He thanked her, signed one and gave it to her. But when she arrived in New York, she couldn't find her passport and she took the next plane home!

Reporter: Have you ever won a competition?
Jenny: Yes, I have. I won a painting competition last year.

LESSON 3 Think about your town, or a large town in your region. Write a paragraph giving suggestions to a visitor.

- Where's the best place to go shopping?
- Which sports teams can you see?
- Where are the best places to eat?
- What can you do in the evenings?

One of the most popular shops in my town is …

LESSON 4 Beautiful places are often crowded with tourists. Write a description of a beautiful place which has too many tourists.

YOUR CHOICE!

WHAT HAVE I DONE?

- Work in a small group. Put eight to ten small objects on a table.
- The group look at the objects and try to remember their positions.
- Student A moves some of the objects while the rest of the group close their eyes.
- The group open their eyes and look at the table. Student A asks *What have I done?* and they try to say what has changed.

You've put the pen on top of the book.

OBSERVATION QUIZ

- Work in pairs and write a ten-question quiz about details of your town. For example:

How many stops are there on bus route 7? How many floors does the department store have? What building is next to the post office? What are the exact words on English signs in the town? How many steps are there from the first to the second floor in the school? When does the bank close? Where is the nearest flower shop to the school?

- Work with another pair and do each other's quizzes.

REVIEW

1 Read and complete. For each number 1–10, choose word or phrase A, B or C.

No singer has had a career like Kylie Minogue and no one ___1___ to more people at the same time. ___2___ the Sydney Olympic Games in 2000 she sang *Dancing Queen* to a worldwide TV audience of four billion people. Today she is one of the most successful singers the world has ___3___ seen, but she started performing as a child actor in soaps on Australian TV.

Kylie Ann Minogue was born in Melbourne, Australia, on 28 May 1968. Her first TV role came when she ___4___ only twelve years old, and six years later she left school and joined *Neighbours*.

A year later, her first single, *Locomotion*, was a Number One hit in Australia. But it was the next song, *I Should Be So Lucky*, released in January 1988, which made ___5___ a world star. 'A new star ___6___ arrived,' the newspapers said. 'It's the first time a singer has ___7___ had a Number One in the UK and Australia at the same time.'

Kylie discovered she had cancer in 2006, but she was performing again by the end of 2007. Over her long career she ___8___ hundreds of awards and she is a household name everywhere. But Kylie herself ___9___ changed. Ask her how many records she has sold or how ___10___ money she has, and she smiles her famous smile. She simply enjoys making people happy and they love her for being herself.

1	**A** sang	**B** sung	**C** has sung
2	**A** At	**B** In	**C** On
3	**A** always	**B** ever	**C** never
4	**A** has been	**B** is	**C** was
5	**A** her	**B** hers	**C** she
6	**A** have	**B** has	**C** had
7	**A** before	**B** ever	**C** never
8	**A** has won	**B** wins	**C** won
9	**A** hasn't	**B** doesn't	**C** wasn't
10	**A** any	**B** many	**C** much

2 🔴 2.44 Ask Carrie questions about future arrangements, like this:

Kristin/return to Switzerland

> When is she returning to Switzerland?

On 31st August.

Listen and write the dates. Now you.

1 Kristin/return to Switzerland *31 August*
2 Leyla/fly home
3 Ramón and Jay/visit Scotland
4 Alexey/go on holiday
5 Emma/go back to school
6 you/get married

Now write sentences.

1 *Kristin is returning to Switzerland on 31st August.*

3 Choose *some* or *any*.

1 I want to buy some/any presents for my family.
2 Could you lend me some/any money for an ice cream?
3 There aren't some/any empty tables in the café.
4 Would you like some/any water with your meal?
5 I haven't got some/any expensive jewellery.
6 Do you sell some/any French newspapers?

4 Complete with *How much/many*, and write the answers.

1 _____ _____ water do you drink every day?
2 _____ _____ meals do you have every day?
3 _____ _____ money do you spend every week?
4 _____ _____ books do you read every month?
5 _____ _____ English words do you learn every week?
6 _____ _____ time do you spend at school every week?
7 _____ _____ sleep do you have every night?
8 _____ _____ times do you wash your hair every week?

5 Emma is talking to Leyla about Saturday evening. Complete with object pronouns.

'This evening, some friends called me from Scotland. I was talking to ___1___ on the phone and Jay was waiting for ___2___. So Carrie gave Jay a map of central London and told ___3___ the way to the Lyceum Theatre. But I don't think Jay listened to ___4___! We looked for the theatre but we couldn't find ___5___, so we asked a police officer to help ___6___. When we ran into the theatre, you were all waiting for ___7___. It was great to see ___8___! And we were just in time for the show – I'm glad I didn't miss ___9___.'

6 Complete with these prepositions.

> across   along   down   into   past   through   to   up

The River Seine runs ___1___ the centre of Paris and there are many famous buildings and attractions ___2___ the river. You can take a boat trip ___3___ the Eiffel Tower, the Louvre, and Notre Dame Cathedral. But don't fall ___4___ the river!

There are lots of bridges over the Seine. Carrie and her boyfriend walked ___5___ a bridge to the Eiffel Tower. She took a lift ___6___ the top of the tower, but her boyfriend climbed ___7___ the steps! He couldn't walk ___8___ the steps because he was exhausted – he took the lift down with Carrie!

7 Write sentences about what's happened this week.

Alexey/play football ✓/tennis ✗
Alexey has played football, but he hasn't played tennis.

1 Jay/speak to his father ✓/mother ✗
2 Kristin and Leyla/have a letter ✗/an email ✓
3 Alexey/buy a CD ✗/a book ✓
4 Emma/write a postcard ✓/a letter ✗
5 Carrie/make a podcast ✓/a film ✗
6 we/go to the cinema ✗/theatre ✓

8 Rewrite the sentences using the present perfect with *just*.

Steve had lunch half an hour ago.
Steve has just had lunch.

1 Leyla had a shower ten minutes ago.
2 Ramón bought some new trainers yesterday.
3 Kristin went to bed five minutes ago.
4 Emma sent a text message a few seconds ago.
5 Leyla and Alexey showed their video an hour ago.
6 Carrie interviewed the President this morning.

9 Ask and answer.

Emma/see the Statue of Liberty ✗
A Has Emma ever seen the Statue of Liberty?
B No, she hasn't.

1 Kristin/made a video before ✗
2 Carrie/visit New York ✓
3 Jay and Emma/be on TV ✓
4 Leyla/meet Eminem ✗
5 Ramón/win a competition ✓
6 Alexey/lose his camera ✗
7 the competition winners/see the Queen ✗
8 Steve/go to Italy ✓

Now write sentences.
Emma has never seen the Statue of Liberty.

10 Complete with *much*, *many* or *enough* and write the answers.

1 Are there too _____ tourists in your town?
2 Is there too _____ traffic in the streets?
3 Have you spent too _____ money this week?
4 Have you watched too _____ TV programmes this week?
5 Have you got too _____ TV channels?
6 Have you got too _____ homework?
7 Do you always have _____ sleep?
8 Do you go to bed early _____?

VOCABULARY

11 Complete with nine of these words.

customer fountain magnet menu park position
route satellite stadium tie track waiter

1 A _____ is someone who works in a restaurant.
2 A _____ is an artificial object in space which goes round the earth.
3 A _____ is someone who buys things in a shop or a meal in a restaurant.
4 A _____ is a list of the food you can order in a restaurant.
5 A _____ is a green open space in a town or city.
6 A _____ is something that a man wears round his neck over a shirt.
7 A _____ is a piece of metal which attracts objects that contain iron.
8 A _____ is a place where people play football.
9 A _____ is a way to get from one place to another.

12 Match these words with their definitions.

ancient dairy produce engine market paradise
queue railway starving statue vegetarian

1 perfect place
2 machine that makes a train, car or plane move
3 very very hungry
4 someone who doesn't eat meat
5 butter and cheese, for example
6 place (often outside) where you can buy things from stalls
7 track that trains travel along
8 opposite of *modern*
9 large stone or metal model of a person or animal
10 line of people waiting for something

13 Match the verbs in list A with the words and phrases in list B.

	A	B
1	cross	a competition
2	give	a meal
3	go	directions
4	order	shopping
5	pull	someone the way
6	tell	someone's leg
7	visit	the road
8	win	the zoo

LEARNER INDEPENDENCE
SELF ASSESSMENT

Look back at Lessons 1–3 in Units 5 and 6.

How good are you at …?	✓ Fine	? Not sure
1 Talking about future arrangements Workbook pp52–53 exercises 1–4	☐	☐
2 Describing a sequence of events Workbook p53 exercise 5	☐	☐
3 Ordering a meal in a restaurant Workbook p54 exercise 1	☐	☐
4 Giving directions Workbook p57 exercises 5–7	☐	☐
5 Talking about recent events Workbook pp64–65 exercises 1–4	☐	☐
6 Talking about experiences Workbook pp66–67 exercises 1–3	☐	☐
7 Saying what's wrong with something Workbook p69 exercises 3 and 4	☐	☐

Not sure? Have a look at Language File pages 117–120 and do the Workbook exercise(s) again.

Now write an example for 1–7

1 We're meeting tomorrow at 11.30.

PREVIEW

UNITS 7–8

COMMUNICATIVE AIMS
LEARNING HOW TO …

1 Express obligation and prohibition
2 Express lack of obligation
3 Make suggestions and express preferences
4 Describe a process
5 Express purpose and consequence
6 Talk about cause and effect
7 Ask for agreement

TOPICS AND VOCABULARY

Household items
Rules
Exhibitions
Animals
Feelings
The Arctic
Body language
Animated films
Jobs and occupations
Digital cameras

They were watching the juggler, weren't they?

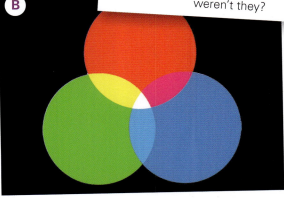

If we mix red and green, we get yellow.

They used computer animation to bring the dinosaurs to life.

1 Match the communicative aims (1–7) with the pictures (A–G).

2 ⊙ 3.01 Listen to extracts 1–3 from Units 7–8. Match each extract with a topic in the box.

3 Put the words into categories.

> **Household items**

> **The Arctic**

> **Body language**

knife smile plate snow winter cup polar bear friendly fork gesture spoon igloo glass ice polite cold kiss shake hands

D

Then they make puppets of the characters and the designer plans the background.

E

I'd rather look at snakes.

F

You don't have to come to the stadium.

G

They mustn't forget the dangers of the jungle.

5 Ask other students questions and complete the chart with eight different names.

Are you scared of spiders?

QUESTIONNAIRE

Find someone who …   **Name**

isn't scared of spiders.

likes doing the washing-up.

prefers cold weather to hot weather.

enjoys animated films.

loves dogs.

is nervous about flying.

would like to climb Mount Everest.

often goes to football matches.

What interesting or surprising things did you find out? Tell another student.

4 Write three more words for each of these categories.

Feelings
surprised _____ _____ _____

Animated films
animation _____ _____ _____

Animals
horse _____ _____ _____

Believe it or not!

The coldest inhabited place is Oymyakon in Siberia, Russia. Its lowest recorded temperature is –71.2°C. The hottest inhabited place is Dallol in northern Ethiopia, with an average temperature of 34°C.

They must eat insects and worms

Expressing obligation and prohibition
must and *mustn't*

I'm A Celebrity –
Get Me Out Of Here!

I'm A Celebrity – Get Me Out Of Here! is a very popular reality TV show. The celebrities who take part in the programme must give up luxuries and spend up to a fortnight in a camp in the Australian jungle. During that time, hidden cameras film everything they do and say, day and night.

Each person can take one 'luxury item', such as a hat, a notebook, or even make-up – but they mustn't take things like mobile phones. The group gets basic supplies: two knives, three spoons, 10 boxes of matches, candles, a chopping board, shampoo, toilet paper, a mirror, paraffin, a cooking pot, and rice and beans. At the centre of the camp is a log fire, and the celebrities must prepare and cook their own food. And they mustn't forget the dangers of the jungle – there are poisonous snakes and spiders in the area! Before they go, they must learn basic survival techniques, such as emergency treatment of snake bites.

In the first week, the celebrities must do different things to win extra food – the TV viewers choose who does the task each day. What kind of things must the contestants do? For example, they must eat insects and worms, or carry live snakes, or spend the whole night alone in the jungle. One person had to walk through water full of crocodiles – the small crocodiles were real, but fortunately the largest crocodile was plastic! In the second week, the viewers decide who leaves the jungle each day. The last person left becomes King or Queen of the Jungle, and wins a lot of money for charity.

Life in the jungle isn't easy for the celebrities. They complain because they're hungry, and they often get bored because they have no contact with the outside world. They only see the show's presenters and film crews who interview them. But not too far away from the camp there are up to 400 people working on the programme!

1 OPENER

Look at the photos. Which of these words do you expect to find in the text?

crocodiles   horses   insects   jungle   knives   log
market   mobile phones   rhinos   snakes   zoo

2 READING

🔴 3.02 Read *I'm A Celebrity – Get Me Out Of Here!*
Would you like to take part in the show?
Why/Why not?

3 AFTER READING

True or false? Correct the false sentences.

1 The celebrities spend up to two weeks in the jungle.
2 They must hide their cameras.
3 They can take any luxury items they want.
4 They must cook on an open fire.
5 The celebrities choose who must do the tasks to win extra food.
6 In one of the tasks, a celebrity must eat live snakes.
7 The King or Queen of the Jungle earns a lot of money.
8 The celebrities aren't always happy in the camp.

Your response Do you watch reality TV shows? What makes celebrities and other people want to appear on them?

4 SPEAKING

You can often get free tickets to TV shows. Read the notice and say what you must and mustn't do in the studio.

> You must do what the director tells you.

> You mustn't use mobile phones.

NOTES FOR VISITORS
Read these notes carefully and enjoy the show.

PLEASE	DON'T
• Do what the director tells you.	• Use mobile phones.
• Stay with your group.	• Smoke.
• Arrive and leave on time.	• Leave litter in the studio.
• Be quiet during filming.	• Ask for autographs.
• Clap when the 'Clap!' sign is on.	• Take flash photographs.

5 SPEAKING

Look at the signs from a TV studio. Ask and answer.

> Can we use a video camera?

> No, you mustn't use a video camera.

Now write a sentence for each sign.

NO PHOTOGRAPHS
NO VIDEO CAMERAS
SILENCE! NO TALKING
NO ENTRY
NO EATING IN THE STUDIO
NO VISITORS IN THIS AREA
DON'T TOUCH THE EQUIPMENT

You mustn't use a video camera.

> **Extension** Think about your school rules. Write six signs saying what to do and what not to do at school. Then write a sentence for each sign.

6 PRONUNCIATION

🔴 3.03 Listen and repeat.

/m/

You must remember my mobile number – you mustn't make a mistake.

7 VOCABULARY

Match the words in box A with the words in box B to make compound words. How many of the compound words can you find in this lesson?

cooking pot

A
cooking ice film make mobile
note snake toilet video

B
bites book camera cream
crew paper phone pot up

> **Extension** Write a list of other compound words which you know. Compare lists. The student with the longest list wins and shares the list with the other students.

8 WRITING

What things must and mustn't you do in your town? Make lists of places and rules. Think about:

on a bus   at the cinema
in a park   at a restaurant

You mustn't smoke at the cinema.
You must wait for a table at a restaurant.

Now compare your lists with other students.

LANGUAGE WORKOUT

Complete.

must and mustn't
The celebrities _____ give up luxuries.
They _____ learn survival techniques.
What kind of things _____ they do?
They _____n't take mobile phones.
They _____n't forget the dangers of the jungle.

We often use *must* and _____ to talk about rules.

The past tense of *must* is *had to*.
One person **had to** walk through water full of crocodiles.

▶**Answers and Practice**
Language File page 120

Do we have to go?

Expressing obligation and lack of obligation
have/has to and *don't/doesn't have to*

1 OPENER

Look at the photo and the title of the lesson.
Why do you think Emma doesn't look pleased?

2 READING

○ 3.04 Read the dialogue. What will Emma miss, and how does she feel about it?

The group are in Covent Garden.

STEVE OK everyone, we have to go now. It's time for our visit to the Emirates Stadium, so we're taking the tube to Arsenal.

EMMA Oh, no! Last time we had to stand all the way because the train was so crowded.

STEVE It's only six stops – we'll be there in no time.

EMMA But I'm not really into football. Do we have to go?

STEVE No, you don't have to come to the stadium. But you'll miss something really exciting.

EMMA I don't care. Anyway, I have to do some more shopping. I want to go to Harrods.

JAY I'll come with you.

EMMA You don't have to – I can go on my own.

JAY I know I don't have to come with you, but I'd like to. All right?

STEVE Have you two finished? Now, for the rest of you, a surprise. After the tour of the stadium, you're going to … meet the players!

RAMÓN Hey, that's terrific!

EMMA What, you're going to meet the Arsenal team?!

STEVE But Emma, you don't really like football!

EMMA Well – oh, never mind.

3 AFTER READING

Choose the best answer.

1 They are going to Arsenal by underground.
   A Yes, they are.   **B** No, they aren't.
   C Don't know.

2 All of the group have to go to the stadium.
   A Yes, they do.   **B** No, they don't.
   C Don't know.

3 Emma has to buy some presents.
   A Yes, she does.   **B** No, she doesn't.
   C Don't know.

4 Jay has to go shopping with Emma.
   A Yes, he does.   **B** No, he doesn't.
   C Don't know.

5 Emma says it's OK for her to go on her own.
   A Yes, she does.   **B** No, she doesn't.
   C Don't know.

6 Steve wants Jay and Emma to
   A go to the stadium.   **B** get ready.
   C be quiet.

Your response Have you ever met a famous sports personality? Which sports team would you most like to meet?

4 WRITING

Match the beginnings with the endings.

You have to …
1 be at the airport
2 be on time
3 get all the answers right
4 pass an examination
5 pay at the checkout
6 wear a seat belt

a to win the competition.
b two hours before take-off.
c in a supermarket.
d for your lessons.
e when you're in a car.
f before you can go to university.

5 LISTENING

○ 3.05 Listen to Carrie talking about the rules for the next World2day competition. Tick (✓) the things you have to do and put a cross (✗) by the things you don't have to do.

1 answer three questions about New York
2 say why World2day is the greatest website
3 pay £5 to enter the competition
4 send a photograph with your answers
5 send your answers by 1 September
6 be an expert
7 know New York very well
8 give your phone number
9 be over 16 to enter the competition

Now tell each other about the competition rules.

> You have to answer three questions about New York.

> You don't have to pay £5 to enter the competition.

6 SPEAKING

What do you have to do every day? Write a short questionnaire. Ask about:

Meals
help with meals   lay the table   do the washing-up
Clothes
wash your own clothes   do the ironing
wear school uniform
Your room
make your bed   put your clothes away   clean your room
School
walk a long way to school   catch a bus to school
do homework every night

Begin like this:

Do you have to help with meals?
Do you have to lay the table?

Ask three students the questions in your questionnaire. Compare the results.

7 PRONUNCIATION

○ 3.06 Listen and repeat.

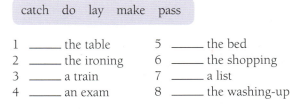

/h/
How hard does a hungry horse have to work before he has some help?

8 VOCABULARY

Complete the phrases with these verbs.

> catch do lay make pass

1 _____ the table
2 _____ the ironing
3 _____ a train
4 _____ an exam
5 _____ the bed
6 _____ the shopping
7 _____ a list
8 _____ the washing-up

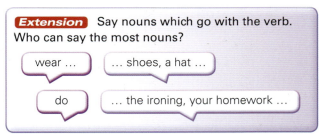

Extension Say nouns which go with the verb. Who can say the most nouns?

> wear …   … shoes, a hat …

> do   … the ironing, your homework …

9 WRITING

Write a paragraph about things you have to do during the week, but don't have to do at weekends. Use the questionnaire you wrote in exercise 6 to help you.

Extension Write a paragraph about things you had to and didn't have to do last weekend.

LANGUAGE WORKOUT

Complete.

have/has to and *don't/doesn't have to*
I _____ _____ do some more shopping.
Emma _____ _____ buy some presents.
You _____ _____ _____ come with me.
Do we _____ _____ go?

We use both *have to* and *must* to express obligation.
don't/doesn't have to = It's not necessary.
mustn't = It's not allowed.

had to is the past of both *have to* and *must*.
We _____ _____ stand all the way.

▶**Answers and Practice**
Language File page 120

3 # Don't be frightened!

Making suggestions and expressing preferences
Participial adjectives ending in *ed/ing*
Relative pronouns: *which/that*
want to/would like to   I'd rather …

These exhibitions are just a few highlights of …

THE NATURAL HISTORY MUSEUM

Dinosaurs

Experience the thrill and danger of life amongst the dinosaurs that lived on our planet for 160 million years! These extraordinary animals became extinct around 65 million years ago, but they come alive in our exciting animated display.

EXCITING!

Fish, amphibians and reptiles

Enjoy an exhibition which is full of surprising fish, amphibians and reptiles, including sea creatures that live so deep they have to provide their own light, and a 150-year-old giant tortoise.

SURPRISING!

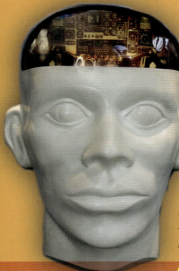

Human biology

Take a really close look at yourself – the most intelligent mammal in the world. You'll be surprised how amazing you are! Test your mind and body, and understand how they grow and develop, in this highly interactive exhibition.

AMAZING!

1 OPENER

Look at the photos. What can you see?

2 READING

3.07 Read the information about the Natural History Museum. Which exhibition is about the past?

3 AFTER READING

Answer the questions.

Which exhibition is best for someone who wants to …
1 visit the jungle?
2 understand how their brain works?
3 see an animated Tyrannosaurus Rex?
4 look at snakes?
5 find out about eruptions?

Your response Which exhibition would you like to go to? Why?

4 VOCABULARY

Match the definitions 1–5 with these words.

> **Word Bank** Animals
>
> amphibians   birds   fish   mammals   reptiles

1 animals which live in water and swim.
2 animals that can live both in water and on land.
3 animals which lay eggs and have short legs or no legs.
4 animals that lay eggs and have feathers and two wings.
5 animals which feed their babies with milk.

5 PRONUNCIATION

3.08 Listen and repeat.

> both   clothes   feather   fourth   other   south
> then   think   thrill   through   together   with

Now write the words under /θ/ or /ð/ in the chart. Then listen and check.

/θ/ earth	/ð/ rather

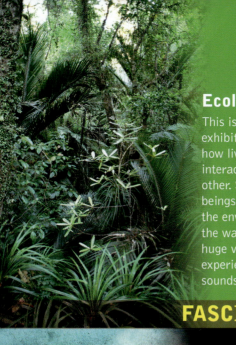

Ecology

This is a fascinating exhibition which shows how living things interact with each other. See how human beings are changing the environment, follow the water cycle on a huge video wall, and experience the sights and sounds of a rainforest.

FASCINATING!

The power within

Find out how shocking an earthquake feels in an earthquake simulator. Don't be frightened – it isn't real! Discover what happens when a volcano erupts and check for yourself where there have been earthquakes in the last week.

SHOCKING!

6 LISTENING

Emma and Jay are in the Natural History Museum. Before you listen, look at the sentences below and guess who says what.

1 I'd like to try the earthquake simulator – it sounds exciting!
2 No way! I think earthquakes are very frightening!
3 I'd rather look at snakes.
4 I'd rather not.
5 I'd rather see the Dinosaurs exhibition.
6 I'm tired of dinosaurs.
7 What about the rainforest?
8 That sounds quite boring.
9 Would you like to go to the museum café?
10 Let's go shopping!

 3.09 Now listen and check.

> **Extension** Make up three-line dialogues about the exhibitions using the language in exercise 5.

7 ROLE PLAY

Act out a conversation between two people who are trying to decide what to do or where to go. Use the phrases in the box and look back at exercise 6.

A

Suggest an activity.

Suggest another activity.

Suggest another activity.

B

Say what you'd rather do.

Say why you don't want to do that.

Agree.

> **Making suggestions and expressing preferences**
> What about …?   How about …?   I'd like to …
> I want to …   Would you like to …?   Let's …
> Do you want to …?   I'd rather …   I'd rather not.

> **Extension** Write a conversation between two people who are trying to decide what to do or where to go.

8 WRITING

A friend sends you this email.

> **Subject**: Cinema
>
> Hi!
> How about going to the cinema at the weekend?
> I want to see the new James Bond movie – would you like to come with me? What about Saturday afternoon?

You'd like to go to the cinema, but you've seen the James Bond movie and you're busy on Saturday afternoon. Write a reply suggesting another film and another time.

LANGUAGE WORKOUT

Complete.

Participial adjectives ending in *ed/ing*
There are lots of surpris___ fish.
You'll be surpris___ by the human body.
Earthquakes are shock___.
Don't be frighten___!

Adjectives ending in *ed* describe a feeling or reaction.
Adjectives ending in *ing* describe the **cause** of the feeling or reaction.

Relative pronouns: *which/that*
Enjoy an exhibition **which** is full of surprising fish.
… amongst the dinosaurs **that** lived on our planet …

We can use either *which* or _____ to refer to things.

▶**Answers and Practice**
Language File pages 120–121

4 Integrated Skills

Describing a journey

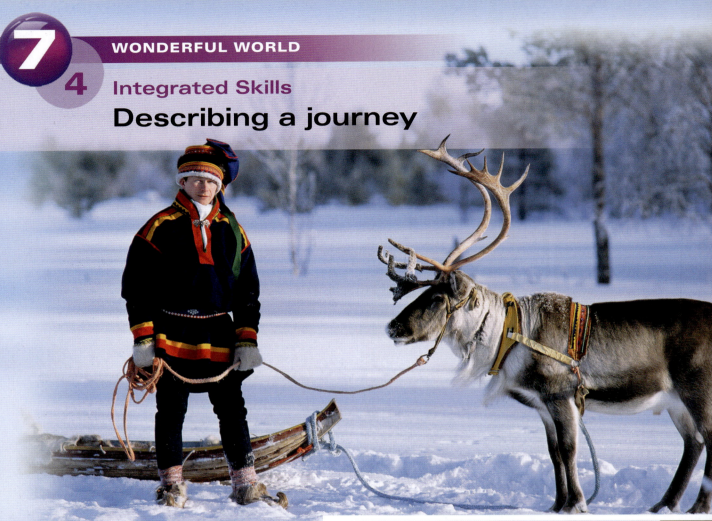

1 OPENER

Look at the photos. Use these words to describe what you can see.

> actor   huskies   ice   reindeer   sled   snow
> stage   theatre   traditional costume

READING

2 Read *Ice Paradise* and complete the text with phrases a–e.

a on the first night the temperature was −31°C
b it's also an important means of transport for the Sami people
c the original inhabitants of the region
d cross-country skiing and 'snowmobile safaris'
e because it melts every spring

🔴 3.10   Now listen and check.

What do you think is the most surprising information in the text?

3 Find the highlighted words in the text which mean:

1 people watching a play *n*
2 area *n*
3 way of life *n*
4 exact copy *n*
5 the way people have usually done something *adv*
6 extremely cold *adj*
7 groups of animals *n*
8 important, big *adj*

Ice Paradise

Lapland is a **region** north of the Arctic Circle, stretching across four countries from Russia in the east, through Finland and Sweden, to Norway in the west. Lapland is the home of the Sami people, ___1___.

Thousands of people now visit Lapland every year. A **major** attraction is the world-famous Ice Hotel, which is 200 kilometres inside the Arctic Circle in a small Swedish town called Jukkasjärvi.

The hotel has an ice bar, ice bedrooms, and an ice church, which is very popular for weddings. They have to rebuild the hotel in November every year ___2___! Most guests stay only one night in the Ice Hotel because it's **freezing**!

And now there is also the Ice Globe, a **replica** of the Globe Theatre in London! The theatre is absolutely stunning. You sit on ice seats covered with reindeer skins, and above the ice stage, the Northern Lights flash across the night sky. All the performances are in the Sami language. The first was Shakespeare's *Hamlet*, a 70-minute version because the **audience** and actors couldn't stand the cold – ___3___!

The Ice Hotel has brought new life to the region and the increased tourism in Lapland is helping to keep the Sami **culture** alive. Jukkasjärvi has become a tourist centre; popular activities include travelling on sleds pulled by husky dogs, ___4___.

The snowmobile is not only for pleasure and fun, ___5___. **Traditionally** the Sami lived by herding reindeer, and they travelled across the ice and snow on sleds pulled by huskies or reindeer. Today they also use snowmobiles to follow the reindeer **herds** and to travel across the tundra.

'I like the cold, I don't like hot places, and I'm interested in dogs, I love dogs, so when I saw an advertisement for an eight-day trip to the Arctic running a team of husky dogs, I thought – this is just too good to miss! I have to do it! But I was worried because I'm very frightened of flying, and I had to fly for the first time in 15 years!'

LISTENING

4  3.11 A woman called Gill Brown travelled to the Arctic for charity. Read the beginning of her story and questions 1–8. Then listen and choose the correct answers.

1 How much money did Gill raise for charity?
A £500   B £5000
2 When did she fly to Sweden?
A 13th March   B 30th March
3 Why was the flight to Sweden frightening?
A It was very windy. B It was very cold.
4 How far did the group have to travel with the dogs?
A 40 kms   B 400 kms
5 How many people were there in the group?
A 14   B 40
6 How many dogs were there in each team?
A 60   B 4
7 How did Gill feel when she fell off her sled?
A Embarrassed.   B Embarrassing.
8 How did she feel at the end of each day?
A Exhausted.   B Exhausting.

5 3.12 Listen to the next part of Gill's story.

Student A

Listen and note down the answers to these questions.

1 Did they stay in different places every night?
2 What time did they get up every morning?
3 How many hours did they travel every day?
4 What was the worst part of the trip?
5 What was one of the best things about the trip?

Student B

Listen and note down the answers to these questions.

1 What did Gill do every evening?
2 What time did they leave in the mornings?
3 When did they stay at the Ice Hotel?
4 Where did Gill see a wonderful Sami performance?
5 Does Gill want to go back to the Arctic?

6 SPEAKING

Students A and B work together. Use your notes from exercise 5 to tell each other about the trip.

7 WRITING

Imagine that you were with the group that went to the Arctic. Write a paragraph describing your trip.

OR Write a paragraph about a different trip – real or imaginary!

● Where did you go?
● How long was the trip?
● How did you get there?
● What did you do?
● What was the best/worst thing about the trip?

LEARNER INDEPENDENCE

8 It's good to try out lots of ways of learning. What is the easiest way for you to learn new words? Order these ways 1–7.

● Using new words in speaking activities.
● Drawing pictures of the new word.
● Looking at the parts of a word.
● Playing games and doing crosswords.
● Writing sentences using the new words.
● Putting words in groups and making word maps.
● Associating the word with something else.

Now compare with another student. Try another way of learning words.

9 Read this list of ways to improve your English.

● I must try to guess the meaning of new words before I look them up.
● I mustn't be embarrassed about making mistakes when I speak English.
● I must learn ten new words a day.
● I must read a graded reader every month.
● I must ask the teacher for help more often.
● I mustn't forget to take my dictionary to class.
● I must keep a vocabulary notebook.

Choose three ways and compare your choices with other students. Try out your choices.

10 3.13 **Phrasebook**: Listen and repeat these useful expressions.

I'm not really into …
I don't care.
That's terrific!
I'd like to try it.
It sounds exciting.
No way!
I'd rather not.
That sounds quite boring.
Would you like to …?
It's freezing.
I like the cold.
It's too good to miss!

Would *you* like to go to the Arctic? Say why or why not. Use some of the expressions in the box.

Inspiration EXTRA!

LANGUAGE LINKS

How many people speak English? Read the text and find out.

English around the world

- About 375 million people speak English as a first language in countries such as the USA, the UK, Canada, Australia and New Zealand. Each of these countries has its own variety of English with its own accent and some different vocabulary.

- Between 500 and 1,000 million people speak English as a second language in many places, including India and countries in Africa and South-east Asia. Some of these areas also have their own varieties of English, which they use in administration, business and education.

- Over 750 million people speak English as a foreign language, learning it in school and using it to communicate with people around the world.

- The estimated total of speakers of English as a first, second and foreign language is two billion, about a third of the world's population. There are now three or four speakers of English as a second or foreign language for every one speaker of English as a first language.

Find out how many people speak English in your country.

SKETCH *Rooms*

🔴 3.14 Read and listen.

BOY	We must find somewhere to stay soon – I'm exhausted.
GIRL	Let's try this hotel – the sign says *Rooms*! *They go into the building.*
MAN	Good evening – can I help you?
GIRL	Yes, we'd like two rooms, please.
MAN	What kind of rooms would you like?
BOY	What kind of rooms?
MAN	Yes – kitchens, sitting rooms, dining rooms …?
BOY	Er – we'd like two bedrooms!
GIRL	With bathrooms.
MAN	Two bedrooms *and* two bathrooms?
GIRL	Yes, and we'd like to have breakfast.
MAN	Breakfast?! But it's six o'clock in the evening!
BOY	We don't want to have breakfast *now*!
MAN	We don't serve breakfast at any time!
GIRL	Oh! But –
MAN	Don't you want to see the rooms? Don't you want to know the prices?
BOY	How much do they cost?
MAN	Two bedrooms and two bathrooms? Oh, about £5,000.
GIRL	£5,000 – for one night! Without breakfast!
BOY	That's absurd! We can't stay here!
MAN	No one has ever wanted to stay here before.
GIRL	I'm not surprised! This hotel is extremely expensive!
MAN	But this isn't a hotel!
BOY	Isn't it?
MAN	No, this is an office – we sell room designs!

Now act out the sketch in groups of three.

Game Desert Island

- Work in groups of three or four.

- You are going to spend six months on a desert island. Each group can only take five things with them, apart from food and clothing. Discuss with your group what you would like to take, and agree on a list of five items.

- Each group explains their choice of items to the class.

- The class votes on the best list.

Limerick

🔴 3.15 Read and listen.

A dinosaur walked into town.

He found a huge chair and sat down.

'Now why did you think

that I was extinct?'

the dinosaur roared with a frown.

REVISION

LESSON 1 Write sentences about things you must and mustn't do in these places:

at a swimming pool
at the theatre   in a library

You must have a shower before you swim.

Look at page 89, exercises 4 and 5 for ideas.

LESSON 2 Look at page 91, exercise 5. Write nine sentences about the rules for the next World2day competition using *have to* and *don't have to*.

You have to answer three questions about New York.

LESSON 3 Look at the text on pages 92 and 93. Choose the two most interesting exhibitions and write sentences saying why you would like to go to them.

LESSON 4 Write a list of as many animals as possible. Put the animals into groups: amphibians, birds, fish, mammals, reptiles.

EXTENSION

LESSON 1 Write a list of things people must and mustn't do in extreme places.

People in very hot places must drink lots of water.

LESSON 2 Imagine that you are flying to London tomorrow. Write sentences about what you have to do before you go.

I have to pack my suitcase.

LESSON 3 Write five sentences saying what you would like/want to do in the next five years. Then exchange sentences with another student. Write responses to your partner's sentences using *I'd rather ... .*

I'd like to visit the USA.
I'd rather go to Brazil.

I want to get a job.
I'd rather go to university.

LESSON 4 Look at pages 94–95 and write sentences about the lesson topics using at least six of these words.

amazed amazing excited exciting fascinated
fascinating frightened frightening interested
interesting surprised surprising tired tiring

The Ice Globe theatre sounds amazing and I'd love to see a performance there.

YOUR CHOICE!

HOW DID YOU FEEL?
- Work in a small group.
- On your own, choose one of these adjectives and think of a time when you felt that way.

  amazed bored excited
  frightened surprised tired
- Make notes about the situation.

  When was it? Where were you? What happened?
- Tell the rest of the group about your experience, but don't say how it made you feel. Can they guess how you felt?

WORDS BEGINNING WITH *EX-*
- Find words in Unit 7 which mean:
  1 extremely tiring *adj*
  2 important test *n*
  3 very unusual and surprising *adj*
  4 public display of art or other interesting things *n*
  5 more than usual, or more than you expect *adj*
- What other words beginning with *ex-* do you know? Check in the Word List.

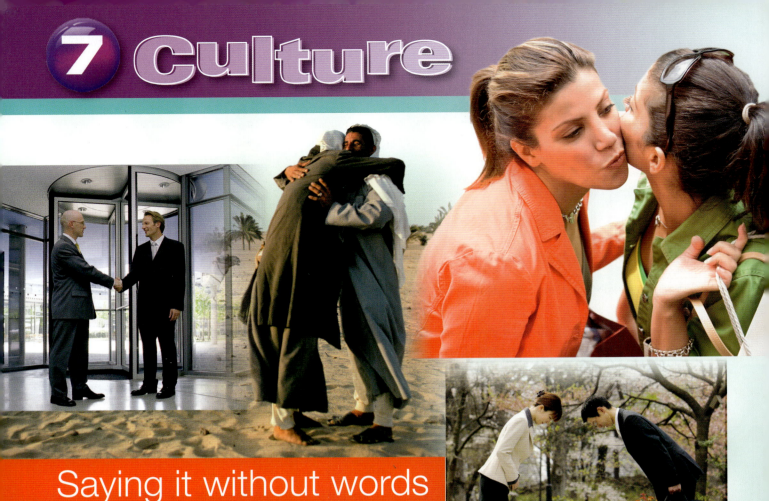

Saying it without words

We use words to communicate with people, but we also use body language – particularly gestures and facial expressions. And different people have different body language …

1 ___

Older people in Britain usually shake hands when they meet for the first time, but young people don't do this very often. In France, many people shake hands every time they see each other – they say the French spend 20 minutes a day shaking hands! In Britain, men often kiss women friends once or twice on the cheek and women sometimes kiss each other too, but men don't usually kiss each other. However, Russian men often kiss each other, and men in the Arab world often hug and kiss each other on the cheek. Meanwhile, in Japan, people bow when they meet each other; neither men nor women kiss in public.

2 ___

Americans usually like people who smile and agree with them, but Australians are often more interested in people who disagree with them or have a different opinion. So sometimes Americans think Australians are rude and unfriendly, and some Australians think polite, friendly Americans are boring! In most of Europe it's friendly to smile at strangers, but in many Asian countries it isn't polite.

3 ___

In Western cultures, young people and adults look each other in the eye during a conversation to show interest and trust, but in many Asian countries, it's rude to look people in the eye, especially a superior, such as a teacher. In Britain and the United States it isn't polite to stare at strangers, but Indians often look long and thoughtfully at people they don't know.

4 ___

In Britain, it's polite to respond during conversations and to make comments to show that you're interested. But in parts of Northern Europe, for example, Finland, it's quite common for people to stay silent when someone is talking to them. In China, Japan, and Korea, young people don't usually start conversations with adults and only speak if an adult speaks to them. In contrast, Americans encourage young people to start conversations.

1 OPENER

We often use our hands to say things without words. What gestures do you use when:

- you want someone to be quiet?
- you say goodbye to people?
- you don't know the answer or don't know what to do?
- you are very surprised or shocked?

2 READING

Read *Saying it without words* and match these headings with paragraphs 1–4.

> Silence   Eye contact
> Greetings   Facial expression

🔘 3.16   Now listen and check.

3 VOCABULARY

Match these words with their definitions.

1	facial *adj*	a	not polite
2	hug *v*	b	look for a long time
3	bow *v*	c	usual
4	rude *adj*	d	of the face
5	superior *n*	e	reply
6	stare *v*	f	bend your body forward
7	respond *v*	g	put your arms round
8	common *adj*	h	someone in a higher position

Which sentences in the text describe what is happening in the photos?

4 AFTER READING

Answer the questions.

In which country or countries do …

1 people shake hands a lot?
2 people not look superiors in the eye?
3 young people wait for adults to talk to them?
4 people sometimes not respond during conversations?
5 men put their arms round each other?
6 people often stare at strangers?

5 SPEAKING

How do you say things without words? For each of the four topics in the text, discuss how people in your country behave.

6 READING

3.17 Do the quiz with another student. Then listen and check.

Do the right thing! QUIZ

Here is some information for visitors to Britain. But half of the statements are false! Can you find the five true statements?

In Britain …

		True	False
1	You must cycle and drive on the left-hand side of the road.	⊘	○
2	When you're waiting for a bus, you don't have to queue.	○	⊗
3	Everyone has eggs and bacon for breakfast.	○	⊘
4	When you've finished eating, you should put your knife and fork together in the centre of the plate.	⊘	○
5	Most people drink tea with milk.	⊘	○
6	When someone invites you to a party, you must arrive five minutes early.	⊘	⊗
7	When you visit someone's home, you have to take off your shoes.	○	⊘
8	Lots of shops are open seven days a week.	⊘	○
9	Girls and boys mustn't kiss on their first date.	○	⊗
10	People can get married when they are 16.	⊘	○

7 AFTER READING AND LISTENING

Match the beginnings with the endings to make *true* sentences about life in Britain.

1 You mustn't
2 You should always stand
3 Many people don't have anything
4 You put your knife and fork together
5 A few people drink
6 It's not polite
7 You don't take off your shoes
8 Lots of people
9 Young people don't
10 People can't

a to show you don't want any more to eat.
b go shopping on Sundays.
c to arrive early for a party.
d get married until they're 16.
e in the queue for a bus.
f have to kiss on their first date.
g drive on the right.
h when you visit people in their home.
i tea without milk.
j to eat for breakfast.

8 MINI-PROJECT
Cultural Information

Work with another student and write some (true!) information for visitors to your country. Use the ideas on this page to help you and think about:

cycling and driving
queueing
typical food and drink
mealtimes and table manners
visiting people
shopping hours
dating and marriage

Read your work carefully and correct any mistakes. Then show your *Cultural Information* to other students.

1 The characters seem to speak

Describing a process
Expressing purpose and consequence
Verb + infinitive
Infinitive of purpose
Linking word: *so*

1 OPENER

Look at the photos. Have you read any books by Roald Dahl or seen any films of his books? What animated films have you seen recently?

2 READING

🔴 3.18 Read the article about animated films. What do the actors do in the films?

ANIMATED FILMS

Adults and children all over the world know the stories of Roald Dahl. There are also films of his books, including some animated films. Dahl's book *Fantastic Mr Fox* came out in 1970. Director Wes Anderson decided to make a film of the book using puppets, and in 2009 *Fantastic Mr Fox* hit cinema screens around the world.

Instead of modern computer animation, Anderson used an older 'stop motion' technique to make the film, with thousands of individual pictures of puppets. The camera takes one picture of a puppet, then the animator moves the puppet a little and the camera takes another picture. The characters in the film are puppets, but the voices are real. Meryl Streep and Bill Murray agreed to perform in it, and George Clooney joined the team to be Mr Fox's voice.

How do they make animated films with puppets?
First the animator draws a storyboard, a series of pictures of the film. The animator uses the storyboard to plan the film in detail.

Then they make puppets of the characters – some of the puppets are life-size and others are no bigger than a thumbnail – and the designer plans the background. Next the director has a rehearsal to make sure that everyone knows what they are doing. After that, they are ready to shoot the film. They record the actors' voices and then the animator moves the puppets' mouths, so the characters seem to speak.

There are 24 pictures for every single second of film, so in one minute each character can move up to 1,440 times! The film-makers often only manage to shoot a few seconds of film a day, so it can take years to make a whole animated film.

3 AFTER READING

Answer the questions.

1 Who directed *Fantastic Mr Fox*?
2 What technique did he use to make the film?
3 What is a storyboard?
4 Why does the director have a rehearsal?
5 Why do the characters seem to speak?
6 Why does it take a long time to make an animated film with puppets?

Your response How do you feel about animated films? Are they just for children or can everyone enjoy them?

4 PRONUNCIATION

🔘 3.19 Mark the stressed syllable.

> animated   animator   background   character
> designer   detail   manage   puppet   storyboard

Now listen and check. Repeat the words.

5 LISTENING

🔘 3.20 Emma, Jay and Ramón are at the World2day goodbye party. Listen and match the beginnings with the endings.

1 Jay wanted	a to get Emma a drink.
2 Emma refused	b not to tell Jay.
3 Ramón offered	c to dance with Jay.
4 Emma agreed	d to stop arguing.
5 Ramón promised	e to dance with Emma.
6 Emma told Ramón and Jay	f to write to Ramón.

Now ask and answer.

A What did Jay want to do?
B He wanted to dance with Emma.

> **Extension** Listen again and note down what the characters actually said for sentences 1–6.

6 ROLE PLAY

Act out a conversation at a party between two friends at the end of a holiday.

A

- Invite B to dance.
- Offer to get B a drink.
- Say how you feel about the end of the holiday.
- Promise. Invite B to visit you.

B

- Refuse and give a reason.
- Thank A but ask for something else.
- Agree. Ask A to promise to do something.
- Accept.

7 GAME

Think about everyday objects and why you use them. Then play the game in pairs.

You use it to eat with.

A knife?

No.

A spoon?

Yes – one point!

8 VOCABULARY

Look at the personal information and match the people with the jobs in the Word Bank. Then say what each person would like to be.

> Jay loves cars, so he'd like to be a mechanic.

- Jay loves cars.
- Leyla is good at languages.
- Ramón likes mathematics.
- Kristin is good at science and likes helping people.
- Alexey likes organising people and events.
- Emma likes cooking.

Word Bank Jobs and occupations

chef   IT consultant   manager
mechanic   surgeon   translator

9 WRITING

Think about what people in your class like or are good at. Write sentences saying what you think they would like to be.

Karl loves blowing whistles, so I think he'd like to be a referee.

LANGUAGE WORKOUT

Complete.

Verb + infinitive
Wes Anderson decided **to make** a film of the book.
Meryl Streep and Bill Murray agreed _____ _____ in it.
They often only manage _____ _____ a few seconds of film.

Infinitive of purpose
Anderson used a 'stop motion' technique **to make** the film.
George Clooney joined the team _____ _____ Mr Fox's voice.
The animator uses the storyboard _____ _____ the film.

We use the infinitive of purpose to say _____ we do something.

Linking word *so*
The animator moves the puppets, **so** the characters seem to speak.

We can use *so* to talk about consequence or result.

▶**Answers and Practice**
Language File page 121

2 If we mix red and green …

Talking about cause and effect
Open conditional with *if/when*

1 OPENER

What photos have you and your friends taken recently?

2 READING

3.21 Read *How a Digital Camera Works*. Name one new fact which you learnt from the article.

HOW A DIGITAL CAMERA WORKS

Digital cameras produce instant photos that you can print at home, share online or send to friends from your phone. They're really simple to use – but how do they actually work?

Unlike traditional cameras, digital cameras don't use a film. Instead they have a computer chip covered in millions of tiny squares called pixels. The more pixels a camera has, the better pictures it takes. When you press the button on the camera, each pixel records the brightness of the light it 'sees'. When the camera records what it sees, it uses numbers, not images.

But the pixels only record light and dark. So do digital cameras only take black and white pictures? No, when you look at digital photos, you see colour pictures. So where does the colour come from?

There are three *primary* colours of light: **red**, **green** and **blue**. What happens if we mix the three primary colours? We get white! If we mix red and green, we get yellow, and so on. This is how your eyes, a computer screen and a digital camera work. In a digital camera there's a filter in front of each pixel, so it 'sees' only one of the three colours.

There's also a computer in your camera which mixes the colours. When you take a picture, the computer compares what each pixel 'sees' with the other pixels around it. During this process, the computer makes millions of calculations in a few seconds.

And the great thing is that if you don't like the pictures, you can always delete them!

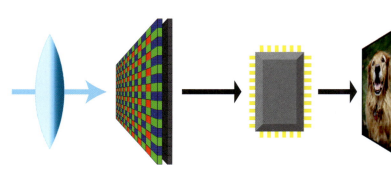

6 LISTENING

🔴 3.23 At the World2day goodbye party Carrie and Emma have a chat. Listen and decide: true or false? Then correct the false sentences.

1 Emma doesn't know what to say to Jay and Ramón.
2 It's not hard for Emma to show her feelings.
3 She's usually nervous when she meets people.
4 She doesn't like it if people tell her what to do.
5 If she's on her own, she doesn't get depressed.
6 Carrie suggests that Emma sees both boys after the holiday.
7 The boys say Emma must choose one of them.

Extension Tell each other what you think of Emma. What do you think she should do about her problem?

7 WRITING

Complete these statements for another student without talking to him/her. Then show them to him/her. How many did you get right? Correct the statements that are wrong.

THIS IS YOU
Your favourite song is …
You are very happy when you …
You don't like it when people …
If you get into trouble, you …
Your favourite food is …
When you meet someone new, you feel …
If you get angry, you …
You feel good if you …
Your favourite colour is …

Extension Complete the statements in the chart for yourself and add five more.

3 AFTER READING

Match the beginnings with the endings.

1 You get instant pictures
2 When you take a picture with a digital camera,
3 A digital camera uses numbers
4 When you look at digital photos,
5 You get white light
6 The computer makes millions of calculations

a if you mix red, green and blue.
b when it records what it sees.
c they are in colour.
d when you use a digital camera.
e when it compares what each pixel 'sees'.
f each pixel records the brightness of the light.

4 VOCABULARY

Match the words with their definitions.

> compare digital instant make calculations
> pixel primary colours

1 when something happens immediately
2 square on a computer chip which records light
3 recording information as numbers
4 you mix them to make other colours
5 see how things are the same or different
6 use mathematics to work out answers

5 PRONUNCIATION

🔴 3.22 Listen and repeat. Which word does not end in the sound /əl/?

> angel animal canal digital inflammable
> local model musical noodle original pixel
> rehearsal simple terrible travel whistle

LANGUAGE WORKOUT

Complete.

Open conditional with *if/when*
If we **mix** red and green, we **get** yellow.
When you **look** at digital photos, you ____ colour pictures.
What ____ if we mix the three primary colours?
When you ____ a picture, the computer compares …
If you don't ____ the pictures, you can delete them.

We use the open conditional to talk about cause and effect.

In open conditional sentences, both verbs are in the ____ ____ tense.

▶**Answers and Practice**
Language File Page 121

You're brilliant, aren't you?

Asking for agreement
Question tags

1 OPENER

Look at the pictures in the *Film and TV Quiz* and tell each other what they show.

2 READING

Read the dialogue and do the quiz.

CARRIE Steve, you're enjoying the party, aren't you?
STEVE Yes, it's great, isn't it?
CARRIE So do you want to try our Film and TV Quiz?
STEVE I'll have a go!

🔘 3.24 Now listen and check your answers.

> **Extension** Write one or two similar quiz questions – make sure you know the right answers. Then give your questions to your teacher and have a class quiz.

3 LISTENING

What do you think Emma will say to Jay and Ramón at the end of the party?

🔘 3.25 Listen and find out. Who are Jay, Emma and Ramón with at the end of the party?

4 PRONUNCIATION

🔘 3.26 Listen and repeat these sentences from the dialogues in exercises 2 and 3.

> Question tags: falling intonation
>
> This is an easy question, isn't it?
>
> You're brilliant, aren't you?
>
> You're coming to Spain, aren't you?
>
> They're very happy together, aren't they?
>
> It was in South America, wasn't it?
>
> We were talking about it, weren't we?

FILM AND TV QUIZ

How much do you know about movies and TV programmes? Find out here!

1 Which actor played James Bond in *Casino Royale*?
A Sean Connery **B** Daniel Craig **C** Roger Moore

2 Who was Romeo in the film of *Romeo and Juliet*?
A Leonardo DiCaprio **B** Sylvester Stallone **C** Brad Pitt

3 Who made the first cartoon film with sound?
A The Lumière Brothers **B** Charlie Chaplin **C** Walt Disney

4 In which series of films does Emma Watson play Hermione?
A *The Lord of the Rings* **B** *Harry Potter* **C** *Star Wars*

5 There are many *Dracula* films – but which novelist created Dracula?
A Charles Dickens **B** Mary Shelley **C** Bram Stoker

6 What is the name of Bart Simpson's father?
A Homer B Ovid C Virgil

7 In which country was Kylie Minogue born?
A the USA B Australia C England

8 Who is the star of the *Pirates of the Caribbean* films?
A Matt Damon B Johnny Depp C Ben Affleck

9 Where was the first broadcast of *Ugly Betty*?
A Brazil B Chile C Colombia

10 One contestant on *I'm A Celebrity – Get Me Out Of Here!*
had to walk through water. What was the water full of?
A Crocodiles B Sharks C Snakes

5 SPEAKING

Say three things about each photo using question tags.
Say who's in the photo, where they were, and what
they were doing.

Photo 1
A Steve is in the photo, isn't he?
B They were near the London Eye, weren't they?
C They were watching the juggler, weren't they?

6 WRITING

Write short descriptions of three film/TV stars. Then
read out your descriptions but don't say the names.
Can the other students guess?

> He's an English film star and he plays a
> vegetarian vampire in the *Twilight* movies.

> It's Robert Pattinson, isn't it?

LANGUAGE WORKOUT

Complete.

Question tags
It's great, **isn't it**?
You're enjoying the party, ____n't you?
It was an American, **wasn't it**?
The questions were quite easy, ____n't they?

▶**Answers and Practice**
Language File page 121

4 Integrated Skills
Describing a process

1 OPENER

Look at the photo. How much do you know about dinosaurs? When did they live? How many different kinds of dinosaur can you name?

2 READING

🔘 3.27 Read *Walking With Dinosaurs* and number the sentences to show the order in which Tim and his crew did things.

A They filmed using people, not dinosaurs.
B They decided which dinosaurs to film.
C They found out as much as possible about the animals.
D They used computer animation to put dinosaurs in the film instead of people.
E They looked for places like those where the dinosaurs lived.

Walking with Dinosaurs

Over 750 million people have seen the amazing TV series *Walking With Dinosaurs* – it's the world's most-watched documentary. It uses dramatic special effects to show these huge animals eating, running and fighting. But the last dinosaur died 65 million years ago. So how did they bring the dinosaurs to life?

'It wasn't easy,' says Tim Haines, the producer of the TV series. 'First we spent two years talking to scientists, and reading everything about the dinosaurs. It's important to remember that dinosaurs lived in a world as real as ours – there was a sun and a moon, day, night, rain, wind and food like today.

Next we chose dinosaurs which people knew a lot about. It's lucky that there are so many dinosaur bones around the world.

Then we found places which look like the world 65 to 230 million years ago. We went all over the world – to Chile and to New Zealand, for example. The dinosaurs are not real, but the trees, the sky, the ground, the rivers and the sea all are. One problem was that when dinosaurs lived there was no grass, so we had to look for places without grass.

After that, we filmed the places with people instead of dinosaurs! The film crew moved things, splashed water, broke trees and so on, in front of the camera just like a dinosaur.

Finally, back in the studio, we used computers to take the people out of the pictures, and put the dinosaurs in. It's called computer animation.'

The TV series inspired a 'live' show, and millions of people worldwide have seen *Walking with Dinosaurs* – The Arena Spectacular. The model dinosaurs in this show, which are up to ten metres tall and weigh as much as a family car, roar and move around the arena just like the real thing!

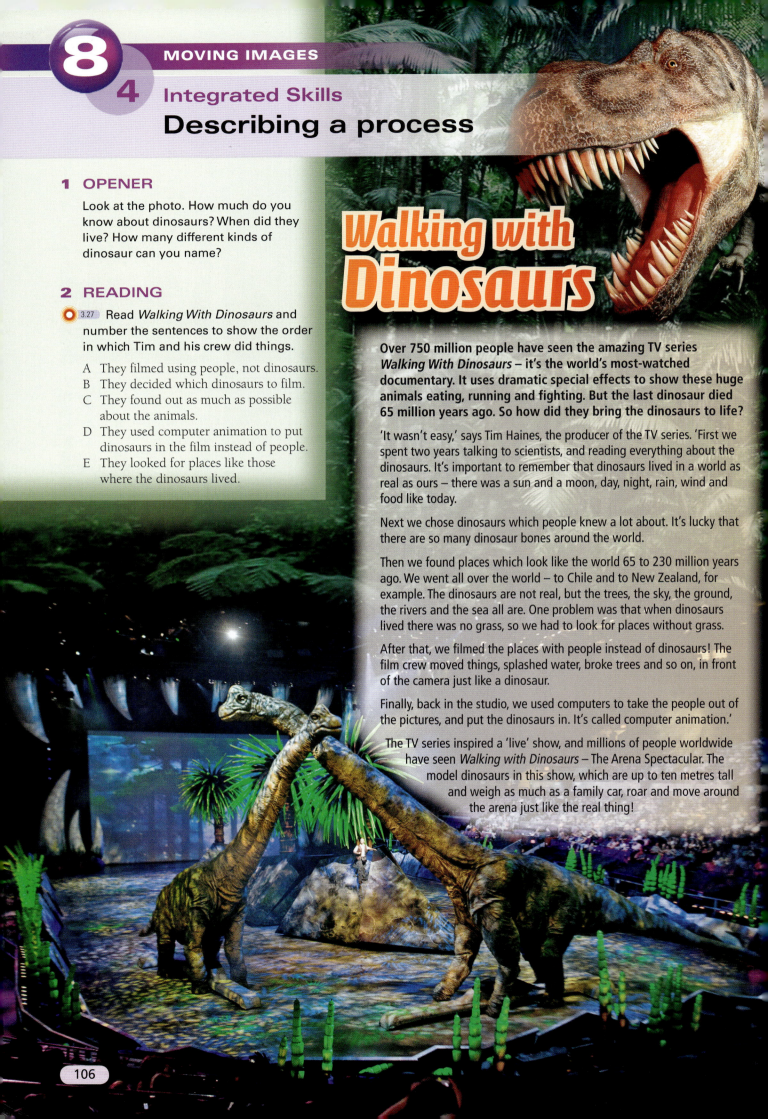

3 LISTENING

3.28 How does computer animation work? Listen to an interview with a producer and number A–E to show the right order.

A Use the computer to make the animal move.
B Scan the model into the computer.
C Put the animal into the film picture.
D Colour the animal's skin.
E Make a white model of the animal.

4 SPEAKING

Look at the pictures and tell each other how to make a computer animation of an animal.

> First you make a white model of the animal …

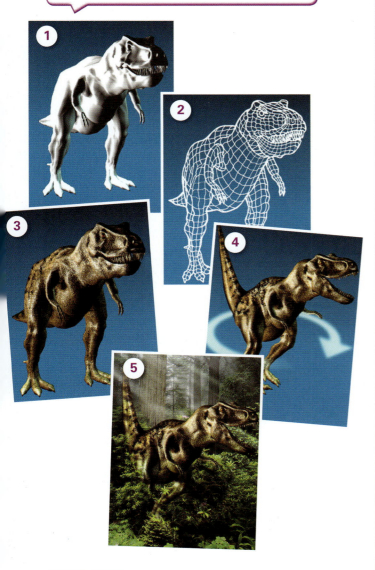

5 WRITING

Complete this process description of how computer animation brought dinosaurs to life.

They used computer animation to bring dinosaurs to life.
First they ___1___. Next they ___2___. Then they ___3___.
After that, they ___4___. Finally they ___5___.

LEARNER INDEPENDENCE

6 If people don't understand you, it's important to be able to explain what you mean. Defining words is a good way to practise this skill. Write definitions of these words and phrases. Then check your definitions in the dictionary.

> animated films chef digital camera
> documentary puppet rehearsal scientist

Now read out your definitions but don't say the word. Can the other students guess?

7 This is the last unit of the book. What can you do to practise English in the holidays? Which of these resources can you use?

> the Internet friends your coursebook
> video camera video or DVD player yourself
> graded readers TV and radio MP3 player

Match the resources with these activities.

1 Talk to yourself in English (silently!) when you are walking somewhere.
2 Watch or listen to English language programmes.
3 Film yourself talking in English and then watch it.
4 Use email to contact other learners of English.
5 Listen to songs in English.
6 Watch recordings of films in English.
7 Read lots of books in English.
8 Look back through the book and revise what you have learnt.
9 Phone a friend every day for five minutes' conversation in English.

Choose resources and activities which you can use in the holidays.

8 **3.29** **Phrasebook**: Listen and repeat these useful expressions.

> I wonder if we could have a word.
> Have you got a minute?
> This sounds silly I know, but …
> But I don't know what to say.
> Yes, that's it.
> To tell the truth, …
> That's a good question.
> I'll have a go.
> It wasn't easy.

Complete these two expressions for yourself.

This sounds silly I know, but …
To tell the truth, …

Now exchange sentences with another student. Write responses to your partner's sentences.

Inspiration EXTRA!

PROJECT *A day to remember*

1 Work with another student and think about what makes a special day – a day to remember. For example, meeting a famous person, or being at an important family event like a wedding.

2 Now make a list of people who you could interview. For example, students or teachers in your school, your family and other people you know outside school. Then choose two people to interview.

3 Make a list of questions to ask:
- Can you tell us about an exciting or unusual day in your life?   When was it?   How old were you?
- What happened?   What did you do?
- What happened next?   How did you feel?
- What do you remember most about that day?

Now interview the people you chose, and note down the answers.

4 Work together and write about the people you interviewed. Read your work carefully and correct any mistakes. Draw pictures or use photographs of the people and what they were doing. Show your work to the other groups.

A day to Remember

It was two years ago and Rick and his parents were staying in a hotel in the north of England. He was 15 and football crazy. They were having tea at the front of the hotel when a big new bus arrived. When the people got off the bus he couldn't believe his eyes – it was the Liverpool football team!

He just sat and stared. He couldn't move. 'Go and get your camera and autograph book! Quick!' his mother said. He ran back to his room and got them. Then his father took photos of him with some of the players. They were really nice and friendly. He felt fantastic and a bit scared at the same time. These were his heroes!

He stayed in the hotel all day, hoping to see them again. But they were working out in the gym and he couldn't go in there. What he remembers most was how tall the players were – much taller than he expected!

Game *Compliments*

- Think about someone you like a lot, perhaps a friend or a member of your family. Note down words to describe the person. Compare your words with other students and write them on the board.

  amazing, easy to talk to, exciting, fantastic, fascinating, friendly, interesting ...

- Use the words on the board to write a sentence or two about another student (don't use their name!) and give it to your teacher.

  She is friendly and warm. She helped me a lot with English.

- Now listen as your teacher reads out the sentences. Guess who they are about and who wrote them.

REVISION

LESSON 1 Look at exercise 5 on page 101. Make questions from sentence beginnings 1–6 using *What ...?* and answer them.

1 Jay wanted ...
What did Jay want to do?
He wanted to dance with Emma.

LESSON 2 Write five sentences beginning *When I ...* using the phrases in the box, and complete them for yourself.

> get hungry   feel tired   feel thirsty
> am bored   am on my own

When I get hungry, I have something to eat.

LESSON 3 Write five sentences about the characters in *New Inspiration 2* beginning ... *is/are from* ... and ending in a question tag.

Leyla is from Izmir, isn't she?

LESSON 4 Put the sentences in the right order. Then complete them with *First ... Next ... Then ... After that, ... Finally ....*

How to record a TV programme

A _____ watch the programme after you have recorded it.
B _____ find a new DVD.
C _____ set the time and channel on the DVD recorder and press 'Record'.
D _____ decide which programme to record.
E _____ put the DVD in the DVD recorder.

EXTENSION

LESSON 1 Read *How do they make animated films with puppets?* on page 100 again. Then close the book and write a description of how they make animated films using these key words:

> storyboard   puppets   rehearsal   shoot
> record   mouths   1,440 times   a few seconds

LESSON 2 Work with another student and look again at the corrected statements in exercise 6 on page 103. Then role play the conversation between Emma and Carrie, using the statements to help you.

LESSON 3 Look at the *Film and TV Quiz* on pages 104–105 and prepare a similar 10-question quiz. Write down the answers. Then ask another student to do your quiz.

LESSON 4 Write a paragraph about what you do every morning from the moment you wake up until you leave for school.

First I turn off the alarm clock ...

YOUR CHOICE!

WORDS IN THE MIND

- Work in a small group.
- Each student makes a list of five interesting words from this unit.
- Take turns to mime or draw your words for the group. Don't say or write the words.
- The first student to guess the word correctly is the winner.

LOOKING BACK AND LOOKING FORWARD

- Work in a small group.
- Have a discussion about your English lessons and *New Inspiration 2*. Talk about:
  - three things you liked about the lessons.
  - activities you would like to do more often.
  - activities you would like to do less often.
  - something you would like to change.
  - what you would like to do in your English lessons next year.
- Now write a letter to your teacher giving the group's opinions.

1 Read and complete. For each number 1–10, choose word or phrase A, B or C.

TOP AIR TRAVEL TIPS

Safety and security are the top priority for all airlines, and flying is the safest way to travel. Each year the world's air travellers make 1.5 billion journeys and on average there are only 50 fatal accidents. But there are lots of things which you can do ___1___ your journey safer and more enjoyable.

→ Pack your suitcase or backpack yourself and never offer ___2___ a packet for someone else.

→ Make sure you check in early. Most airlines say you ___3___ to check in at least two hours before a short flight and three hours before intercontinental flights. However, security checks and baggage X-rays can ___4___ a long time and you don't want ___5___ your flight, so allow an extra half-hour.

→ Remember that you ___6___ have sharp things like scissors or knives in your hand baggage.

→ On the plane you ___7___ stay in your seat all the time. It's good to walk around and stretch your legs.

→ You ___8___ wear a seat belt for take-off and landing, but it's a good idea to keep it on all the time you are in your seat.

→ You ___9___ listen carefully to the safety instructions so that if there ___10___ an accident, you know how to get out of the plane quickly.

1	**A** make	**B** making	**C** to make
2	**A** take	**B** taking	**C** to take
3	**A** have	**B** must	**C** can
4	**A** be	**B** take	**C** make
5	**A** miss	**B** to miss	**C** missing
6	**A** don't have to	**B** have to	**C** mustn't
7	**A** have to	**B** don't have to	**C** mustn't
8	**A** must	**B** have	**C** can
9	**A** don't have to	**B** can	**C** must
10	**A** be	**B** is	**C** was

2 Choose *must* or *mustn't*.

WORLD2DAY Competition Rules
You (1) must/mustn't be over 12 and under 21. Competitors under 16 (2) must/mustn't have their parents' permission. You (3) must/mustn't cheat and you (4) must/mustn't send in more than one entry. You (5) must/mustn't answer all the questions. You (6) must/mustn't send your entry to World2Day and it (7) must/mustn't arrive after 1 August. Winners (8) must/mustn't be ready to travel to London in August.

3 Make true sentences.

You have to	buy a ticket take exercise phone the restaurant have lights look left and right wear trainers be polite speak English	when/if you	want to keep fit. cross the road. cycle at night. talk to teachers. visit London. go to the cinema. want to book a table. go to the gym.

4 Carrie's sister, Jenny, is on a painting course in France. Ask and answer questions beginning *Does she have to …?*

speak French ✓

> Does she have to speak French?   Yes, she does.

1 paint for four hours a day ✓
2 telephone home every day ✗
3 read a lot of books ✗
4 go to all the classes ✓
5 eat French food ✓
6 share a room ✗

5 Choose the correct adjective.

1 Gill is very interested/interesting in dogs.
2 Her flight from London to Sweden was very frightened/frightening.
3 Her first day on the sled was terrified/terrifying.
4 She was really embarrassed/embarrassing when she fell off the sled.
5 She found the whole trip absolutely exhausted/exhausting.
6 The Northern Lights were amazed/amazing.
7 Gill was surprised/surprising how much she enjoyed the trip.

6 Complete with *I'd like* or *I'd rather*.

1 Jay: '_____ to try the earthquake simulator.'
2 Emma: '_____ go shopping.'
3 Jay: '_____ not look at the snakes.'
4 Jay: '_____ to go to the museum café.'
5 Emma: '_____ go to the museum shop.'

7 Alexey was very busy on his last day in London. Match the places in the box with the phrases and write sentences saying where he went and why.

bank   chemist's   cinema   hairdresser's
post office   travel agency

book   some medicine
buy   a film
change   a haircut
see   some money
send   a flight
have   some postcards

Alexey went to the bank to change some money.

8 Complete with the infinitive of these verbs.

> get go have see wait write

1 Emma promised _____ to Ramón.
2 Would you like _____ a pizza?
3 Jay managed _____ Emma an ice cream.
4 Steve told the group _____ for him.
5 Kristin decided _____ to the cinema.
6 Leyla didn't want _____ a film.

9 Match the beginnings with the endings.

1 When you send someone a text message,
2 If you press the red button,
3 When you add two and two,
4 If you warm up snow,
5 When you scan a picture,

a you get water.
b you see it on your computer screen.
c their mobile makes a noise.
d the TV comes on.
e you get four.

10 🔘 3.30 Listen and add question tags to ask for agreement.

Jay is American.
Jay is American, isn't he?

1 Jay is American.
2 The Great Fire was in 1666.
3 Shakespeare's plays were extremely popular.
4 You're from Switzerland.
5 Tamsin was nervous about singing.
6 We're lost.
7 It's freezing in winter.
8 You're pulling my leg.
9 Emma was really angry.
10 We were all at the party.

VOCABULARY

11 Complete with ten of these words.

> autograph candle clap depressed
> earthquake empty grass journey litter
> mammal primary shampoo surgeon

1 We went to the park and had a picnic on the _____.
2 A _____ is a doctor who does operations in a hospital.
3 I asked the star to write her name in my book. Now I've got her _____.
4 Look at all those bits of paper on the ground – what a lot of _____.
5 An _____ is a sudden shaking movement of the ground.
6 The _____ from the hotel to the theatre takes about half an hour.
7 At the end of the show everyone started to _____.
8 There's nothing in the fridge – it's completely _____.
9 Red and blue are _____ colours.
10 Some people get _____ when the weather is bad.

12 Match these words with their definitions.

> animated films celebrity checkout equipment
> luxury second sled storyboard technique

1 way of doing something using a skill
2 something you use to travel across snow or ice
3 something you enjoy but do not really need
4 series of pictures showing scenes from a film
5 someone who is very well-known, perhaps from TV
6 where you pay in a supermarket
7 machines or things you need to do a job
8 they use moving models or drawings, not actors
9 extremely short time, one sixtieth of a minute

13 Match the verbs in list A with the words and phrases in list B.

	A	B
1	arrive	a technique
2	bring	time
3	catch	on time
4	enter	something to life
5	lay	a competition
6	learn	a train
7	make	the table
8	spend	your feelings
9	show	a calculation

LEARNER INDEPENDENCE
SELF ASSESSMENT

Look back at Lessons 1–3 in Units 7 and 8.

How good are you at …?	✓ Fine	? Not sure
1 Expressing obligation and prohibition Workbook pp76–77 exercises 2 and 3	☐	☐
2 Expressing lack of obligation Workbook pp78–79 exercises 1, 2 and 4	☐	☐
3 Making suggestions and expressing preferences Workbook p81 exercise 4	☐	☐
4 Expressing purpose and consequence Workbook pp88–89 exercises 2, 3 and 5	☐	☐
5 Talking about cause and effect Workbook pp90–91 exercises 1–3	☐	☐
6 Asking for agreement Workbook pp92–93 exercises 2 and 3	☐	☐
7 Describing a process Workbook pp94–95 exercises 1–3	☐	☐

Not sure? Have a look at Language File pages 120–121 and do the Workbook exercise(s) again.

Now write an example for 1–7

1 You mustn't smoke in the studio.

LANGUAGE FILE

Present simple: *be*

WELCOME!

Affirmative		Questions
Full forms	**Contractions**	
I am	I'm	am I?
you are	you're	are you?
he is	he's	is he?
she is	she's	is she?
it is	it's	is it?
we are	we're	are we?
you are	you're	are you?
they are	they're	are they?

Negative	
I am not	I'm not
you are not	you aren't
he is not	he isn't
she is not	she isn't
it is not	it isn't
we are not	we aren't
you are not	you aren't
they are not	they aren't

- In questions, the verb *be* comes before the subject:
  Is she English?
  Where is he from?
- We make the negative by adding *not*.
- We use the full form in affirmative short answers and the contraction in negative short answers:
  Yes, she is.   No, she isn't.

Present simple

UNIT 1 LESSON 1

Affirmative	Negative	
	Full forms	**Contractions**
I like	I do not like	I don't like
you like	you do not like	you don't like
he like**s**	he **does** not like	he **doesn't** like
she like**s**	she **does** not like	she **doesn't** like
it like**s**	it **does** not like	it **doesn't** like
we like	we do not like	we don't like
you like	you do not like	you don't like
they like	they do not like	they don't like

Questions	Short answers	
Do you like ...?	Yes, I do.	No, I don't.
	Yes, we do.	No, we don't.
Does he like ...?	Yes, he **does**.	No, he **doesn't**.
Does she like ...?	Yes, she **does**.	No, she **doesn't**.
Does it like ...?	Yes, it **does**.	No, it **doesn't**.
Do they like ...?	Yes, they do.	No, they don't.

- We use the present simple to describe states, routines, timetables and regular activities:
  I go to the cinema on Saturdays.
  She loves horses.
  Emma speaks Italian.
  What languages do you speak?
  Do you really speak Chinese?
  I don't often go to the movies.
  She doesn't speak Chinese.
- We also use the present simple to talk about what people do in their jobs and occupations:
  What does she do? (= What's her job?)
  She's a reporter. She writes news stories.
- The verb does not change in the present simple affirmative except after *he, she, it*:
  *he live**s**   she live**s**   it live**s***
- **Spelling**: third person singular
  Most verbs add *s*:
  *know**s**   live**s**   speak**s***
  Verbs ending in *o, ch, sh, ss, x* and *z* add *es*:
  *go**es**   teach**es**   finish**es**   guess**es**   relax**es**   whizz**es***
  Verbs ending in a consonant + *y* change the *y* to *i* and add *es*:
  *fl**y** – fl**ies**   carr**y** – carr**ies***
  But verbs ending in a vowel + *y* just add *s*:
  *buy**s**   enjoy**s**   play**s***
  Note the irregular verb *have* – **has**

PRACTICE: Present simple

1 Complete with the correct form of the present simple.

1. Kristin _____ horses. (love)
2. She _____ to the cinema on Saturdays. (go)
3. Emma _____ horses at all. (not like)
4. Jay _____ to people online. (chat)
5. He _____ computer games. (not play)
6. Emma and Kristin _____ yoga. (do)
7. _____ they _____ lots of films? (see)
8. _____ Emma _____ Chinese? (speak)
9. Why _____ birds _____ south? (fly)
10. _____ you _____ the answer? (know)

Present continuous

UNIT 1 LESSON 2

Affirmative	
Full forms	**Contractions**
I am helping	I'm helping
you are helping	you're helping
he is helping	he's helping
she is helping	she's helping
it is helping	it's helping
we are helping	we're helping
you are helping	you're helping
they are helping	they're helping

Negative

Full forms	Contractions
I am not helping	I'm not helping
you are not helping	you aren't/you're not helping
he is not helping	he isn't/he's not helping
she is not helping	she isn't/she's not helping
it is not helping	it isn't/it's not helping
we are not helping	we aren't/we're not helping
you are not helping	you aren't/you're not helping
they are not helping	they aren't/they're not helping

Questions	Short answers
Are you helping?	Yes, I am.
	No, I'm not.
	Yes, we are.
	No, we aren't. No, we're not.
Is he/she/it helping?	Yes, he/she/it is.
	No, he/she/it isn't.
	No, he's/she's/it's not.
Are they helping?	Yes, they are.
	No, they aren't. No, they're not.

- We use the present continuous to talk about temporary events and what is happening now:
    You're standing on my foot.
    He's wearing a blue jacket.
    They're holding hands.
    What are they doing?
    Is he helping her?
    He isn't helping her.
    They aren't holding hands.
- **Spelling**: verb + *ing*
  Most verbs add *ing*:
    hold – holding   play – playing   carry – carrying
  Verbs ending in *e* drop the *e* and add *ing*:
    take – taking   leave – leaving
  Verbs of one syllable ending in a single vowel and single consonant double the final consonant before *ing*:
    swim – swimming   run – running
    put – putting   shop – shopping
- See also Unit 5 Lesson 1 **Present continuous: future**.

PRACTICE: Present continuous

2 Write sentences using the present continuous.

Emma/wear/black trousers

Emma is wearing black trousers.

1 Steve/talk/about the London Eye.
2 Leyla/visit/London for the first time.
3 Jay and Leyla/look/at the map?
4 Alexey and Kristin/not hold/hands!
5 the thin man/steal/the girl's wallet?
6 Jay/hold/an umbrella.
7 Kristin/watch/the juggler.
8 Ramón/not listen/to Steve.
9 why/Emma and Ramón/run?
10 I/not/take photos at the moment.

Relative pronouns: *who/that*
UNIT 1 LESSON 2

- We can use either *who* or *that* to refer to people:
    … the thin man who's/that's standing behind the girl …
    He's the one who's/that's wearing a blue jacket.
- See also Unit 7 Lesson 3 **Relative pronouns: *which/that***.

Possessive adjectives and pronouns
UNIT 1 LESSON 3

Possessive adjectives		Possessive pronouns	
my	our	mine	ours
your	your	yours	yours
his/her/its	their	his/hers/its	theirs

- Possessive adjectives do not change with plural nouns:
    my book   **my** book**s**
- We do not use *the* before possessive pronouns.
    *This book is ~~the~~ **mine**.*
- We use *Whose* to ask about possessions:
    Whose is this book? OR *Whose book is this?*
    Whose are the glasses?

PRACTICE: Possessive pronouns

3 Complete with possessive pronouns.

It isn't his camera. It's her camera.
The camera isn't *his*. It's *hers*.

1 This isn't your map. It's my map.
  The map isn't _____. It's _____.
2 These aren't our CDs. They're their CDs.
  These CDs aren't _____. They're _____.
3 It isn't her dog. It's his dog.
  The dog isn't _____. It's _____.
4 They aren't your books. They're our books.
  The books aren't _____. They're _____.

Possessive *'s* and *s'*
UNIT 1 LESSON 3

- Singular nouns add *'s* (apostrophe *s*):
    *my sister**'s** birthday   Anna**'s** guitar*
- Plural nouns add *s'*:
    *celebritie**s'** lives   the girl**s'** bags*
- Irregular plural nouns add *'s*:
    *people**'s** problems   the women**'s** bags*

PRACTICE: Possessive *'s* and *s'*

4 Write phrases using *'s* or *s'*.

Emma + her cats   *Emma's cats*

1 my parents + their car
2 the teacher + her glasses
3 the children + their school
4 your doctor + his name
5 his sisters + their books
6 the people + their clothes
7 students + their work
8 Alexey + his watch

Comparative and superlative adjectives

UNIT 2 LESSON 1

Adjective 1 syllable	Comparative	Superlative
small	small**er**	the small**est**
large	larg**er**	the larg**est**

1 syllable ending in single vowel + single consonant		
big	big**ger**	the big**gest**
hot	hot**ter**	the hot**test**

2 syllables ending in *y*		
nois**y**	nois**ier**	the nois**iest**
sill**y**	sill**ier**	the sill**iest**

2 or more syllables		
famous	**more** famous	the **most** famous
exciting	**more** exciting	the **most** exciting
expensive	**less** expensive	the **least** expensive

Irregular		
good	better	the best
bad	worse	the worst

- Some two-syllable adjectives add *er/est* or *r/st*:
  clever clever**er** the clever**est**
  simple simpl**er** the simpl**est**
- The opposite of *more* is *less*:
  It's less expensive than Rio!
- The opposite of *most* is *least*:
  They stayed in the least expensive hotel.

PRACTICE: Comparative and superlative adjectives

5 Complete with comparative or superlative adjectives.

1 The carnival in Rio is _____ than Notting Hill carnival. (large)
2 Notting Hill Carnival is the _____ carnival in Europe. (big)
3 *Cariocas* think that Rio has the _____ carnival in the world. (good)
4 Rio is the _____ carnival in the world. (exciting)
5 It's _____ for Europeans to go to Notting Hill Carnival. (expensive)
6 Ramón is a _____ dancer than Alexey. (good)
7 Alexey isn't the _____ dancer in the world! (bad)
8 The carnival parades in Rio last _____ than in Notting Hill. (long)
9 The _____ place in Rio at carnival time is the giant samba stadium. (noisy)
10 People who don't have a lot of money look for the _____ hotel. (expensive)

should and *shouldn't*

UNIT 2 LESSON 2

- We can use *should* and *shouldn't* (*should not*) to express advice:
  We should stay together.
  You should tell me where you're going.
  You shouldn't go off on your own.
  Why should they tell Steve?
- *should* is a modal auxiliary verb:
  – it does not change with *he/she/it*.
  – we use *should* + infinitive without *to*:
  You should to take flowers.

PRACTICE: *should* and *shouldn't*

6 Read *Carnival Dos and Don'ts*. Then complete the sentences with *should* or *shouldn't*.

> **CARNIVAL DOS AND DON'TS**
> ✗ Don't get lost – stay with your group.
> ✓ Walk in the same direction as the crowd.
> ✗ Don't carry lots of money.
> ✓ Look after children.
> ✗ Don't wear expensive jewellery.

1 You _____ carry lots of money.
2 You _____ look after children.
3 You _____ get lost – you _____ *should* stay with your group.
4 You _____ wear expensive jewellery.
5 You _____ walk in the same direction as the crowd.

Prepositions of place

UNIT 2 LESSON 2

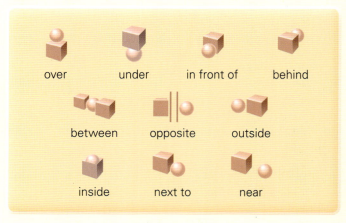

over   under   in front of   behind
between   opposite   outside
inside   next to   near

- *over* is the opposite of *under*:
  *There are lots of bridges **over** the River Thames.*
- *in front of* is the opposite of *behind*:
  *Ramón can't see because Emma is **in front of** him.*
- *outside* is the opposite of *inside*:
  You can get a taxi outside the station.

Verb/Preposition + gerund

UNIT 2 LESSON 3

- A gerund (-*ing* form) is a noun formed from a verb. We can use a gerund after *love, enjoy, like, mind, hate* and *can't stand*:
  *I love go**ing** to festivals.*
  *Bands enjoy play**ing** at Glastonbury.*
  *They like queu**ing** for burgers in the rain.*
  *They don't mind get**ting** covered in mud.*
  *If you hate get**ting** lost …*
  *If you can't stand be**ing** in a crowd …*
- We can also use a gerund after prepositions:
  *Some people are good **at** get**ting** backstage.*
  *We're not interested **in** earn**ing** a lot of money.*

PRACTICE: Verb/Preposition + gerund

7 Complete with the correct form of the verb.

1 He likes _being_ able to see the band. (be)
2 She's good at _dancing_ (dance)
3 What do you hate _doing_? (do)
4 I can't stand _waiting_ for people. (wait)
5 Does she enjoy _camp_? (camp)
6 They love _listen_ to reggae. (listen)
7 He's interested in _talking_ to the band members. (talk)
8 We aren't bad at _____ English! (speak) _speaking_

Past simple

UNIT 3 LESSONS 1 AND 2

be

Affirmative	Negative
I/he/she/it was	I/he/she/it wasn't (was not)
we/you/they were	we/you/they weren't (were not)

Questions	Short answers
Were you …?	Yes, I was.
	No, I wasn't.
	Yes, we were.
	No, we weren't.
Was he/she/it …?	Yes, he/she/it was.
	No, he/she/it wasn't.
Were they …?	Yes, they were.
	No, they weren't.

- There are only two past simple forms of *be*:
  Everything was very dry.
  The people were asleep.
  The fire wasn't near his house.
  There weren't many buildings left.
- In questions, the subject comes after *was/were*:
  Was Alexey asleep all morning?
  Were they exhausted?

Regular verbs

Affirmative		Negative	
I		I	
you		you	
he/she/it	started	he/she/it	didn't start
we		we	(did not start)
you		you	
they		they	

Questions	Short answers
Did you start?	Yes, I/we did.
	No, I/we didn't. (did not)
Did he/she/it start?	Yes, he/she/it did.
	No, he/she/it didn't.
Did they start?	Yes, they did.
	No, they didn't.

- **Spelling**: affirmative forms of regular verbs
  Most verbs add *ed*:
    *start – start**ed**   destroy – destroy**ed***
  Verbs ending in *e* add *d*:
    *escape – escape**d**   die – die**d***
  Verbs ending in a consonant + *y* change the *y* to *i* and add *ed*:
    *carry – carr**ied**   marry – marr**ied***
- Past simple negative: subject + *didn't* + infinitive without *to*:
  The fire didn't cross the river.
- Past simple questions: *did* + subject + infinitive without *to*:
  What did you do?
  How did they cross the river?
  Did you have fun?
  Did they see a play?

Irregular verbs

- There is a complete list of all the irregular verbs in *New Inspiration 2* on page 127.
- Irregular verbs form the negative and questions in the same way as regular verbs:
  They didn't have time to take a lot with them.

PRACTICE: Past simple

8 Complete with the past simple of the verbs. Then look back at page 38 and answer the questions.

1 Where _did_ the group _went_ first? (go)
2 What _did_ they _saw_ at the Globe Theatre? (see)
3 When _was_ the first performance in the new Globe? (be)
4 _Did_ they _cross_ the Millennium Bridge? (cross)
5 When _did_ the bridge _open_? (open)
6 _Did_ they _spent_ two hours in St Paul's Cathedral? (spend)
7 When _did_ the old cathedral _burn_ down? (burn)
8 _Did_ Jay and Kristin _climb_ the Monument? (climb)
9 _Was_ Emma thirsty? (be)
10 _Did_ Emma _have_ a hot drink? (have)
11 _Was_ the others exhausted when they came down? (be)
12 _Were_ there thousands of steps? (be)

Adverbial phrases of time
UNIT 3 LESSON 2

- We use *on* for days and dates:
  on Saturday (morning) *on 21 August*
- We use *in* for periods during the day (except *night*), months, seasons and years:
  in the morning *in August* *in summer* *in 1666*
- We use *at* for specific times:
  at 9am *at noon/midnight*
  and in certain fixed expressions:
  at night *at the weekend*

Past continuous
UNIT 3 LESSON 3

Affirmative	Negative
I/he/she/it was walking	I/he/she/it wasn't walking
we/you/they were walking	we/you/they weren't walking

Questions	Short answers
Were you walking?	Yes, I was.
	No, I wasn't.
	Yes, we were.
	No, we weren't.
Was he/she/it walking?	Yes, he/she/it was.
	No, he/she/it wasn't.
Were they walking?	Yes, they were.
	No, they weren't.

- We use the past continuous to describe what was happening at a particular time in the past, to give the background to an event:

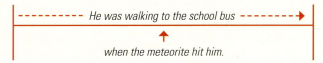

He was walking to the school bus

when the meteorite hit him.

- We form the past continuous with *was/were* + *-ing* form:
  He was walking to the school bus when he saw a ball of light.
  It was travelling at about 500 km/h when it hit him.
  My ears were ringing for hours.
  She wasn't feeling well.
  What was he doing?
  Was she reading? No, she wasn't.

> **PRACTICE: Past continuous**
>
> **9** Look back at the photos on pages 38–39. Complete the sentences with the past continuous of the verbs in brackets.
>
> 1 The photos show the group when they _____ famous places in London. (visit)
> 2 Emma _____ near the Monument. (sit)
> 3 Jay _____ over the bridge. (not/walk)
> 4 Ramón and Kristin _____ at the camera. (smile)
> 5 They _____ at the river. (not/look)
> 6 _____ Kristin _____ next to Jay? (stand) Yes, she _____.
> 7 _____ Emma _____ a banana? (eat) No, she _____.
> 8 _____ everyone _____ fun? (have) Yes, they _____.
> 9 _____ Alexey _____ photos? (take) No, he _____.
> 10 _____ it _____? (rain) No, the sun _____. (shine)

Why? because
UNIT 3 LESSON 3

- We use the conjunction *because* to introduce clauses of reason or cause which answer the question *Why ...?*
  Why was she asleep on the sofa?
  She was asleep on the sofa because she wasn't feeling well.

going to: future
UNIT 4 LESSON 1

Affirmative		Negative	
I'm		I'm not	
you're		you aren't/you're not	
he's		he isn't/he's not	
she's	going to	she isn't/she's not	going to
it's	help	it isn't/it's not	help
we're		we aren't/we're not	
they're		they aren't/they're not	

Questions	Short answers
Are you going to help?	Yes, I am. Yes, we are.
	No, I'm not. No, we aren't.
	No, we're not.
Is he/she/it going to help?	Yes, he/she/it is.
	No, he/she/it isn't.
	No, he's/she's/it's not.
Are they going to help?	Yes, they are.
	No, they aren't.
	No, they're not.

- We use *going to* + infinitive to talk about future plans and intentions:
  He's going to star in a musical.
  She's going to study in the USA.
  He isn't going to go to university.
  Is JK Rowling going to write any more Harry Potter novels?
  What is Dan going to do next?
- We also use *going to* + infinitive to predict the future when we can see that something is likely to happen:
  Look at those black clouds – it's going to rain.

> **PRACTICE: *going to*: future**
>
> **10** Complete with the correct form of *going to*.
>
> 1 Steve _____ take them on a tour of the studio.
> 2 We _____ stay here all afternoon.
> 3 What time _____ they _____ have lunch?
> 4 She _____ not _____ meet Daniel Radcliffe.
> 5 When _____ you _____ start the rehearsal?
> 6 I _____ not _____ miss the party.

Future simple: *will/won't*
UNIT 4 LESSON 2

- We can use *will* and *won't* (*will not*) to say what we predict or hope about the future:

    MP3 players will soon replace CDs.
    We won't know the answer for a few years.
    What will replace MP3 players?
    Which will we choose?

- We often use the future simple after these verbs and phrases:

    believe   be sure   expect   hope   know   suppose   think

- *will* is a modal auxiliary verb:
    – it does not change with *he/she/it*.
    – we use *will* + infinitive without *to*:
        I think she will ~~to~~ say it's a great idea.

PRACTICE: *will/won't*

11 Complete with *will* or *won't*.

1   What do you think _____ happen?
2   I don't think Jay _____ say he's afraid of dogs.
3   I'm sure Emma _____ miss a chance to go shopping.
4   Leyla _____ wear the black T-shirt because she loves black.
5   It's raining, so they _____ have a picnic in the park.
6   They _____ go to an expensive restaurant because they haven't got a lot of money.

Adverbs of manner
UNIT 4 LESSON 3

Regular		Irregular	
Adjective	**Adverb**	**Adjective**	**Adverb**
bad	bad**ly**	early	early
normal	normal**ly**	fast	fast
proper	proper**ly**	good	well
quick	quick**ly**	hard	hard
comforta**ble**	comforta**bly**	late	late
ang**ry**	angr**ily**		
happ**y**	happ**ily**		

- We use adverbs of manner to describe **how** we do something.
    You spoke too fast.
    Actors work extremely hard.
- **Spelling**:
    Most adjectives add *ly*:
        *normal – normal**ly**   proper – proper**ly***
    Adjectives ending in *y* change the *y* to *i* and add *ly*:
        *happ**y** – happ**ily**   angr**y** – angr**ily***
    Adjectives ending in *ble* drop the *e* and add *y*:
        *comforta**ble** – comforta**bly**   terri**ble** – terri**bly***

PRACTICE: Adverbs of manner

12 Complete with adverbs of manner. You can look back at page 52.

1   Are you sitting _____?
2   Steve thought that the group acted very _____.
3   They spoke _____ but the director thought they spoke too _____.
4   There wasn't time for them to rehearse _____.
5   The director thought the group acted _____.
6   Actors work _____ doing drama exercises.

Present continuous: future
UNIT 5 LESSON 1

- We can use the present continuous to talk about future arrangements, and we often say the time and/or place:

    Steve is taking people to the Science Museum.
    We're returning to the hotel at 5.30pm.
    They aren't having lunch at the hotel.
    What time are they having lunch?
    Who is taking them to the Science Museum?
    How long are they spending at the museums?

- See also Unit 1 Lesson 2 **Present continuous**.

PRACTICE: Present continuous: future

13 Write sentences about future arrangements using the present continuous.

they/have lunch/at quarter past one

They're having lunch at quarter past one.

1   Steve/visit/the Science Museum/tomorrow.
2   he/not spend/all afternoon at the museum.
3   they/visit/the museums/in the morning?
4   we/take/a boat trip/before lunch.
5   what time/they/return/to the hotel?
6   we/not go/to the show/tonight.
7   you/come/to my party/this evening?
8   I/meet my friends/in the café at 6.30.

Sequencing adverbs
UNIT 5 LESSON 1

First they're visiting London Zoo.
Next they're walking along Regent's Canal.
Then they're having lunch.
After that, they're going shopping.
Finally they're taking a canal boat trip.

- We use sequencing adverbs to describe a sequence of events.
- We can use *next*, *then*, and *after that* in any order. We always put a comma after *after that*.

some and *any*

UNIT 5 LESSON 2

- We use *some* and *any* with both plural and uncountable nouns.
- We use *some* in affirmative sentences, and in requests and questions when we want/expect the answer 'yes':
  I'd like some garlic bread.
  Could I borrow some money?
  Would you like some water?
- We use *any* in negative sentences and neutral questions:
  I don't want any olives/meat.
  Have you got any pizzas with mushrooms?

PRACTICE: *some* and *any*

14 Complete with *some* or *any*.

1 Can I have _some_ water, please?
2 I'm sorry, we haven't got _any_ ice cream.
3 There aren't _any_ glasses on the table.
4 I'd like _some_ extra cheese on my pizza.
5 Could I have _some_ bread and butter, please?
6 He hasn't got _any_ money.
7 There are _some_ nice pizzas on the menu.
8 She doesn't want _any_ garlic.
9 Is there _any_ spinach in it?
10 Can I have _some_ more mushrooms, please?

How much/many?

UNIT 5 LESSON 2

- We use *How much …?* with uncountable nouns:
  How much money have you got?
  How much bread do you want?
- We use *How many …?* with plural countable nouns:
  How many colas?
  How many people are there?

PRACTICE: *How much/many?*

15 Complete with *much* or *many*.

1 How _____ people are there in the restaurant?
2 How _____ drinks do they order?
3 How _____ money does Jay need?
4 How _____ bread does Kristin want?
5 How _____ pizzas are there on the menu?

Countable and uncountable nouns

UNIT 5 LESSON 2

- Countable nouns have a singular and a plural form:
  a tomato – tomatoes   an olive – olives
- We don't use *a/an* with uncountable nouns:
  We like cheese.   Do you want some bread?
- Uncountable nouns are singular:
  It's rice.   Spaghetti comes from Italy.

Object pronouns

UNIT 5 LESSON 3

Singular	Plural
me	us
you	you
him, her, it	them

- We use object pronouns after verbs and prepositions:
  *Why do people use **them**?*
  *Can you help **me**?*
  *Listen to **her**.*
  *I'm waiting for **him**.*

PRACTICE: Object pronouns

16 Complete with object pronouns.

1 Where are Kristin and Alexey? I'm looking for _____.
2 Steve told Leyla the way and he gave _____ a map.
3 We're looking for the shop but we can't find _____.
4 Excuse _____, we're lost. Can you tell _____ the way to the museum?
5 Jay was making a phone call, so Emma waited for _____.
6 Hurry up, Jay! I'm waiting for _____!

Verb + indirect and direct object

UNIT 5 LESSON 3

- Many verbs can have two objects:
  Can you tell me the way?
  (me = indirect object; the way = direct object)
  … they give you directions.
  (you = indirect object; directions = direct object)
  … show them their position.
  (them = indirect object; their position = direct object)
- The following verbs can have indirect and direct objects:
  ask bring buy give send show sing take tell write
- The indirect object with a preposition can come after the direct object:
  She bought a present for him. = She bought him a present.
  I'll give the map to you. = I'll give you the map.

PRACTICE: Verb + indirect and direct object

17 Put the words in the right order to make sentences.

1 asked   the   we   way   someone .
2 email   me   send   you   could   an ?
3 bought   present   he   her   a .
4 us   joke   will   tell   a   you ?
5 them   I   a   thank-you   wrote   letter .
6 flowers   gave   they   me   some .

Prepositions of direction
UNIT 5 LESSON 3

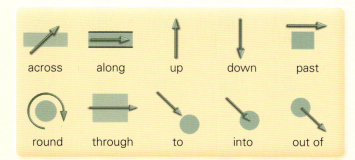

across	along	up	down	past
round	through	to	into	out of

- Note these examples with *across* and *through*:

	the bridge		the trees
	the river		the crowd
across	the street	**through**	the door
	the room		the window
	the road		the rain

- We often use *down*, and sometimes *up*, to mean *along* when there is no hill!

    We ran **down the road** to the bus stop.
    He walked **up the path** to the front door.

Present perfect
UNIT 6 LESSONS 1 AND 2

Affirmative

Full forms	Contractions
I/you/we/they **have** worked	I/you/we/they**'ve** worked
he/she/it **has** worked	he/she/it**'s** worked

Negative

I/you/we/they **have not** worked	I/you/we/they **haven't** worked
he/she/it **has not** worked	he/she/it **hasn't** worked

Questions / Short answers

Questions	Short answers
Have you worked?	Yes, I/we have.
	No, I/we haven't.
Has he/she/it worked?	Yes, he/she/it has.
	No he/she/it hasn't.
Have they worked?	Yes, they have.
	No, they haven't.

- We can use the present perfect to talk about recent completed actions or events, which often have an effect on the present:

    I have tried to talk to her.
    She has been horrible to me.
    Have you recorded anything? Yes, I have.
    Have you had an argument with her? No, I haven't.

- We don't say the exact time of the action or event, but we can refer to an unfinished period of time, for example *all day, today, this week/month/year*.

    She hasn't said a word to me all day. (It's now 6pm.)
    Have you had fun this week? (It's now Friday.)

- We can use the present perfect with *just* to talk about very recent events:

    I've just worked out how to use the camera.
    I've just filmed you two.

- We can also use the present perfect, often with *ever/never*, to talk about experiences at an indefinite time in the past.

- *ever* = at any time. It is used mainly in questions:

    Have you ever been on a high-speed train?
    Have you ever played with two magnets?

- *ever* is also used in affirmative statements after superlatives:

    It's the best film I've ever seen.

- *never* = at no time:

    The world has never had so many fast trains.
    There has never been so much interest in it before.

- We form the present perfect with *have/has* + past participle.

- For regular verbs the past participle is the same as the past simple tense: *work, worked, worked*

- For some irregular verbs the past participle is the same as the past simple tense, but for many it is different: *be, was/were, been*. There is a complete list of all the irregular verbs in *New Inspiration 2* on page 127.

- The past participle of *go* can be *gone* or *been* (= *gone* and *returned*):

    He's gone to Rio. = He's in Rio now.
    He's been to Rio. = He's visited Rio but he's not there now.

PRACTICE: Present perfect

18 Write sentences about recent events using the present perfect.

1 Emma/just/film/Ramón and Kristin.
2 she/record/everything they said.
3 she/not say/anything to Ramón today.
4 Ramón/be/rude to Emma?
5 they/just/have/an argument?
6 we/not break/anything.

19 Complete with *ever* or *never*.

1 Alexey has _____ been to London before.
2 Have Jay and Emma _____ been to Covent Garden?
3 Have you _____ made a video?
4 I've _____ felt so stupid.
5 Has Leyla _____ met anyone famous?
6 She has _____ been on a high-speed train.

Indefinite pronouns and adverbs
UNIT 6 LESSON 2

Indefinite pronouns		Indefinite adverbs
anyone	anything	anywhere
everyone	everything	everywhere
no one	nothing	nowhere
someone	something	somewhere

- We use *anyone, anything* and *anywhere* in negative sentences and questions.

    I've never met anyone famous.
    Have you ever lost anything important?
    Have you ever flown anywhere?

- Indefinite pronouns are singular, so they all take verbs in the singular form.

    Everyone in the group was making a video.

- Alternative forms for indefinite pronouns ending in *one*:

    anybody   everybody   nobody   somebody

PRACTICE: Indefinite pronouns and adverbs

20 Complete with indefinite pronouns and adverbs.

Carrie is ___1___ who has been ___2___, seen ___3___ and met ___4___. There isn't ___5___ who doesn't like her and there isn't ___6___ she can't do. But how can she be so perfect? Is there ___7___ she hasn't been, ___8___ she hasn't met or ___9___ she hasn't done? ___10___ knows!

PRACTICE: *must* and *mustn't*

22 Complete with *must* or *mustn't*.

1 The celebrities _____ cook their own meals.
2 They _____ go too far from the camp.
3 They _____ be careful in the jungle.
4 What _____ they do to win extra food?
5 They _____ complain too much!

too much/too many and (not) enough

UNIT 6 LESSON 3

- We use *too much* with uncountable nouns:
  They cost too much money.
  Don't make too much noise.
- We use *too many* with plural countable nouns:
  There are too many tourists.
  There are too many queues.
- We put *enough* before nouns:
  There isn't enough time.
  and after adjectives and adverbs:
  Is that loud enough?

PRACTICE: *too much/too many* and (*not*) *enough*

21 Complete with *much, many* or *enough*.

1 There are too _____ visitors in London.
2 Buses move slowly because there is too _____ traffic.
3 Sometimes there are too _____ people on the trains.
4 There isn't _____ time to go shopping.
5 I think there's too _____ sport on TV.
6 They haven't got _____ money for a ticket.
7 There are too _____ cars on the road.
8 Are you old _____ to drive?

must and mustn't

UNIT 7 LESSON 1

- We use *must* to express present and future obligation, often when talking about rules:
  The celebrities must give up luxuries.
  They must learn survival techniques.
  What kind of things must they do?
- We use *mustn't* (*must not*) for prohibition:
  They mustn't take mobile phones.
  They mustn't forget the dangers of the jungle.
- *must* is a modal auxiliary verb:
  – it does not change with *he/she/it.*
  – we use *must* + infinitive without *to*:
  They must ~~to~~ eat insects and worms.
- The past tense of *must* is *had to*:
  One person had to walk through water full of crocodiles.
- *must* is stronger than *should.*

have/has to and don't/doesn't have to

UNIT 7 LESSON 2

- We also use *have/has to* to talk about present and future obligation:
  I have to do some more shopping.
  Emma has to buy some presents.
  Do we have to go?
- We use *don't/doesn't have to* to express lack of obligation:
  You don't have to come with me.
- *have to* and *must* in the affirmative both express obligation. But:
  – *don't/doesn't have to* = *It's not necessary.*
  – *mustn't* = *It's not allowed.*
- The past tense of both *must* and *have to* is *had to*:
  We had to stand all the way.
  I didn't have to walk to school.
  Did you have to catch a bus?

PRACTICE: *have/has to* and *don't/doesn't have to*

23 Rewrite the sentences replacing the words in italics with the correct form of *have to*.

1 *The law says that you must* wear a seat belt in a car.
2 *You don't need to* study every night.
3 *It's necessary to* do what the teacher says.
4 *It was necessary for me to* phone the doctor.
5 *The law says that you must* buy a ticket when you catch a train.
6 *They didn't need to* wait long for a bus.

Participial adjectives ending in ed/ing

UNIT 7 LESSON 3

- Adjectives ending in *ed* describe a feeling or reaction:
  You'll be surprised by the human body.
  Don't be frightened!
- Adjectives ending in *ing* describe the **cause** of the feeling or reaction:
  There are lots of surprising fish.
  Earthquakes are shocking.
- The following are common participial adjectives:
  amazed – amazing   bored – boring   excited – exciting
  fascinated – fascinating   frightened – frightening
  interested – interesting   shocked – shocking
  surprised – surprising   tired – tiring

PRACTICE: Participial adjectives ending in *ed/ing*

24 Choose the correct adjective.

1 The museum has some *fascinated/fascinating* exhibitions.
2 The human biology exhibition is very *interested/interesting*.
3 We were *amazed/amazing* to see the animated dinosaurs.
4 I'm not *frightened/frightening* of snakes.
5 The earthquake simulator is *excited/exciting*.
6 They were *tired/tiring* after four hours in the museum.

Now write sentences using the remaining six adjectives.

We were fascinated by the Tyrannosaurus Rex.

Relative pronouns: *which/that*

UNIT 7 LESSON 3

- We can use either *which* or *that* to refer to things:
  Enjoy an exhibition which is full of surprising fish.
  … amongst the dinosaurs that lived on our planet …
- See also Unit 1 Lesson 2 **Relative pronouns: *who/that***.

Verb + infinitive

UNIT 8 LESSON 1

- We use *to* + infinitive after these verbs and phrases:
  agree ask decide know how learn manage mean
  need offer pretend promise refuse seem teach
  tell want would like
  Wes Anderson decided to make a film of the book.
  Meryl Streep and Bill Murray agreed to perform in it.
  They often only manage to make a few seconds of film.

Infinitive of purpose

UNIT 8 LESSON 1

- We use the infinitive of purpose to say **why** we do something:
  Anderson used a 'stop motion' technique to make the film.
  George Clooney joined the team to be Mr Fox's voice.
  The animator uses the storyboard to plan the film.

PRACTICE: Infinitive of purpose

25 Match the words in list A with the phrases in list B and write sentences: *You use a(n) … to …*

	A	B
1	camera	make a recording
2	computer	take photographs
3	map	listen to music
4	microphone	wash your hair
5	MP3 player	carry things on your back
6	rucksack	find the way
7	shampoo	send email

Linking word: *so*

UNIT 8 LESSON 1

- We use the conjunction *so* to talk about consequence or result.
  Jay loves cars, so he'd like to be a mechanic.

Open conditional with *if/when*

UNIT 8 LESSON 2

- We use the open conditional to talk about general truths, and cause and effect:
  If we mix red and green, we get yellow.
  If you don't like the pictures, you can delete them.
  When you look at digital photos, you see colour pictures.
- In open conditional sentences, both verbs are in the present simple tense.
- The *if/when* clause can follow the main clause:
  What happens if we mix the three primary colours?
  When you take a picture, the computer compares …

PRACTICE: Open conditional with *if/when*

26 Match the beginnings with the endings.

1 If you mix blue, yellow and light green,
2 When I go to bed late,
3 If you take five from thirteen,
4 When people shout,
5 If your phone rings,

a you can check who's calling you.
b you get eight.
c you get brown.
d I don't listen to them.
e I feel tired the next day.

Question tags

UNIT 8 LESSON 3

- We can use question tags with **falling** intonation to ask for agreement when we are sure about something:
  It's great, **isn't it**?
  You're enjoying the party, **aren't you**?
  It was an American, **wasn't it**?
  The questions were quite easy, **weren't they**?
- When the statement in the first part of the sentence is affirmative, the question tag is negative.
- We can use question tags with **rising** intonation to ask real questions:
  It's nearly 7 o'clock, **isn't it**?

PRACTICE: Question tags

27 Complete with six of these question tags.

isn't he? isn't she? aren't I? aren't they?
wasn't it? wasn't he? weren't they? weren't you?

1 Steve and Carrie are English, _____
2 Leyla is from Turkey, _____
3 Alexey is packing his suitcase, _____
4 Emma and Jay were in the museum, _____
5 Ramón was excited to meet the team, _____
6 It was a great holiday, _____

WORD LIST

★ = fairly common words   ★★ = very common words   ★★★ = the most common and basic words

UNIT 1

bell (n) ★★	/bel/
celebrity (n) ★	/sə'lebrəti/
Christmas Day (n)	/ˌkrɪsməs 'deɪ/
coach (n) ★	/kəʊtʃ/
column (n) ★★★	/'kɒləm/
double-decker bus (n)	/ˌdʌb(ə)ldekə 'bʌs/
exactly (adv) ★★★	/ɪg'zæk(t)li/
fire (n) ★★★	/faɪə/
flower (n) ★★★	/'flaʊə/
gymnastics (n pl)	/dʒɪm'næstɪks/
in fact (adv)	/ɪn 'fækt/
karate (n)	/kə'rɑːti/
life (pl lives) (n) ★★★	/laɪf/
lunch break (n)	/'lʌntʃ ˌbreɪk/
model (n) ★★★	/'mɒd(ə)l/
passenger (n) ★★★	/'pæsɪndʒə/
permission (n) ★★	/pə'mɪʃ(ə)n/
pickpocket (n)	/'pɪkˌpɒkɪt/
power station (n)	/'paʊə ˌsteɪʃn/
salt (n) ★★	/sɔːlt/
sky (n) ★★★	/skaɪ/
stethoscope (n)	/'steθəˌskəʊp/
stone (n) ★★★	/stəʊn/
sunshine (n) ★★	/'sʌnˌʃaɪn/
thief (n) ★★	/θiːf/
thin (n) ★★★	/θɪn/
tonne (n) ★★	/tʌn/
tree (n) ★★★	/triː/
truth (n) ★★★	/truːθ/
work (of art) (n) ★★★	/wɜːk/
yoga (n)	/'jəʊgə/

ADJECTIVES

far (adj) ★★★	/fɑː/
high (adj & adv) ★★★	/haɪ/
important (adj) ★★★	/ɪm'pɔːt(ə)nt/
interested (in) (adj) ★★★	/'ɪntrəstɪd/
interesting (adj) ★★★	/'ɪntrəstɪŋ/
modern (adj) ★★★	/'mɒd(ə)n/
present (adj) ★★★	/'prez(ə)nt/
quick (adj) ★★★	/kwɪk/
simple (adj) ★★★	/'sɪmp(ə)l/
successful (adj) ★★★	/sək'sesf(ə)l/
tall (adj & adv) ★★★	/tɔːl/
unusual (adj) ★★★	/ʌn'juːʒʊəl/

CLOTHES AND ACCESSORIES

bag (n) ★★★	/bæg/
baseball cap (n)	/'beɪsbɔːl ˌkæp/
boots (n pl) ★★★	/buːts/
camera (n) ★★★	/'kæmrə/
coat (n) ★★★	/kəʊt/
clothes (n pl) ★★★	/kləʊðz/
dress (n) ★★★	/dres/
glasses (n pl) ★	/'glɑːsɪz/
hat (n) ★★★	/hæt/
jacket (n) ★★★	/'dʒækɪt/
jeans (n pl) ★	/dʒiːnz/
pocket (n) ★★★	/'pɒkɪt/
pullover (n) ★	/'pʊləʊvə/
shirt (n) ★★★	/ʃɜːt/
shoes (n pl) ★★★	/ʃuːz/
shorts (n pl) ★	/ʃɔːts/
skirt (n) ★★	/skɜːt/
sweatshirt (n)	/'swetˌʃɜːt/
top (n) ★★★	/tɒp/
trainers (n pl) ★	/'treɪnəz/
trousers (n pl) ★★	/'traʊzəz/
T-shirt (n) ★	/'tiːˌʃɜːt/
umbrella (n) ★	/ʌm'brelə/
wallet (n)	/'wɒlɪt/

COMMUNICATION TECHNOLOGY

account (n) ★★★	/ə'kaʊnt/
character (n) ★★★	/'kærɪktə/
email address (n)	/'iːmeɪl əˌdres/
Internet (n) ★★★	/'ɪntəˌnet/
laptop (n)	/'læpˌtɒp/
message (n) ★★★	/'mesɪdʒ/
microphone (n) ★	/'maɪkrəˌfəʊn/
mobile phone (n) ★★	/ˌməʊbaɪl 'fəʊn/
network (n) ★★★	/'netˌwɜːk/
online (adv) ★★	/ɒn'laɪn/
password (n) ★	/'pɑːsˌwɜːd/
sign up (v)	/ˌsaɪn 'ʌp/
social networking site (n)	/ˌsəʊʃ(ə)l 'netwɜːkɪŋ saɪt/
surf (the Web) (v) ★	/sɜːf/
text message (n)	/'teks ˌmesɪdʒ/
tweet (n)	/twiːt/
username (n)	/'juːzəˌneɪm/
website (n) ★★	/'webˌsaɪt/

JOBS AND OCCUPATIONS

actor (n) ★★★	/'æktə/
artist (n) ★★★	/'ɑːtɪst/
boss (n) ★★★	/bɒs/
busker (n)	/'bʌskə/
doctor (n) ★★★	/'dɒktə/
film star (n)	/'fɪlm ˌstɑː/
juggler (n)	/'dʒʌglə/
king (n) ★★★	/kɪŋ/
musician (n) ★★	/mjuːˈzɪʃ(ə)n/
nurse (n) ★★★	/nɜːs/
office (n) ★★★	/'ɒfɪs/
PA (personal assistant) (n)	/ˌpiː 'eɪ/
photographer (n) ★★	/fə'tɒgrəfə/
pilot (n) ★★★	/'paɪlət/
queen (n) ★★★	/kwiːn/
receptionist (n) ★	/rɪ'sepʃ(ə)nɪst/
reporter (n) ★	/rɪ'pɔːtə/
teacher (n) ★★★	/'tiːtʃə/
tour guide (n)	/'tʊə ˌgaɪd/
vet (n)	/vet/
waiter (n) ★	/'weɪtə/

TOURIST ATTRACTIONS

aquarium (n)	/ə'kweəriəm/
art gallery (n)	/'ɑːt ˌgæləri/
big wheel (n)	/ˌbɪg 'wiːl/
cathedral (n) ★★	/kə'θiːdrəl/
church (n) ★★★	/tʃɜːtʃ/
clock tower (n)	/'klɒk ˌtaʊə/
exhibition (n) ★★★	/ˌeksɪ'bɪʃ(ə)n/
market (n) ★★★	/'mɑːkɪt/
monument (n) ★★	/'mɒnjʊmənt/
museum (n) ★★★	/mjuːˈziːəm/
sightseeing (n)	/'saɪtˌsiːɪŋ/

VERBS

add (v) ★★★	/æd/
bet (v) ★★	/bet/
chat (v) ★★	/tʃæt/
climb (v) ★★★	/klaɪm/
create (v) ★★★	/kri'eɪt/
finish (v) ★★★	/'fɪnɪʃ/
follow (v) ★★★	/'fɒləʊ/
interview (v) ★★	/'ɪntəˌvjuː/
miss (v) ★★★	/mɪs/
perform (v) ★★★	/pə'fɔːm/
rebuild (v) ★★	/ˌriː'bɪld/
relax (v) ★★★	/rɪ'læks/
sell (v) ★★★	/sel/
weigh (v) ★★	/weɪ/
whisper (v) ★★	/'wɪspə/

EXPRESSIONS

as soon as possible	/əz 'suːn əz ˌpɒsəbl/
hold hands	/ˌhəʊld 'hændz/
How about ...?	/ˌhaʊ ə'baʊt/
It depends.	/ˌɪt dɪ'pendz/
look forward to	/ˌlʊk 'fɔːwəd tuː/
take a picture/photo	/ˌteɪk ə 'pɪktʃə / 'fəʊtəʊ/
What about ...?	/ˌwɒt ə'baʊt/
What else?	/ˌwɒt 'els/

UNIT 2

arrival (n) ★★★	/ə'raɪv(ə)l/
atmosphere (n) ★★	/'ætməsˌfɪə/
backstage (adv)	/ˌbæk'steɪdʒ/
cheek (= face) (n) ★★	/tʃiːk/
contact (n) ★★★	/'kɒntækt/
crowd (n) ★★★	/kraʊd/
dragon (n)	/'drægən/
envelope (n) ★★	/'envələʊp/
fan (= person) (n) ★★	/fæn/
flight (n) ★★★	/flaɪt/
front (n) ★★★	/frʌnt/
guest (n) ★★★	/gest/
haircut (n) ★	/'heəˌkʌt/
immediately (adv) ★★★	/ɪ'miːdiətli/
judge (n) ★★★	/dʒʌdʒ/
medicine (n) ★★	/'med(ə)s(ə)n/
mud (n) ★★	/mʌd/
once (adv) ★★★	/wʌns/
poem (n) ★★★	/'pəʊɪm/
purse (n) ★	/pɜːs/
region (n) ★★★	/'riːdʒ(ə)n/
rest (= others) (n pl) ★★★	/rest/
rubbish (n) ★★	/'rʌbɪʃ/
safety (n) ★★★	/'seɪfti/
security (n) ★★★	/sɪ'kjʊərəti/
size (n) ★★★	/saɪz/
stall (n) ★★	/stɔːl/
stamp (n) ★★	/stæmp/
start (n) ★★★	/stɑːt/
suitcase (n) ★	/'suːtˌkeɪs/
telephone (n) ★★★	/'telɪˌfəʊn/
tent (n) ★★	/tent/
tradition (n) ★★★	/trə'dɪʃ(ə)n/
twice (adv) ★★★	/twaɪs/
underwear (n) ★	/'ʌndəˌweə/
usual (as usual) (adj) ★★★	/'juːʒʊəl/
wave (= sea) (n) ★★★	/weɪv/

ADJECTIVES

bad (at) (adj) ★★★	/bæd/
cheap (adj) ★★★	/tʃiːp/
close (adj) ★★★	/kləʊs/
cold (adj) ★★★	/kəʊld/
colourful (adj) ★	/'kʌləf(ə)l/
cool (adj) ★	/kuːl/
cosmopolitan (adj)	/ˌkɒzmə'pɒlɪt(ə)n/
dangerous (adj) ★★★	/'deɪndʒərəs/
dry (adj) ★★★	/draɪ/
exciting (adj) ★★	/ɪk'saɪtɪŋ/
exotic (adj) ★	/ɪg'zɒtɪk/
expensive (adj) ★★★	/ɪk'spensɪv/
foreign (adj) ★★★	/'fɒrɪn/
friendly (adj) ★★★	/'fren(d)li/
full (of) (adj) ★★★	/fʊl/
giant (adj) ★★	/'dʒaɪənt/
good (at) (adj) ★★★	/gʊd/
hot (adj) ★★★	/hɒt/
large (adj) ★★★	/lɑːdʒ/
loud (adj) ★★	/laʊd/
lovely (adj) ★★★	/'lʌvli/
noisy (adj) ★	/'nɔɪzi/
non-stop (adj)	/ˌnɒn 'stɒp/
old (adj) ★★★	/əʊld/
open-air (adj)	/ˌəʊpən'eə/
popular (adj) ★★★	/'pɒpjʊlə/
quiet (adj) ★★★	/'kwaɪət/
safe (adj) ★★★	/seɪf/
smart (adj) ★★	/smɑːt/
spectacular (adj) ★★	/spek'tækjʊlə/
traditional (adj) ★★★	/trə'dɪʃ(ə)nəl/
valuable (adj) ★★★	/'væljʊb(ə)l/
warm (adj) ★★★	/wɔːm/
well-known (adj) ★★	/ˌwel'nəʊn/
wet (adj) ★★★	/wet/

FESTIVALS AND CELEBRATIONS

ball (= dance) (n) ★★★	/bɔːl/

candle (n) ★★ /ˈkænd(ə)l/
carnival (n) /ˈkɑːnɪv(ə)l/
celebrate (v) ★★★ /ˈseləˌbreɪt/
celebration (n) ★★ /ˌseləˈbreɪʃ(ə)n/
costume (n) /ˈkɒstjuːm/
dancer (n) ★★ /ˈdɑːnsə/
festival (n) ★★★ /ˈfestɪv(ə)l/
fireworks (n pl) ★ /ˈfaɪəwɜːks/
greetings card (n) /ˈgriːtɪŋz ˌkɑːd/
New Year's Eve (n) ★★ /ˌnjuː jɪəz ˈiːv/
parade (n) ★ /pəˈreɪd/
party (n) ★★★ /ˈpɑːti/
present (n) ★★★ /ˈprez(ə)nt/
show (n) ★★★ /ʃəʊ/
stage (n) ★★★ /steɪdʒ/

FOOD AND DRINK

burger (n) ★ /ˈbɜːgə/
champagne (n) /ˌʃæmˈpeɪn/
grape (n) ★ /greɪp/
lentils (n pl) /ˈlentlz/
noodles (n pl) /ˈnuːdlz/
rice (n) ★★ /raɪs/
soup (n) ★★ /suːp/
wine (n) ★★★ /waɪn/

MUSIC

drummer (n) /ˈdrʌmə/
heavy metal (n) /ˌhevi ˈmetl/
hip-hop (n) /ˈhɪpˌhɒp/
jazz (n) ★ /dʒæz/
lead singer (n) /ˌliːd ˈsɪŋə/
live music (n) /ˌlaɪv ˈmjuːzɪk/
pop (n) ★ /pɒp/
punk (n) ★ /pʌŋk/
rap (n) /ræp/
reggae (n) /ˈregeɪ/
rock (n) ★★★ /rɒk/
salsa (n) /ˈsælsə/
samba (n) /ˈsæmbə/
soul (n) ★★★ /səʊl/
sound system (n) /ˈsaʊnd ˌsɪstəm/
techno (n) /ˈteknəʊ/
world (n) ★★★ /wɜːld/

PREPOSITIONS OF PLACE

behind (prep) ★★★ /bɪˈhaɪnd/
between (prep) ★★★ /bɪˈtwiːn/
in front of (prep) /ɪn ˈfrʌnt əv/
inside (prep) ★★★ /ˌɪnˈsaɪd/
near (prep) ★★★ /nɪə/
next to (prep) /ˈneks ˌtuː/
opposite (prep) ★★★ /ˈɒpəzɪt/
outside (prep) ★★★ /ˌaʊtˈsaɪd/
over (prep) ★★★ /ˈəʊvə/
under (prep) ★★★ /ˈʌndə/

TOWN FACILITIES

bank (n) ★★★ /bæŋk/
bookshop (n) ★ /ˈbʊkˌʃɒp/
café (n) ★★ /ˈkæfeɪ/
chemist's (n) ★★ /ˈkemɪsts/
flower shop (n) /ˈflaʊə ˌʃɒp/
hairdresser's (n) ★ /ˈheəˌdresəz/
hotel (n) ★ /həʊˈtel/
newsagent's (n) /ˈnjuːzˌeɪdʒənts/
police station (n) ★ /pəˈliːs ˌsteɪʃn/
post office (n) ★★ /ˈpəʊst ˌɒfɪs/
stadium (n) ★ /ˈsteɪdiəm/
supermarket (n) ★★ /ˈsuːpəˌmɑːkɪt/
travel agency (n) /ˈtrævl ˌeɪdʒənsi/

VERBS

book (v) ★★ /bʊk/
bring (v) ★★★ /brɪŋ/
burn (v) ★★★ /bɜːn/
camp (v) ★ /kæmp/
cover (v) ★★★ /ˈkʌvə/
last (v) ★★★ /lɑːst/
light (v) ★★★ /laɪt/
queue (v) ★ /kjuː/
ring (v) ★★★ /rɪŋ/
sleep (v) ★★★ /sliːp/
throw (v) ★★★ /θrəʊ/

EXPRESSIONS

a long way (from) /ə ˈlɒŋ weɪ (frəm)/
be able to /bi ˈeɪbl tuː/
change money /ˌtʃeɪndʒ ˈmʌni/
earn money /ˌɜːn ˈmʌni/
get up early /ˌget ʌp ˈɜːli/
Good luck! /ˌgʊd ˈlʌk/
Happy New Year! /ˌhæpi njuː ˈjɪə/
How long? /ˌhaʊ ˈlɒŋ/
I can't stand it. /aɪ ˌkɑːnt ˈstænd ɪt/
I don't mind it. /aɪ ˌdəʊnt ˈmaɪnd ɪt/
look after someone /ˌlʊk ˈɑːftə sʌmwʌn/
make friends /ˌmeɪk ˈfrendz/
make a wish /ˌmeɪk ə ˈwɪʃ/
on time /ˌɒn ˈtaɪm/
shake hands /ˌʃeɪk ˈhændz/
stay up late /ˌsteɪ ʌp ˈleɪt/

UNIT 3

acting company (n) /ˈæktɪŋ ˌkʌmp(ə)ni/
actually (adv) ★★★ /ˈæktʃuəli/
ages (n pl) ★★★ /ˈeɪdʒəz/
art school (n) /ˈɑːt ˌskuːl/
ball of light (n) /ˌbɔːl əv ˈlaɪt/
ball-point pen (n) /ˌbɔːlpɔɪnt ˈpen/
bang (n) ★ /bæŋ/
bestseller (n) /ˌbestˈselə/
biscuit (n) ★★ /ˈbɪskɪt/
brandy (n) ★ /ˈbrændi/
bridge (n) ★★★ /brɪdʒ/
butter (n) ★★ /ˈbʌtə/
car park (n) /ˈkɑː ˌpɑːk/
career (n) ★★★ /kəˈrɪə/
case (= example) (n) ★★★ /keɪs/
chance (n) ★★★ /tʃɑːns/
classmate (n) /ˈklɑːsˌmeɪt/
close (adv) ★★★ /kləʊs/
death (n) ★★★ /deθ/
diary (n) ★★ /ˈdaɪəri/
emergency (n) ★★★ /ɪˈmɜːdʒ(ə)nsi/
enough (adv) ★★★ /ɪˈnʌf/
expert (n) ★★★ /ˈekspɜːt/
extremely (adv) ★★★ /ɪkˈstriːmli/
factory (n) ★★★ /ˈfæktri/
fame (n) ★★ /feɪm/
flame (n) ★★ /fleɪm/
forest (n) ★★★ /ˈfɒrɪst/
fortune (n) ★★ /ˈfɔːtʃən/
grammar (n) ★★ /ˈgræmə/
ground (n) ★★★ /graʊnd/
guys (n pl) ★★ /gaɪz/
harbour (n) ★★ /ˈhɑːbə/
hard (= with force)
  (adv) ★★★ /hɑːd/
hole (n) ★★★ /həʊl/
iron (= metal) (n) ★★ /ˈaɪən/
luckily (adv) ★ /ˈlʌkɪli/
meteorite (n) /ˈmiːtiəˌraɪt/
nearly (adv) ★★★ /ˈnɪəli/
nightclothes (n pl) /ˈnaɪtˌkləʊðz/
noise (n) ★★★ /nɔɪz/
nonsense (n) ★★ /ˈnɒns(ə)ns/
novel (n) ★★★ /ˈnɒv(ə)l/
oil (n) ★★★ /ɔɪl/
overboard (adv) /ˈəʊvəˌbɔːd/
pain (n) ★★★ /peɪn/
part-owner (n) /ˌpɑːtˈəʊnə/
payment (n) ★★★ /ˈpeɪmənt/
performance (n) ★★★ /pəˈfɔːməns/
play (n) ★★★ /pleɪ/
railway (n) ★★★ /ˈreɪlweɪ/
rock (= stone) (n) ★★★ /rɒk/
roof (n) ★★★ /ruːf/
rubbish (n) ★★ /ˈrʌbɪʃ/
schoolboy (n) /ˈskuːlˌbɔɪ/
smoke (n) ★★ /sməʊk/
sofa (n) ★ /ˈsəʊfə/
space (n) ★★★ /speɪs/
step (n) ★★★ /step/
strike (n) ★★★ /straɪk/
studio (= film) (n) ★★★ /ˈstjuːdiəʊ/
success (n) ★★★ /səkˈses/
sugar (n) ★★★ /ˈʃʊgə/

theme park (n) /ˈθiːm ˌpɑːk/
thunder (n) ★ /ˈθʌndə/
tragedy (n) ★★ /ˈtrædʒədi/
will (=document) (n) ★★★ /wɪl/
wind (n) ★★★ /wɪnd/

ADJECTIVES

asleep (adj) ★★ /əˈsliːp/
brilliant (adj) ★★★ /ˈbrɪljənt/
complete (adj) ★★★ /kəmˈpliːt/
enormous (adj) ★★★ /ɪˈnɔːməs/
exhausted (adj) /ɪgˈzɔːstɪd/
inflammable (adj) /ɪnˈflæməb(ə)l/
lazy (adj) ★★ /ˈleɪzi/
magnetic (adj) ★ /mægˈnetɪk/
major (adj) ★★★ /ˈmeɪdʒə/
original (adj) ★★★ /əˈrɪdʒ(ə)nəl/
public (adj) ★★★ /ˈpʌblɪk/
rare (adj) ★★★ /reə/
red-hot (adj) ★ /ˌredˈhɒt/
rich (adj) ★★★ /rɪtʃ/
thatched (adj) /θætʃt/
tired (adj) ★★★ /ˈtaɪəd/
tiny (adj) ★★★ /ˈtaɪni/

JOBS AND OCCUPATIONS

architect (n) ★★ /ˈɑːkɪˌtekt/
baker (n) ★ /ˈbeɪkə/
explorer (n) /ɪkˈsplɔːrə/
housewife (n) ★ /ˈhaʊsˌwaɪf/
novelist (n) ★ /ˈnɒvəlɪst/
playwright (n) /ˈpleɪˌraɪt/
writer (n) ★★★ /ˈraɪtə/

TIME REFERENCE WORDS

after (prep) ★★★ /ˈɑːftə/
afterwards (adv) ★★★ /ˈɑːftəwədz/
ago (prep) ★★★ /əˈgəʊ/
at first (adv) /ˌət ˈfɜːst/
between (prep) ★★★ /bɪˈtwiːn/
by (prep) ★★★ /baɪ/
finally (adv) ★★★ /ˈfaɪn(ə)li/
first (adv) ★★★ /fɜːst/
for (prep) ★★★ /fə, fɔː/
in (prep) ★★★ /ɪn/
later (adv) ★★★ /ˈleɪtə/
next (adj) ★★★ /nekst/
on (prep) ★★★ /ɒn/
soon (adv) ★★★ /suːn/
still (adv) ★★★ /stɪl/
suddenly (adv) ★★★ /ˈsʌd(ə)nli/
then (adv) ★★★ /ðen/
until (conj & prep) ★★★ /ənˈtɪl/
when (conj) ★★★ /wen/

TRANSPORT

bicycle (n) ★★ /ˈbaɪsɪk(ə)l/
boat (n) ★★★ /bəʊt/
car (n) ★★★ /kɑː/
helicopter (n) ★★ /ˈhelɪˌkɒptə/
rocket (n) ★ /ˈrɒkɪt/
ship (n) ★★★ /ʃɪp/
spaceship (n) /ˈspeɪsˌʃɪp/
speedboat (n) /ˈspiːdˌbəʊt/

VERBS

be born (v) /ˌbi ˈbɔːn/
become (v) ★★★ /bɪˈkʌm/
build (v) ★★★ /bɪld/
burn down (v) /ˌbɜːn ˈdaʊn/
burn up (v) /ˌbɜːn ˈʌp/
bury (v) ★★ /ˈberi/
collect (v) ★★★ /kəˈlekt/
contain (v) ★★★ /kənˈteɪn/
continue (v) ★★★ /kənˈtɪnjuː/
describe (v) ★★★ /dɪˈskraɪb/
design (v) ★★★ /dɪˈzaɪn/
destroy (v) ★★★ /dɪˈstrɔɪ/
escape (n & v) ★★★ /ɪˈskeɪp/
fall (v) ★★★ /fɔːl/
hit (v) ★★★ /hɪt/
invent (v) ★★ /ɪnˈvent/
land (v) ★★★ /lænd/
marry (v) ★★★ /ˈmæri/

/pæk/
/plæn/
/prɪnt/
/ˈpʌblɪʃ/
/riːtʃ/
...ceive (v) ★★★ /rɪˈsiːv/
rescue (v) ★★ /ˈreskjuː/
return (v) ★★★ /rɪˈtɜːn/
sink (v) ★★ /sɪŋk/
survive (v) ★★★ /səˈvaɪv/
whistle (v) ★ /ˈwɪs(ə)l/

EXPRESSIONS

as far as we know /əz ˌfɑː əz wiː ˈnəʊ/
be (really) keen on /ˌbiː (rɪəli) ˈkiːn ɒn/
feel well /ˌfiːl ˈwel/
make a phone call /ˌmeɪk ə ˈfəʊn kɔːl/
have fun /ˌhæv ˈfʌn/
on fire /ˌɒn ˈfaɪə/
spend time /ˌspend ˈtaɪm/
tell a story /ˌtel ə ˈstɔːri/

UNIT 4

businessman (n) ★★ /ˈbɪznəsmæn/
coordination (n) ★ /kəʊˌɔːdɪˈneɪʃ(ə)n/
dyspraxia (n) /dɪsˈpræksiə/
education (n) ★★★ /ˌedjʊˈkeɪʃ(ə)n/
episode (n) ★★ /ˈepɪsəʊd/
few (n) ★★★ /fjuː/
future (n) ★★★ /ˈfjuːtʃə/
handwriting (n) ★ /ˈhændˌraɪtɪŋ/
height (n) ★★★ /haɪt/
illness (n) ★★★ /ˈɪlnəs/
invention (n) ★★ /ɪnˈvenʃ(ə)n/
manner (n) ★★★ /ˈmænə/
murderer (n) ★ /ˈmɜːdərə/
ourselves (pron) ★★★ /aʊəˈselvz/
patient (n) ★★★ /ˈpeɪʃ(ə)nt/
politician (n) ★★★ /ˌpɒləˈtɪʃ(ə)n/
prison (n) ★★★ /ˈprɪz(ə)n/
romance (n) ★ /rəʊˈmæns/
satire (n) /ˈsætaɪə/
series (n) ★★★ /ˈsɪəriːz/
setting (n) ★★★ /ˈsetɪŋ/
thought (n) ★★★ /θɔːt/
trouble (n) ★★★ /ˈtrʌb(ə)l/
university (n) ★★★ /ˌjuːnɪˈvɜːsəti/
unlike (prep) ★★ /ʌnˈlaɪk/
voice (n) ★★★ /vɔɪs/
wizard (n) /ˈwɪzəd/

ADJECTIVES

absurd (adj) ★ /əbˈsɜːd/
action-packed (adj) /ˈækʃnˌpækt/
attractive (adj) ★★★ /əˈtræktɪv/
available (adj) ★★★ /əˈveɪləb(ə)l/
clever (adj) ★★ /ˈklevə/
extraordinary (adj) ★★ /ɪkˈstrɔːd(ə)n(ə)ri/
fast-moving (adj) /ˈfɑːstˌmuːvɪŋ/
flat (adj) ★★★ /flæt/
frightening (adj) ★ /ˈfraɪt(ə)nɪŋ/
imaginary (adj) ★ /ɪˈmædʒɪnəri/
intelligent (adj) ★★ /ɪnˈtelɪdʒ(ə)nt/
little-known (adj) /ˈlɪtlˌnəʊn/
medical (adj) ★★★ /ˈmedɪk(ə)l/
middle-class (adj) ★ /ˌmɪdlˈklɑːs/
ordinary (adj) ★★★ /ˈɔːd(ə)n(ə)ri/
pretty (adj) ★★ /ˈprɪti/
recent (adj) ★★★ /ˈriːs(ə)nt/
serious (adj) ★★★ /ˈsɪəriəs/
teen (adj) /tiːn/

ADVERBS OF MANNER

angrily (adv) /ˈæŋɡrəli/
badly (adv) ★★★ /ˈbædli/
carefully (adv) /ˈkeəfəli/
comfortably (adv) /ˈkʌmftəbli/
easily (adv) ★★★ /ˈiːzɪli/
fantastically (adv) /fænˈtæstɪkli/
fast (adv) ★★★ /fɑːst/
happily (adv) ★★ /ˈhæpɪli/
hard (adv) ★★★ /hɑːd/
hungrily (adv) /ˈhʌŋɡrəli/

late (adv) ★★★ /leɪt/
loudly (adv) /ˈlaʊdli/
neatly (adv) /ˈniːtli/
nervously (adv) /ˈnɜːvəsli/
normally (adv) ★★★ /ˈnɔːm(ə)li/
politely (adv) ★ /pəˈlaɪtli/
properly (adv) ★★★ /ˈprɒpəli/
quickly (adv) ★★★ /ˈkwɪkli/
quietly (adv) ★★★ /ˈkwaɪətli/
rudely (adv) /ˈruːdli/
sadly (adv) ★★ /ˈsædli/
slowly (adv) ★★★ /ˈsləʊli/
thirstily (adv) /ˈθɜːstəli/
well (adv) ★★★ /wel/

FEELINGS

afraid (of) (adj) ★★★ /əˈfreɪd/
angry (adj) ★★★ /ˈæŋɡri/
comfortable (adj) ★★★ /ˈkʌmftəb(ə)l/
happy (adj) ★★★ /ˈhæpi/
nervous (adj) ★★ /ˈnɜːvəs/
pleased (adj) ★★ /pliːzd/
sad (adj) ★★★ /sæd/
sensitive (adj) ★★★ /ˈsensətɪv/

GRAMMAR WORDS

adjective (n) ★ /ˈædʒɪktɪv/
adverb (n) ★ /ˈædvɜːb/
gerund (n) /ˈdʒerənd/
infinitive (n) ★ /ɪnˈfɪnətɪv/
noun (n) ★ /naʊn/
preposition (n) ★ /ˌprepəˈzɪʃ(ə)n/
pronoun (n) ★ /ˈprəʊnaʊn/
verb (n) ★ /vɜːb/

PERFORMANCE

actor (n) ★★★ /ˈæktə/
band (n) ★★★ /bænd/
character (n) ★★★ /ˈkærɪktə/
concert (n) ★★ /ˈkɒnsət/
co-star (n) /ˈkəʊˌstɑː/
drama (n) ★★★ /ˈdrɑːmə/
director (n) ★★★ /dəˈrektə/, /daɪˈrektə/
film (n & v) ★★★ /fɪlm/
musical (n) /ˈmjuːzɪk(ə)l/
musician (n) ★★ /mjuːˈzɪʃ(ə)n/
play (n & v) ★★★ /pleɪ/
rehearsal (n) ★ /rɪˈhɜːs(ə)l/
rehearse (v) ★ /rɪˈhɜːs/
scene (n) ★★★ /siːn/
show (n) ★★★ /ʃəʊ/
stage (n) ★★★ /steɪdʒ/
studio (n) ★★★ /ˈstjuːdiəʊ/
theatre (n) ★★★ /ˈθɪətə/

RECORDED MUSIC

cassette (n) ★ /kəˈset/
CD (compact disc) (n) ★★ /ˌsiː ˈdiː/
cylinder (n) ★ /ˈsɪlɪndə/
disc (n) ★★ /dɪsk/
LP (long playing record) (n) /ˌel ˈpiː/
MP3 player (n) /ˌempiːˈθriː pleɪə/
phonograph (n) /ˈfəʊnəɡrɑːf/, /ˈfəʊnəɡræf/
record (n & v) ★★★ /ˈrekɔːd/
tape (n) ★★★ /teɪp/
tape recorder (n) /ˈteɪp rɪˌkɔːdə/

TV PROGRAMMES

broadcast (n) ★ /ˈbrɔːdˌkɑːst/
cartoon (n) ★ /kɑːˈtuːn/
chat show (n) ★ /ˈtʃæt ˌʃəʊ/
drama (n) ★★★ /ˈdrɑːmə/
documentary (n) ★ /ˌdɒkjʊˈment(ə)ri/
game show (n) /ˈɡeɪm ʃəʊ/
music programme (n) /ˈmjuːzɪk ˌprəʊɡræm/
news programme (n) /ˈnjuːz ˌprəʊɡræm/
reality show (n) /riːˈæləti ˌʃəʊ/
science fiction programme (n) /ˌsaɪəns ˈfɪkʃn ˌprəʊɡræm/
sitcom (n) /ˈsɪtˌkɒm/
soap (opera) (n) ★★ /səʊp/
sports programme (n) /ˈspɔːts ˌprəʊɡræm/

talent show (n) /ˈtælənt ˌʃəʊ/
thriller (n) ★ /ˈθrɪlə/

VERBS

affect (v) ★★★ /əˈfekt/
appear (v) ★★★ /əˈpɪə/
bully (v) ★ /ˈbʊli/
introduce (v) ★★★ /ˌɪntrəˈdjuːs/
need (v) ★★★ /niːd/
overtake (v) ★ /ˌəʊvəˈteɪk/
prefer (v) ★★★ /prɪˈfɜː/
replace (v) ★★★ /rɪˈpleɪs/
star (n & v) ★★★ /stɑː/
substitute (v) ★★ /ˈsʌbstɪˌtjuːt/
succeed (v) ★★★ /səkˈsiːd/
suffer (from) (v) ★★★ /ˈsʌfə/
surf (v) ★ /sɜːf/

EXPRESSIONS

do up (your shoes) /ˌduː ˈʌp (jə ʃuːz)/
have a party /ˌhæv ə ˈpɑːti/
I'm afraid (= I'm sorry) /ˌaɪm əˈfreɪd/
make sense /ˌmeɪk ˈsens/
take place /ˌteɪk ˈpleɪs/
take someone seriously /ˌteɪk sʌmwʌn ˈsɪəriəsli/
What a shame! /ˌwɒt ə ˈʃeɪm/

UNIT 5

above (prep) ★★★ /əˈbʌv/
accuracy (n) ★★ /ˈækjʊrəsi/
adventure holiday (n) /ədˈventʃə ˌhɒlɪdeɪ/
advice (n) ★★★ /ədˈvaɪs/
arrangement (n) ★★★ /əˈreɪndʒmənt/
atomic clock (n) /əˌtɒmɪk ˈklɒk/
backpack (n) /ˈbækˌpæk/
backpacking (n) /ˈbækˌpækɪŋ/
canal (n) ★★ /kəˈnæl/
certainly (adv) ★★★ /ˈsɜːt(ə)nli/
cheaply (adv) /ˈtʃiːpli/
classical music (n) ★ /ˌklæsɪkl ˈmjuːzɪk/
cliff (n) ★★ /klɪf/
customer (n) ★★★ /ˈkʌstəmə/
daypack (n) /ˈdeɪˌpæk/
definitely (adv) ★★ /ˈdef(ə)nətli/
directions (n pl) /dɪˈrekʃənz/, /daɪˈrekʃənz/
edge (n) ★★★ /edʒ/
exam (n) ★★ /ɪɡˈzæm/
fashion (n) ★★★ /ˈfæʃ(ə)n/
fashion designer (n) /ˈfæʃn dɪˌzaɪnə/
freedom (n) ★★★ /ˈfriːdəm/
GPS (Global Positioning System) (n) /ˌdʒiː piː ˈes/
guy (n) ★★ /ɡaɪ/
honestly (adv) ★★ /ˈɒnɪs(t)li/
independence (n) ★★★ /ˌɪndɪˈpendəns/
instead (of) (adv) ★★★ /ɪnˈsted/
kid (n) ★★★ /kɪd/
mainly (adv) ★★★ /ˈmeɪnli/
minibus (n) /ˈmɪniˌbʌs/
natural history (n) /ˌnætʃ(ə)rəl ˈhɪst(ə)ri/
paperback (n) ★ /ˈpeɪpəˌbæk/
percentage (n) ★★ /pəˈsentɪdʒ/
playing cards (n pl) /ˈpleɪɪŋ ˌkɑːdz/
position (n) ★★★ /pəˈzɪʃ(ə)n/
postcard (n) /ˈpəʊs(t)ˌkɑːd/
responsibility (n) ★★★ /rɪˌspɒnsəˈbɪləti/
room (=space) (n) ★★★ /ruːm/
route (n) ★★★ /ruːt/
satellite (n) ★★ /ˈsætəˌlaɪt/
satnav (satellite navigation system) (n) /ˈsætˌnæv/
second (n) ★★★ /ˈsekənd/
souvenir (n) /ˌsuːvəˈnɪə/
spider (n) ★ /ˈspaɪdə/
stuff (n) ★★★ /stʌf/
suggestion (n) ★★★ /səˈdʒestʃ(ə)n/
third (n) /θɜːd/
tip (= suggestion) (n) ★★ /tɪp/
underground (n) /ˈʌndəˌɡraʊnd/
user (n) ★★★ /ˈjuːzə/

waste (n) ★★★ /weɪst/
zoo (n) ★ /zuː/

ADJECTIVES

accurate (adj) ★★ /ˈækjʊrət/
addictive (adj) /əˈdɪktɪv/
exact (adj) ★★ /ɪgˈzækt/
healthy (adj) ★★★ /ˈhelθi/
hopeless (adj) ★ /ˈhəʊpləs/
latest (= most recent) /ˈleɪtɪst/
  (adj) ★★★
massive (adj) ★★★ /ˈmæsɪv/
perfect (adj) ★★★ /ˈpɜːfɪkt/
starving (adj) /ˈstɑːvɪŋ/
total (adj) ★★★ /ˈtəʊt(ə)l/
upset (adj) ★★ /ʌpˈset/
vegetarian (adj) /ˌvedʒəˈteəriən/

CLOTHES AND MATERIALS

artificial (adj) ★★ /ˌɑːtɪˈfɪʃ(ə)l/
cloth (n) ★★ /klɒθ/
cotton (adj & n) ★★ /ˈkɒt(ə)n/
designer clothes (n pl) /dɪˌzaɪnə ˈkləʊðz/
lightweight (adj) /ˈlaɪtˌweɪt/
material (n) ★★★ /məˈtɪəriəl/
polyester (adj & n) /ˌpɒliˈestə/
raincoat (n) /ˈreɪnˌkəʊt/
suit (n) ★★★ /suːt/
sweater (n) ★ /ˈswetə/
swimming trunks (n pl) /ˈswɪmɪŋ ˌtrʌŋks/
tie (n) ★★ /taɪ/
waterproof (adj) ★ /ˈwɔːtəˌpruːf/
wool (adj & n) ★★ /wʊl/

DICTIONARY WORDS

abbreviation (n) ★ /əˌbriːviˈeɪʃ(ə)n/
adjective (n) ★ /ˈædʒɪktɪv/
adverb (n) ★ /ˈædvɜːb/
auxiliary verb (n) /ɔːgˈzɪliəri ˌvɜːb/
countable (adj) /ˈkaʊntəb(ə)l/
plural (adj) ★ /ˈplʊərəl/
singular (adj) ★ /ˈsɪŋjʊlə/
somebody (pron) ★★★ /ˈsʌmbədi/
something (pron) ★★★ /ˈsʌmθɪŋ/
uncountable (adj) /ʌnˈkaʊntəb(ə)l/

FOOD

cheese (n) ★★ /tʃiːz/
dairy produce (n) /ˈdeəri ˌprɒdjuːs/
diet (n) ★★★ /ˈdaɪət/
(fried) egg (n) ★★★ /(fraɪd) ˈeg/
garlic (n) ★ /ˈgɑːlɪk/
ham (n) ★ /hæm/
meat (n) ★★★ /miːt/
mushroom (n) ★ /ˈmʌʃruːm/
olive (n) ★ /ˈɒlɪv/
onion (n) ★★ /ˈʌnjən/
pepper (n) ★ /ˈpepə/
pineapple (n) /ˈpaɪnˌæp(ə)l/
pizza (n) ★ /ˈpiːtsə/
spinach (n) /ˈspɪnɪdʒ/
steak (n) ★ /steɪk/
tomato (n) ★★ /təˈmɑːtəʊ/

PREPOSITIONS OF DIRECTION

across (prep) ★★★ /əˈkrɒs/
along (prep) ★★★ /əˈlɒŋ/
down (prep) ★★★ /daʊn/
into (prep) ★★★ /ˈɪntə/, /ˈɪntʊ/, /ˈɪntuː/
past (prep) ★★★ /pɑːst/
round (prep) ★★★ /raʊnd/
through (prep) ★★★ /θruː/
to (prep) ★★★ /tə/, /tʊ/, /tuː/
up (prep) ★★★ /ʌp/

VERBS

afford (v) ★★★ /əˈfɔːd/
carry on (v) /ˌkæri ˈɒn/
dry (v) ★★ /draɪ/
end up (v) /ˌend ˈʌp/
explain (v) ★★★ /ɪkˈspleɪn/
fit (v) ★★★ /fɪt/
organise (v) ★★★ /ˈɔːgəˌnaɪz/

revise (v) ★ /rɪˈvaɪz/
treat (v) ★★★ /triːt/
trust (v) ★★★ /trʌst/
wave (v) ★★ /weɪv/
work out (= calculate) (v) /ˌwɜːk ˈaʊt/

EXPRESSIONS

catch a bus/train /ˌkætʃ ə ˈbʌs/ˈtreɪn/
get stuck /ˌget ˈstʌk/
get on (with /ˌget ˈɒn (wɪð
  someone) ˈsʌmwʌn)/
keep going /ˌkiːp ˈgəʊɪŋ/
keep in touch /ˌkiːp ɪn ˈtʌtʃ/
last but not least /ˌlɑːst bət nɒt ˈliːst/
make a list /ˌmeɪk ə ˈlɪst/
Never mind. /ˌnevə ˈmaɪnd/
order a meal /ˌɔːdər ə ˈmiːl/
pass the time /ˌpɑːs ðə ˈtaɪm/
spend money /ˌspend ˈmʌni/
take a (boat) trip /ˌteɪk ə (bəʊt) ˈtrɪp/
turn left/right /ˌtɜːn ˈleft/ˈraɪt/
You can't miss it! /jə kɑːnt ˈmɪs ɪt/

UNIT 6

absolutely (adv) ★★★ /ˈæbsəluːtli,
  ˌæbsəˈluːtli/
air (n) ★★★ /eə/
angel (n) ★★ /ˈeɪndʒ(ə)l/
brakes (n pl) ★ /breɪks/
channel (=TV) (n) ★★★ /ˈtʃænl/
cushion (n) ★ /ˈkʊʃ(ə)n/
danger (n) ★★★ /ˈdeɪndʒə/
dream (n) ★★★ /driːm/
farm (n) ★★★ /fɑːm/
grass (n) ★★★ /grɑːs/
interest (n) ★★★ /ˈɪntrəst/
jewellery (n) ★★ /ˈdʒuːəlri/
library (n) ★★★ /ˈlaɪbrəri/
lift (=in a building) (n) ★★ /lɪft/
magnet (n) /ˈmægnɪt/
magnetic levitation (n) /mægˌnetɪk leviˈteɪʃn/
open space (n) /ˌəʊpən ˈspeɪs/
paradise (n) ★ /ˈpærədaɪs/
pole (n) ★★ /pəʊl/
queue (n) ★ /kjuː/
reality (n) ★★★ /riˈæləti/
reason (n) ★★★ /ˈriːz(ə)n/
satellite TV (n) /ˌsætəlaɪt tiːˈviː/
side (n) ★★★ /saɪd/
simulator (n) /ˈsɪmjʊˌleɪtə/
species (n) ★★★ /ˈspiːʃiːz/
speed (n) ★★★ /spiːd/
technology (n) ★★★ /tekˈnɒlədʒi/
whole (n) ★★★ /həʊl/
wildlife (n) ★★ /ˈwaɪldˌlaɪf/
wing (n) ★★★ /wɪŋ/
wonder (n) ★★ /ˈwʌndə/

ADJECTIVES

ancient (adj) ★★★ /ˈeɪnʃ(ə)nt/
average (adj) ★★★ /ˈæv(ə)rɪdʒ/
commercial (adj) ★★★ /kəˈmɜːʃ(ə)l/
crowded (adj) ★ /ˈkraʊdɪd/
electric (adj) ★★ /ɪˈlektrɪk/
empty (adj) ★★★ /ˈempti/
horrible (adj) ★★ /ˈhɒrəb(ə)l/
limited (adj) ★★ /ˈlɪmɪtɪd/
powerful (adj) ★★★ /ˈpaʊəf(ə)l/
right-hand (adj) /ˈraɪtˌhænd/
rude (adj) ★★ /ruːd/
steep (adj) ★★ /stiːp/
stunning (adj) ★ /ˈstʌnɪŋ/
wild (adj) ★★★ /waɪld/
world-famous (adj) /ˌwɜːldˈfeɪməs/

ANIMALS

cow (n) ★★ /kaʊ/
deer (n) ★ /dɪə/
duck (n) ★★ /dʌk/
giraffe (n) ★ /dʒəˈrɑːf/
goat (n) ★ /gəʊt/
hippo (n) /ˈhɪpəʊ/
lion (n) ★★ /ˈlaɪən/

monkey (n) ★ /ˈmʌŋki/
pig (n) ★★ /pɪg/
sheep (n) ★★★ /ʃiːp/
squirrel (n) /ˈskwɪrəl/
tiger (n) ★ /ˈtaɪgə/

FAMOUS LANDMARKS

fortress (n) /ˈfɔːtrəs/
fountain (n) ★ /ˈfaʊntɪn/
lighthouse (n) /ˈlaɪtˌhaʊs/
mountain (n) ★★★ /ˈmaʊntɪn/
palace (n) ★★ /ˈpæləs/
ruins (n pl) ★ /ˈruːɪnz/
sight (n) ★★★ /saɪt/
statue (n) ★★ /ˈstætʃuː/
temple (n) ★★ /ˈtemp(ə)l/
waterfall (n) ★ /ˈwɔːtəˌfɔːl/

INDEFINITE PRONOUNS AND ADVERBS

anyone (pron) ★★★ /ˈeniˌwʌn/
anything (pron) ★★★ /ˈeniˌθɪŋ/
anywhere (adv) ★★★ /ˈeniˌweə/
everyone (pron) ★★★ /ˈevriˌwʌn/
everything (pron) ★★★ /ˈevriˌθɪŋ/
everywhere (adv) ★★★ /ˈevriˌweə/
no one (pron) ★★★ /ˈnəʊ ˌwʌn/
nothing (pron) ★★★ /ˈnʌθɪŋ/
nowhere (adv) ★★ /ˈnəʊweə/
someone (pron) ★★★ /ˈsʌmwʌn/
something (pron) ★★★ /ˈsʌmθɪŋ/
somewhere (adv) ★★★ /ˈsʌmweə/

TRANSPORT

airport (n) ★★★ /ˈeəˌpɔːt/
bus driver (n) /ˈbʌs ˌdraɪvə/
bus station (n) /ˈbʌs ˌsteɪʃn/
bus stop (n) /ˈbʌs ˌstɒp/
bus ticket (n) /ˈbʌs ˌtɪkɪt/
bus timetable (n) /ˈbʌs ˌtaɪmteɪbl/
car driver (n) /ˈkɑː ˌdraɪvə/
car engine (n) /ˈkɑː ˌendʒɪn/
car park (n) /ˈkɑː ˌpɑːk/
ferry (n) ★ /ˈferi/
high-speed train (HST) (n) /ˌhaɪspiːd ˈtreɪn/
railway engine (n) /ˈreɪlweɪ ˌendʒɪn/
railway line (n) ★ /ˈreɪlweɪ ˌlaɪn/
railway station (n) /ˈreɪlweɪ ˌsteɪʃn/
railway track (n) /ˈreɪlweɪ ˌtræk/
train driver (n) /ˈtreɪn ˌdraɪvə/
train station (n) /ˈtreɪn ˌsteɪʃn/
train ticket (n) /ˈtreɪn ˌtɪkɪt/
train timetable (n) /ˈtreɪn ˌtaɪmteɪbl/
tram (n) /træm/
tube (n) ★★ /tjuːb/

VERBS

attract (v) ★★★ /əˈtrækt/
break (v) ★★★ /breɪk/
float (v) ★★ /fləʊt/
imagine (v) ★★★ /ɪˈmædʒɪn/
joke (v) ★★ /dʒəʊk/
link (v) ★★★ /lɪŋk/
practise (v) ★★ /ˈpræktɪs/
protect (v) ★★★ /prəˈtekt/
push away (v) /ˌpʊʃ əˈweɪ/
repel (v) /rɪˈpel/
stand for (v) /ˈstænd ˌfɔː/
stick (together) (v) ★★★ /stɪk/

EXPRESSIONS

as you know /ˌəz juː ˈnəʊ/
Cheer up! /ˌtʃɪər ˈʌp/
have an argument /ˌhæv ən ˈɑːgjʊmənt/
have a shower /ˌhæv ə ˈʃaʊə/
in advance /ˌɪn ədˈvɑːns/
make a noise /ˌmeɪk ə ˈnɔɪz/
pull someone's leg /ˌpʊl sʌmwʌnz ˈleg/

UNIT 7

advertisement (n) ★★ /ədˈvɜːtɪsmənt/
amongst (prep) /əˈmʌŋst/
animated display (n) /ˌænɪmeɪtɪd dɪˈspleɪ/

	/ˈɔːdiəns/
	/ˈɔːtəˌgrɑːf/
	/ˈbeɪbi/
	/ˈbeɪkən/
	/bɑː/
...s (n pl) ★★	/biːnz/
bite (n) ★	/baɪt/
brain (n) ★★★	/breɪn/
camp (n) ★★★	/kæmp/
charity (n) ★★★	/ˈtʃærəti/
checkout (n)	/ˈtʃekaʊt/
comment (n) ★★★	/ˈkɒment/
contestant (n)	/kənˈtestənt/
cross-country skiing (n)	/ˌkrɒskʌntri ˈskiːɪŋ/
date (= arrangement)	/deɪt/
(n) ★★★	
earthquake (n) ★	/ˈɜːθˌkweɪk/
environment (n) ★★★	/ɪnˈvaɪrənmənt/
equipment (n) ★★★	/ɪˈkwɪpmənt/
eruption (n)	/ɪˈrʌpʃ(ə)n/
feather (n) ★	/ˈfeðə/
film crew (n)	/ˈfɪlm ˌkruː/
flash photograph (n)	/flæʃ ˈfəʊtəgrɑːf/
fortnight (n) ★★	/ˈfɔːtnaɪt/
fortunately (adv) ★★	/ˈfɔːtʃənətli/
highlight (n) ★	/ˈhaɪˌlaɪt/
human being (n) ★★★	/ˌhjuːmən ˈbiːɪŋ/
in contrast (n)	/ˌɪn ˈkɒntrɑːst/
inhabitant (n) ★★	/ɪnˈhæbɪtənt/
jungle (n) ★	/ˈdʒʌŋg(ə)l/
litter (n) ★	/ˈlɪtə/
log (n) ★	/lɒg/
luxury (n)	/ˈlʌkʃəri/
make-up (n) ★★	/ˈmeɪkˌʌp/
means of transport (n)	/ˌmiːnz əv ˈtrænspɔːt/
mind (n) ★★★	/maɪnd/
opinion (n) ★★★	/əˈpɪnjən/
power (n) ★★★	/ˈpaʊə/
rainforest (n) ★	/ˈreɪnˌfɒrɪst/
replica (n)	/ˈreplɪkə/
seat belt (n)	/ˈsiːt ˌbelt/
silence (n) ★★★	/ˈsaɪləns/
skin (n) ★★★	/skɪn/
sled (n)	/sled/
snow (n) ★★★	/snəʊ/
snowmobile (n)	/ˈsnəʊməˌbiːl/
stranger (n) ★★	/ˈstreɪndʒə/
superior (n) ★	/suˈpɪəriə/
supplies (n pl) ★★★	/səˈplaɪz/
survival technique (n)	/səˌvaɪvl tekˈniːk/
table manners (n pl)	/ˈteɪbl ˌmænəz/
take-off (n)	/ˈteɪkˌɒf/
task (n) ★★★	/tɑːsk/
thoughtfully (adv)	/ˈθɔːtf(ə)li/
thrill (n)	/θrɪl/
tourism (n) ★★	/ˈtʊərɪz(ə)m/
tourist centre (n)	/ˈtʊərɪst ˌsentə/
traditionally (adv)	/trəˈdɪʃn(ə)li/
treatment (n) ★★★	/ˈtriːtmənt/
trust (n) ★★★	/trʌst/
tundra (n)	/ˈtʌndrə/
version (n) ★★★	/ˈvɜːʃ(ə)n/
viewer (n) ★★	/ˈvjuːə/
volcano (n) ★	/vɒlˈkeɪnəʊ/
water cycle (n)	/ˈwɔːtə ˌsaɪkl/
wedding (n) ★★★	/ˈwedɪŋ/

ADJECTIVES

alive (adj) ★★★	/əˈlaɪv/
basic (adj) ★★★	/ˈbeɪsɪk/
common (adj) ★★★	/ˈkɒmən/
deep (adj) ★★★	/diːp/
exhausting (adj)	/ɪgˈzɔːstɪŋ/
extinct (adj) ★	/ɪkˈstɪŋkt/
fascinating (adj) ★★	/ˈfæsɪneɪtɪŋ/
freezing (adj) ★	/ˈfriːzɪŋ/
increased (adj) ★★★	/ɪnˈkriːst/
interactive (adj)	/ˌɪntərˈæktɪv/
live (adj)	/laɪv/
poisonous (adj) ★	/ˈpɔɪz(ə)nəs/
shocking (adj) ★	/ˈʃɒkɪŋ/
silent (adj) ★★★	/ˈsaɪlənt/

surprising (adj) ★★★	/səˈpraɪzɪŋ/
terrifying (adj)	/ˈterəfaɪŋ/
tiring (adj)	/ˈtaɪərɪŋ/
unfriendly (adj) ★	/ʌnˈfren(d)li/

ANIMALS

amphibian (n)	/æmˈfɪbiən/
creature (n) ★★★	/ˈkriːtʃə/
crocodile (n)	/ˈkrɒkəˌdaɪl/
dinosaur (n) ★	/ˈdaɪnəˌsɔː/
herd (n & v) ★	/hɜːd/
husky (dog) (n)	/ˈhʌski/
insect (n) ★★	/ˈɪnsekt/
mammal (n) ★	/ˈmæm(ə)l/
reindeer (n)	/ˈreɪnˌdɪə/
reptile (n) ★	/ˈrepˌtaɪl/
rhino (n)	/ˈraɪnəʊ/
snake (n) ★	/sneɪk/
tortoise (n)	/ˈtɔːtəs/
worm (n) ★	/wɜːm/

BODY LANGUAGE

clap (v) ★	/klæp/
frown (n) ★	/fraʊn/
bend (n) ★★	/bend/
bow (v) ★	/baʊ/
facial expression (n)	/ˌfeɪʃl ɪkˈspreʃn/
gesture (n) ★★	/ˈdʒestʃə/
hug (v) ★	/hʌg/
stare (v) ★★★	/steə/

FEELINGS

amazed (adj)	/əˈmeɪzd/
bored (adj) ★★	/bɔːd/
embarrassed (adj) ★	/ɪmˈbærəst/
excited (adj) ★★	/ɪkˈsaɪtɪd/
fascinated (adj)	/ˈfæsɪneɪtɪd/
frightened (adj) ★	/ˈfraɪt(ə)nd/
worried (adj) ★★★	/ˈwʌrid/

HOUSEHOLD ITEMS

chopping board (n)	/ˈtʃɒpɪŋ ˌbɔːd/
cooking pot (n)	/ˈkʊkɪŋ ˌpɒt/
matches (n pl) ★★★	/ˈmætʃɪz/
mirror (n) ★★★	/ˈmɪrə/
paraffin (n)	/ˈpærəfɪn/
shampoo (n)	/ʃæmˈpuː/
toilet paper (n)	/ˈtɔɪlət ˌpeɪpə/

VERBS

communicate (v) ★★	/kəˈmjuːnɪˌkeɪt/
complain (v) ★★★	/kəmˈpleɪn/
develop (v) ★★★	/dɪˈveləp/
disagree (v) ★★	/ˌdɪsəˈgriː/
encourage (v) ★★★	/ɪnˈkʌrɪdʒ/
enter (v) ★★★	/ˈentə/
erupt (v)	/ɪˈrʌpt/
experience (v) ★★★	/ɪkˈspɪəriəns/
feed (v) ★★★	/fiːd/
flash (v) ★★	/flæʃ/
give up (v)	/ˌgɪv ˈʌp/
grow (v) ★★★	/grəʊ/
hide (v) ★★★	/haɪd/
interact (v) ★	/ˌɪntərˈækt/
provide (v) ★★★	/prəˈvaɪd/
put away (v)	/ˌpʊt əˈweɪ/
respond (v) ★★★	/rɪˈspɒnd/
roar (v) ★	/rɔː/
smoke (v) ★★	/sməʊk/
stretch (v) ★★★	/stretʃ/

EXPRESSIONS

be into something	/biː ˈɪntə sʌmθɪŋ/
do the ironing	/ˌduː ði ˈaɪənɪŋ/
do the shopping	/ˌduː ðə ˈʃɒpɪŋ/
do the washing-up	/ˌduː ðə wɒʃɪŋ ˈʌp/
I don't care	/aɪ ˌdəʊnt ˈkeə/
I'd rather (not)	/aɪd ˌrɑːðə (ˈnɒt)/
lay eggs	/ˌleɪ ˈegz/
lay the table	/ˌleɪ ðə ˈteɪbl/
make the bed	/ˌmeɪk ðə ˈbed/
No way!	/ˌnəʊ ˈweɪ/

pass an exam(ination)	/ˌpɑːs ən ɪgˈzæm(ɪˈneɪʃn)/
raise money	/ˌreɪz ˈmʌni/
take off (your shoes)	/ˌteɪk ˈɒf (jə ʃuːz)/
take part (in)	/ˌteɪk ˈpɑːt (ɪn)/

UNIT 8

arena (n) ★	/əˈriːnə/
bone (n) ★★★	/bəʊn/
depressed (adj) ★★	/dɪˈprest/
dramatic (adj) ★★★	/drəˈmætɪk/
DVD player (n)	/diːviːˈdiː ˌpleɪə/
graded reader (n)	/ˌgreɪdɪd ˈriːdə/
individual (adj) ★★★	/ˌɪndɪˈvɪdʒuəl/
instant (adj) ★★	/ˈɪnstənt/
life-size (adj)	/ˈlaɪfˌsaɪz/
mathematics (n) ★★	/ˌmæθəˈmætɪks/
process (n) ★★★	/ˈprəʊses/
screen (n) ★★★	/skriːn/
square (n) ★★★	/skweə/
thumbnail (n)	/ˈθʌmˌneɪl/
whistle (n) ★	/ˈwɪs(ə)l/
worldwide (adv) ★	/ˌwɜːldˈwaɪd/

ANIMATED FILMS

animation (n)	/ˌænɪˈmeɪʃ(ə)n/
animator (n)	/ˈænɪˌmeɪtə/
background (n) ★★★	/ˈbækˌgraʊnd/
puppet (n)	/ˈpʌpɪt/
scan (v) ★★	/skæn/
scanner (n) ★	/ˈskænə/
shoot (a film) (v) ★★★	/ʃuːt/
special effects (n pl)	/ˌspeʃl ɪˈfekts/
storyboard (n)	/ˈstɔːriˌbɔːd/
stop-motion technique (n)	/stɒpˈməʊʃn tekˌniːk/

DIGITAL CAMERAS

brightness (n)	/ˈbraɪtnəs/
button (n) ★★	/ˈbʌt(ə)n/
calculation (n) ★★	/ˌkælkjʊˈleɪʃ(ə)n/
computer chip (n)	/kəmˈpjuːtə ˌtʃɪp/
digital photo (n)	/ˌdɪdʒɪtl ˈfəʊtəʊ/
filter (n) ★★	/ˈfɪltə/
image (n) ★★★	/ˈɪmɪdʒ/
pixel (n)	/ˈpɪks(ə)l/
primary colour (n)	/ˌpraɪməri ˈkʌlə/

JOBS AND OCCUPATIONS

chef (n) ★	/ʃef/
designer (n) ★★	/dɪˈzaɪnə/
film-maker (n)	/ˈfɪlmˌmeɪkə/
IT consultant (n)	/aɪˈtiː kənˌsʌltənt/
manager (n) ★★★	/ˈmænɪdʒə/
mechanic (n) ★	/mɪˈkænɪk/
producer (n) ★★★	/prəˈdjuːsə/
referee (n) ★★	/ˌrefəˈriː/
surgeon (n) ★★	/ˈsɜːdʒ(ə)n/
translator (n)	/trænsˈleɪtə/

VERBS

argue (v) ★★★	/ˈɑːgjuː/
blow (v) ★★★	/bləʊ/
colour (v) ★★	/ˈkʌlə/
contact (v) ★★★	/ˈkɒntækt/
delete (v) ★★	/dɪˈliːt/
inspire (v) ★★	/ɪnˈspaɪə/
manage (to do something) (v) ★★★	/ˈmænɪdʒ/
mix (v) ★★★	/mɪks/
press (v) ★★★	/pres/
produce (v) ★★★	/prəˈdjuːs/
promise (v) ★★★	/ˈprɒmɪs/
refuse (v) ★★★	/rɪˈfjuːz/
set (v) ★★★	/set/
splash (v) ★	/splæʃ/

EXPRESSIONS

bring to life	/ˌbrɪŋ tə ˈlaɪf/
have a go	/ˌhæv ə ˈgəʊ/
in detail	/ˌɪn ˈdiːteɪl/
tell the truth	/ˌtel ðə ˈtruːθ/

IRREGULAR VERBS

Infinitive	Past simple	Past participle
be	was, were	been
become	became	become
begin	began	begun
bend	bent	bent
bet	bet	bet
bite	bit	bitten
blow	blew	blown
break	broke	broken
bring	brought	brought
broadcast	broadcast	broadcast
build	built	built
burn	burnt/burned	burnt/burned
buy	bought	bought
catch	caught	caught
choose	chose	chosen
come	came	come
cost	cost	cost
cut	cut	cut
do	did	done
draw	drew	drawn
drink	drank	drunk
drive	drove	driven
eat	ate	eaten
fall	fell	fallen
feed	fed	fed
feel	felt	felt
fight	fought	fought
find	found	found
fit	fitted/fit	fitted/fit
fly	flew	flown
forget	forgot	forgotten
freeze	froze	frozen
get	got	got
give	gave	given
go	went	gone/been
grow	grew	grown
have	had	had
hear	heard	heard
hide	hid	hidden
hit	hit	hit
hold	held	held
hurt	hurt	hurt
keep	kept	kept
know	knew	known
lay	laid	laid
learn	learnt/learned	learnt/learned
leave	left	left
lend	lent	lent
let	let	let

Infinitive	Past simple	Past participle
lie	lay	lain
light	lit	lit
lose	lost	lost
make	made	made
mean	meant	meant
meet	met	met
overtake	overtook	overtaken
pay	paid	paid
put	put	put
read /riːd/	read /red/	read /red/
rebuild	rebuilt	rebuilt
rewrite	rewrote	rewritten
ride	rode	ridden
ring	rang	rung
run	ran	run
say	said	said
see	saw	seen
sell	sold	sold
send	sent	sent
set	set	set
shake	shook	shaken
shine	shone	shone
shoot	shot	shot
show	showed	shown
sing	sang	sung
sink	sank	sunk
sit	sat	sat
sleep	slept	slept
smell	smelt/smelled	smelt/smelled
speak	spoke	spoken
spell	spelt/spelled	spelt/spelled
spend	spent	spent
stand	stood	stood
steal	stole	stolen
stick	stuck	stuck
swim	swam	swum
take	took	taken
teach	taught	taught
tell	told	told
think	thought	thought
throw	threw	thrown
understand	understood	understood
wake	woke	woken
wear	wore	worn
win	won	won
write	wrote	written

PRONUNCIATION GUIDE

Vowels	
/aː/	arm, large
/æ/	cap, bad
/aɪ/	ride, fly
/aɪə/	diary, science
/aʊ/	how, mouth
/aʊə/	our, shower
/e/	bed, head
/eɪ/	day, grey
/eə/	hair, there
/ɪ/	give, did
/i/	happy, taxi
/iː/	we, heat
/ɪə/	ear, here
/ɒ/	not, watch
/əʊ/	cold, boat
/ɔː/	door, talk
/ɔɪ/	point, boy
/ʊ/	foot, could
/uː/	two, food
/ʊə/	sure, tourist
/ɜː/	bird, heard
/ʌ/	fun, come
/ə/	mother, actor

Consonants	
/b/	bag, rubbish
/d/	desk, cold
/f/	fill, laugh
/g/	girl, big
/h/	hand, home
/j/	yes, young
/k/	cook, back
/l/	like, fill
/m/	mean, climb
/n/	new, want
/p/	park, happy
/r/	ring, borrow
/s/	say, this
/t/	town, city
/v/	very, live
/w/	water, away
/z/	zoo, his
/ʃ/	shop, machine
/ʒ/	usually, television
/ŋ/	thank, doing
/tʃ/	cheese, picture
/θ/	thing, north
/ð/	that, clothes
/dʒ/	jeans, bridge

Macmillan Education
4 Crinan Street
London N1 9XW
A division of Macmillan Publishers Limited
Companies and representatives throughout the world

ISBN 978-0-230-40848-7

Text © Judy Garton-Sprenger and Philip Prowse 2011
Design and illustration © Macmillan Publishers Limited 2011

First published 2011

Original design by Giles Davies
Page make-up by Giles Davies
Illustrated by Kate Sheppard (pp18, 44, 70r, 96), Martin Sanders (pp25, 67, 76), John Taylor (pp70l, 89, 99), Nadine Wickenden (pp41, 91)
Cover design by Designers Collective
Cover photos by **Alamy**/ Blaine Harrington III (tc), Alamy/ Steven May (tr); **Brand X** (bcl); **Corbis**/ Carlos Dominguez/ The Merlin Entertainments London Eye (bl), Corbis/ Image Source (br); **Digital Vision** (tl); **Getty** (bcr).

Authors' acknowledgements
The authors would like to thank all the team at Macmillan Education in the UK and worldwide for everything they have done to create *New Inspiration*. We are most grateful to Celia Bingham for editing the Student's Book, to Helena Gomm for revising the Workbook, and to Rachel Bladon and Anna Cole for the Teacher's Book. We would also like to thank James Richardson for his usual great skill in producing the recorded material, and the actors who appear on the recordings and bring the book to life.

We owe an enormous debt of gratitude to teenage students and their teachers in many different countries who welcomed us into their classrooms and contributed so much to the formation of *New Inspiration*. In particular we would like to thank teachers and classes in Argentina, Greece, Italy, Poland, Spain, Switzerland, Turkey and Uruguay. We are equally indebted to all those participants on teacher training courses in Europe, South America and elsewhere from whom we have learnt so much, in particular British Council courses in the UK and overseas, and courses at the University of Durham and NILE in Norwich.

The authors and publishers would like to express their great thanks to all those who commented on syllabus and materials for *New Inspiration* and provided feedback on their use of *Inspiration*, in particular: Fatiha Ajaoui, Mª Angeles Ramiro Alvarez, Alejandro De Angelis, Asun Armendáriz, Roseli Franco Babora, Cristina Ceratti Bo, Monika Bucher, Barbara Chuck, Bilsev Demir, Anastasia Egorova, Yolanda Elsener-Fischer, Pia Ettlin, Nadine Fesseler, Katharina Fischer, Joe Hediger, Lisbeth Heinzer-Föhn, Alda Heloisa Santoyo Garcia, Anna Häfliger-Schmidlin, Mgr.Jana Hanesova, Katharina Hofmann, Corinna Iaizzo, Daniela Iskerková, Estrella Gómez Jiménez-Tusset, Bulent Karababa, Figen Kılıçarslan, Antonia Köppel, Svetlana Korostelyova, Lycia Lourenço Lacerda, Carmelia Loher, Pilar García López-Tello, Zuzana Lovasova, Monika Mižáková, Fabiane R. Montanari, Andrea Cristina Neiger, Clara González O'Sullivan, Ingrid Rizzi Razente, Brigitte Reber, Peach Richmond, Alfonsa Pliego Romera, Jean Rüdiger-Harper, Karl Russi, Monica Cristina Sales, Susanna Schwab, Adilson Geraldo Da Silva, Monica Dolores Sosa, Geraldo de Souza Jr, Janine Strub-Dittli, Maria Vertiletskaya, Mª Rosa Pradilla Vicente, Maria Luisa Villarruel, Menekşe Yildiz, Andrea Zeiger.

The authors and publishers would like to thank the following for permission to reproduce their photographic material: **Alamy**/ Ambient Images Inc p46, Alamy/ Amana Images inc p28(c), Alamy/ Nathan Benn p98(c), Alamy/ Big Cheese Photo LLC pp72, 73, Alamy/ Blend Images p98(tr), Alamy/ Peter Bowater pp60(c), 76(ct), Alamy/ David Cook/ blueshiftstudios p9(trainers), Alamy/ Tony Cordoza p9(cap), Alamy/ David Doyeol p15(l), Alamy/ Louise Batalla Duran p32(c), Alamy/ Chad Ehlers p68(l), Alamy/ Greg Balfour Evans p37(cr), Alamy/ Form Advertising pp8(c background), 12-13(background), 86(t background), 105(tl background), Alamy/ Blaine Harrington III p80(br), Alamy/ Juice Images p51(t), Alamy/ Justin Kaze zsixz p39(bl background),

45(bl), Alamy/ Russell Kord p29, Alamy/ Steven May pp9(festival), 26-27, Alamy/ Motoring Picture Library pp37(Benz), 45(tl), Alamy/ Nagelestock. com p28(b), Alamy/ Forget Patrick/ Sagaphoto.com pp10-11(background), 19(background), Alamy/ PhotoAlto p14(tc), Alamy/ Pictorial Press Ltd p48(t), Alamy/ RIA Novosti p30(bl), Alamy/ Friedrich Saurer pp34(t), 41, Alamy/ Alex Segre pp61(tl), 78(br), 83(r), Alamy/ Robert Stainforth pp60(b), 62(t), Alamy/ Homer W Sykes p20(9), Alamy/ tbkmedia.de pp68-69, 71(br), Alamy/ The Print Collector p44(t), Alamy/ UK City Images pp87(cl background), 90(background), 105(cr background), Alamy/ Worldwide Photo p14(t); **Bananastock**/ pp48(t), 49(t), 108(bl); **Bridgeman Art Library**/ Guildhall Library, City of London pp35(tr), 36; **CEN**/ Europics pp36(b) & 40; **Corbis**/ p56(tl), Corbis/ A. Chederros/ Onoky p55, Corbis/ Carlos Dominguez pp20(4), 62(b), Corbis/ Leo Fiedler pp92(l), 97(l), Corbis/ Andrew Fox p66(tl), Corbis/ Sven Hagolani p98(br), Corbis/ Rune Hellestad p78(bl), Corbis/ John Henley p96, Corbis/ So Hing-Keung p28(e), Corbis/ Jorma Jaemsen p94(t), Corbis/ Frantzesco Kangaris/ epa p32(r), Corbis/ Cedric Lim/AsiaPix p14(b), Corbis/ George Logan pp8(l), 22-23, Corbis/ Paul Miller/ epa pp62(cb), 71(tr), Corbis/ Kelly Redinger/ Design Pics p39(r), Corbis/ Travel Pix Collection/ JAI p21(5), Corbis/ Steven Vidler/ Eurasia Press p80(tr), Corbis/ Olix Wirtinger pp34(c), 51(b); **Digital Stock**/ Corbis p82(ct); **Getty**/ pp8(t), 21(6), 26(tl), 27(insert), 32(l), 64(t), 87(br), 92(tr), 94-95(t), 97(r), 108(br), Getty/ George Doyle p14(bc), Getty/ Alain Evrard p28(f), Getty/ Steve Gorton p9(sweater), Getty/ Andrew Holt p63, Getty/ Dave King p9(jacket), Getty/ Moment p58, Getty/ Steve Shott p37(br), Getty/ SSPL p37(bcl & tr), Getty/ Ian Waldie p18(l), Getty/ WireImage p56(br); **Goodshoot**/ p82(tl); **Image Source**/ pp9(br), 37(biro), 80(bl), 81, 82(tr), 83(bl), 98(tl); **John Foxx Images**/ p75(l); **London Transport Museum**/ p77(tr & tl); **Macmillan Australia**/ pp102(b), 108(tl); **Mary Evans Picture Library**/ pp44(b), 47(b & t), 50(t & c), 104(cb); **Medio Images**/ p61(br); **Natural History Museum Picture Library, London** p92(br), Natural History Museum Picture Library, London/ Kokoro pp87(tr), 106(inset); **Nature Picture Library**/ John Cancalosi p75(r); **Photoalto**/ p93(t); **Photodisc**/ pp75(ct), 93(b); **Photolibrary**/ Age Fotostock p18(r), Photolibrary/ Britain on View pp9(tr background), 24(background), 77(br), 105(tr background), Photolibrary/ ComStock p50(r), Photolibrary/ Image Source p56(c), Photolibrary/ David Jerome p78(tl), Photolibrary/ Javier Larrea p80(cr), Photolibrary/ Moodboard RF p9(trousers), Photolibrary/ Museum of London p20(l), Photolibrary/ Tetra Images p15(r); **Photoshot**/ Imagebrokers p30(r), Photoshot/ JTB p76(cb), Photoshot/ WPM pp28(a), 30(tl); **Rex Features**/ pp84, 104(c), 105(ct), Rex Features/ 20ᵗʰ C. Fox/ Everett pp42(t), 54(br), 57(r), 104(t), 105(tr), Rex Features/ ABC/ Everett pp54(cr), 57(l), 105(cb), Rex Features/ Alex J Berliner/ BEI p31, Rex Features/ China Span Keren SU/ Sunset p76(t), Rex Features/ Columbia/ Everett p43(b), Rex Features/ Ian Daniels pp87(tl), 100(b), Rex Features/ David Fisher pp34(b), 48(l), Rex Features/ FoxSearch/ Everett pp100(t), 109(r), Rex Features/ Robert Hallam p13(juggler), Rex Features/ Michael Holder p80(tl), Rex Features/ ITV pp87(bl), 88, 105(b), Rex Features/ Mark Leech p78(tr), Rex Features/ Alisdair Macdonald p20(2), Rex Features/ Ken McKay/ Talkback Thames p56(tr), Rex Features/ Dean Murray p26(bl), Rex Features/ Erik C. Pendzich p106, Rex Features/ NBCU Photobank pp54(tl), 54(tr), 57(l), Rex Features/ Pekka Sakki p37(tl), Rex Features/ Alex Segre p62(ct), Rex Features/ Micha Theiner p20(3); **Science and Society Picture Library**/ The Science Museum p37(bl & helicopter); **Science Photo Library**/ ESA/ CE/ Eurocontrol p66(tr), Science Photo Library/ GE Astro Space p66(b); **Stockbyte**/ p75(cb); **Superstock**/ pp20(8), 42(b), 43(t), 45(b), Superstock/ Age Fotostock p28(d); **Topfoto**/ The Print Collector p82(b).

Commissioned photography by Stuart Cox pp6/7, 8(c), 9(f,g,h), 10/11, 12/13, 16, 17, 19, 20/21(b), 24, 35(d), 38, 39(t,b), 45, 52, 53, 60(a), 61(r), 64/65, 71(l), 74, 83(t), 86(a), 87(f), 90, 105(1-6), 109(portrait).

Thanks to Bradley, Charlotte A, Charlotte H, Dominic, Nicole, Matthew.

The author and publishers are grateful for permission to reprint the following copyright material: Material about *I'm a Celebrity – Get Me Out Of Here!*, reprinted by permission of ITV Press Office. Material from *'Schoolboy survives direct hit by meteorite travelling at 30,000mph'* by Eddie Wrenn, first appeared in *The Daily Mail* 14/06/09, reprinted by permission of the publisher.

Dictionary extracts taken from Macmillan Essential Dictionary copyright © Macmillan Publishers Limited 2003 and Macmillan English Dictionary 2nd Edition copyright © Macmillan Publishers Limited 2007

Printed and bound in Thailand

2017 2016 2015 2014
16 15 14 13 12 11